The End of Accounting and The Path Forward for Investors and Managers

The Wiley Finance series contains books written specifically for finance and investment professionals as well as sophisticated individual investors and their financial advisors. Book topics range from portfolio management to e-commerce, risk management, financial engineering, valuation and financial instrument analysis, as well as much more. For a list of available titles, visit our website at www.WileyFinance.com.

Founded in 1807, John Wiley & Sons is the oldest independent publishing company in the United States. With offices in North America, Europe, Australia, and Asia, Wiley is globally committed to developing and marketing print and electronic products and services for our customers' professional and personal knowledge and understanding.

The End of Accounting and The Path Forward for Investors and Managers

BARUCH LEV
FENG GU

WILEY

Published by John Wiley & Sons, Inc., Hoboken, New Jersey.

Published simultaneously in Canada.

For general information on our other products and services or for technical support, please contact our Customer Care Department within the United States at (800) 762-2974, outside the United States at (317) 572-3993 or fax (317) 572-4002.

Wiley publishes in a variety of print and electronic formats and by print-on-demand. Some material included with standard print versions of this book may not be included in e-books or in print-on-demand. If this book refers to media such as a CD or DVD that is not included in the version you purchased, you may download this material at http://booksupport.wiley.com. For more information about Wiley products, visit www.wiley.com.

Library of Congress Cataloging-in-Publication Data:

Names: Lev, Baruch, author. | Gu, Feng, 1968- author.
Title: The end of accounting and the path forward for investors and managers / Baruch Lev, Feng Gu.
Description: Hoboken, New Jersey : John Wiley & Sons, Inc., 2016. | Series: Wiley finance series | Includes index.
Identifiers: LCCN 2016007850 (print) | LCCN 2016015075 (ebook) | ISBN 9781119191094 (hardback) | ISBN 9781119190998 (pdf) | ISBN 9781119191087 (epub)
Subjects: LCSH: Financial statements. | Investments—Decision making. | Finance. | BISAC: BUSINESS & ECONOMICS / Finance.
Classification: LCC HG4028.B2 L49 2016 (print) | LCC HG4028.B2 (ebook) | DDC 332.63/2042—dc23
LC record available at http://lccn.loc.gov/2016007850

Cover Design: Wiley
Cover Image: © Sergey Nivens/Shutterstock

Printed in the United States of America

10 9 8 7 6 5 4

To Ilana, Eli, and Racheli
Rui, Elizabeth, and Isabella

Contents

Acknowledgments

In recent decades, corporate financial information, conveyed by those voluminous and increasingly complex quarterly and annual reports, has lost most of its usefulness to investors—the major intended users—and is urgently in need of revitalization and restructuring. In this book, we empirically prove the former (information relevance lost) and perform the latter: propose a new and actionable information paradigm for twenty-first century investors.

In this we were very ably assisted by various colleagues and experts to whom we express our deep gratitude. Gene Epstein, Barron's economics editor, provided important guidance and insight (though was disappointed that we didn't change the book title to The Death of Accounting). Our colleague, Stephen Ryan, provided numerous comments and suggestions on accounting and statistical issues. Win Murray, Director of Research, Harris Associates; Philip Ryan, Chairman, Swiss Re Americas; and Allister Wilson, Global Audit Partner at Ernst & Young, all provided valuable comments on parts of the book. Zvika Zelikovitch, a superb artist, and Ayala Lev, creative and loving, furnished useful ideas for the book cover. Our colleagues Mary Billings, Massimiliano Bonacchi, Matthew Cedergren, Jing Chen, Justin Deng, Ilia Dichev, Dan Gode, William Greene, John Hand, Doron Nissim, Suresh Radhakrishnan, and Paul Zarowin enlightened us with numerous suggestions and insights.

Our trusted assistant, Shevon Estwick, highly professional and dedicated, provided invaluable administrative support in handling the manuscript. Nancy Kleinrock, not only edited the book very skillfully, but offered numerous constructive comments and suggestions. Jessica Neville, Executive Director of Communications at NYU's Stern School of Business, provided valuable marketing advice, and Wiley Finance Editor, William Falloon, accepted the book almost at face value and guided it smoothly and efficiently through the long production process, providing important advice. He was ably assisted by his Wiley editorial and production team.

We are deeply indebted to all, and to our families, of course.

The Book in a Nutshell

THE FADING USEFULNESS OF INVESTORS' INFORMATION

Corporate financial reports—balance sheets, income and cash flow statements, as well as the numerous explanatory footnotes in quarterly and annual reports and IPO prospectuses—form the most ubiquitous source of information for investment and credit decisions. Many stocks and bonds investors, individuals and institutions, as well as lenders to business enterprises look for financial report information to guide them where and when to invest or lend. Major corporate decisions, such as business restructuring or mergers & acquisitions, are also predicated on financial report indicators of profitability and solvency. Responding to such widespread demand, the supply of corporate financial information, tightly regulated all over the world, keeps expanding in scope and complexity. Who would have imagined, for example, that the accounting rules determining when a sale of a product should be recorded as revenue in the income statement would extend over 700 (!) pages?[1] Eat your heart out, IRS. Its complexity notwithstanding, financial information is widely believed to move markets and businesses. But does it?

Like a *Consumer Reports* evaluation, we examine in the first part of this book the usefulness of financial (accounting) information to investors and, regrettably, provide an unsatisfactory report, to put it mildly. Based on a comprehensive, large-sample empirical analysis, spanning the past half century, we document a fast and continuous deterioration in the usefulness and relevance of financial information to investors' decisions. Moreover, the pace of this usefulness deterioration has accelerated in the past two decades. Hard to believe, despite all of regulators' efforts to improve accounting and corporate transparency, financial information no longer reflects the factors—so important to investors—that create corporate value and confer on businesses the vaunted sustained competitive advantage. In fact, our analysis (Chapter 4) indicates that today's financial reports provide a trifling 5 percent of the information relevant to investors.

To avoid undue reader suspense, Part II of the book identifies, again with full empirical support, the three major reasons for the surprising accounting fade, thereby laying the foundation for the main part of the book: our new disclosure proposal outlined in Part III, which directs investors with specificity to the information they should seek for substantially improved investment decisions. Our proposed disclosure to investors is primarily based on nonaccounting information, focusing on the enterprise's strategy (business model) and its execution, and highlighting fundamental indicators, such as the number of new customers and churn rate of Internet and telecom enterprises, accidents' frequency and severity—as well as policy renewal rates—of car insurers, clinical trial results of pharma and biotech companies, changes in proven reserves of oil and gas firms, or the book-to-bill (order backlog) ratio of high-tech companies, to name a few fundamental indicators that are more relevant and forward-looking inputs to investment decisions than the traditional accounting information, like earnings and asset values, conveyed by corporate financial reports. Such reports, moreover, are outright misleading for important sectors of the economy, such as fast-growing technology and science-based companies, often portraying innovative and high-potential enterprises as losing, asset-starved business failures.

In short, based on our evidence, we grade the ubiquitous corporate financial report information as largely unfit for twenty-first-century investment and lending decisions, identify the major causes for this accounting fade, and provide a remedy for investors. But wait.

WHO CARES?

So what if financial (accounting) information lost much of its relevance to investors in recent decades? Who besides accountants, and accounting educators like us, should care about that? With modern information technologies, the proliferation of data vendors (Bloomberg, FactSet), and the ubiquity of financial social media sites, investors can surely supplement the relevance-challenged accounting data with more pertinent and timely information. So, why bother about the fading usefulness of financial information? Why this book?

For the simple and compelling reason that there aren't and never will be good substitutes for corporate-issued information, since corporate managers are always substantially better informed about their business than outsiders. Managers are privy, for example, to recent sales and cost trends, the progress of drugs or software products under development, customer defection rate (churn), new contracts signed, and emerging markets penetration rate, among many other important business developments. No information vendor, Internet chat room, or even a sophisticated analyst can provide investors such "inside" information. No advances in information technology and investors' processing capacity (Edgar, XBRL) can overcome the fundamental information asymmetry—managers know more than investors—inherent to capital markets. You might not like it, but that's how it is and will be.

In fact, in subsequent chapters we provide empirical evidence suggesting that the quality of the overall information used by investors continuously deteriorates and share prices reveal less of companies' value and future prospects. Not the buzz, hype, and financial Internet chatter, which are surely deafening; rather the hard, fundamental data so crucial for investors' decisions. So who cares? Investors, policy makers, and even corporate managers should be highly concerned with our findings of the fast-diminishing relevance of financial (accounting) information.

But our book doesn't end with this downer. Far from it. In Part III of the book—its main part—we propose a new, comprehensive information paradigm for twenty-first-century investors: the Strategic Resources & Consequences Report. For clarity, we demonstrate this information system on four key economic sectors: media and entertainment, insurance, pharmaceutics and biotech, and oil and gas. The focus of this Resources & Consequences Report is on the strategic, value-enhancing resources (assets) of modern enterprises, like patents, brands, technology, natural resources, operating licenses, customers, business platforms available for add-ons, and unique enterprise relationships, rather than on the commoditized plant, machines, or inventory, which are prominently displayed on corporate balance sheets. The main purpose of the proposed information system is to provide investors and lenders (and managers, too) with actionable, up-to-date information required for today's investment decisions. It directs every investor and lender to seek from companies the information that really matters, rather than the information regulators believe is good for you. So, what you get in this book is a package deal: comprehensive evidence that the information you used to rely on lost much of its usefulness, along with the reasons for this relevance lost, and a clear articulation of the information you should seek and use to assess the performance of business enterprises and chart their future potential. The book concludes with three important chapters: How exactly can our radical change proposals be implemented (Chapter 16); how should the current accounting and reporting systems be restructured to advance them to the twenty-first century (Chapter 17); and how should investors and analysts transform their investment routines in light of this book's message (Chapter 18).

In short, this is an *operating instructions* book for investors, directing them with specificity to the information leading to successful investment and lending decisions, as well as guiding corporate managers, many of whom intuitively realize the serious shortcomings of financial information, how to enhance their information disclosure. Importantly, while this book deals with highly complex, often confusing financial information, and is fully backed by large-sample empirical evidence, you don't have to be an accountant or a statistician to fully comprehend it. In contrast with typical academic courses, there are no prerequisites for this book. Common sense, intuition, and a strong desire to improve your investment performance are all that is required for reaping the benefits of this book. Open admission, so to speak (except for diehard accountants whose peace of mind might not endure this book's message).

NOT ONLY FOR INVESTORS

While the intended readers of this book are mainly investors and lenders, alerted here to the hazards of using outdated, inadequate financial report information in making investment and lending decisions, the implications of our findings are far reaching and of considerable interest to wider audiences: corporate managers, accountants, and capital market regulatory agencies. These widespread implications stem from the unique role of the corporate accounting and reporting systems in the economy.[2] To fully grasp this role, and the implications of our findings, we have to briefly consider the impact of financial information on economic growth and the perplexing uniqueness of accounting regulation. Bear with us, you don't get this in business school.

FINANCIAL INFORMATION, A MAJOR DRIVER OF ECONOMIC GROWTH

While you surely heard, and perhaps even personally experienced, that accounting is outright boring, it's nevertheless vitally important. Here is why. No economy can grow and prosper without an active and deep capital market that channels the savings of individuals and business organizations to the most productive investment uses by the private sector.[3] Promising biotech companies, software producers, energy startups, and healthcare enterprises rely on the stock and bond markets to raise the much-needed funds to finance their capital investment and R&D, and attract talent by offering shares and stock options. In capital markets, investors' funds chase corporate growth opportunities and, vice versa, desert failing businesses. The "fuel" running this sophisticated capital accumulation and allocation "machine" is information: the information available to investors and lenders on the prospects of business enterprises, translated to expected risks and returns on investments, directing investors' capital to its most productive uses. Poor information, in contrast, seriously distorts investors' decisions by misdirecting their capital to failed enterprises, while starving worthy ones. The economic "growth machine" falters with the contaminated fuel of low-quality information.

For years, Enron's and WorldCom's glowing—yet misleading—financial reports masked the operational failures of these companies and drove investors to plow billions of dollars into them, only to see their fortunes go down the drain, and, more seriously, depriving other worthy investments of much-needed capital.[4] But note, it's not only fraudulent information that impedes investment and growth; it's mainly the poor quality of "honest" financial reports, legitimately disclosed under the current, universally used accounting system, that seriously harms the capital allocation system and economic growth. Consider:

Biotech companies developing promising drugs and medical instruments, as well as high-tech and Internet startups, often report heavy losses because their investments in R&D, brands, and customer acquisition are treated by accountants as regular, income-reducing expenses, rather than assets generating future benefits. Many such enterprises encounter difficulties in raising money by going public, or, once public, in getting additional funds in the capital or debt markets because promising investments are erroneously perceived by investors as enterprises awash in red ink.[5] For established enterprises, important business events—like increases in customers' "churn rate" (termination) of telecom, Internet, and insurance companies, which is a leading indicator of serious operating problems—aren't reported to investors. Nor is there full and timely disclosure to investors of the success or failure of clinical trials for drugs under development by pharma companies. As for the information conveyed by corporate reports, it's often subject to serious biases, like reflecting the costs of restructuring without its benefits (conservatism, in the accounting parlance), and uncertainty due to heavy reliance on managerial forecasts and estimates that are subjective and sometimes unreliable. These, and other reporting shortcomings are detailed in Part II. All in all, a largely deficient source of information for investors. No wonder that privately held companies, which are not affected by investors' decisions based on low-quality information, invest considerably more and grow faster than publicly held companies.[6]

Given the crucial role of financial (accounting) information in fostering prosperity and growth of business enterprises and the economy at large, the serious deficiencies of this information, documented in the following chapters, should be of great concern not only to investors—the primary users of the information—but also to managers, accountants, and policy makers. Corporate managers, in particular, should be concerned with the deteriorating usefulness of financial information, since the consequent increasing opaqueness of companies elevates investors' risk and companies' cost of capital, and reduces share values.[7] Contaminated fuel at gas pumps would have caused a public uproar and triggered regulatory actions. Contaminated information, capital markets' "fuel," should likewise draw general concern and action.

UNIQUE AMONG REGULATIONS

Accounting's usefulness deserves critical examination, not only because of its central economic role, but also due to its unique, yet little known, institutional status. Did you know that those, rather obscure, accounting rules and procedures underlying financial information are like the law of the land? They have, in fact, a legal status, because public companies have to follow them to the letter in generating financial information.[8] But what makes accounting regulation unique and imposes a heavy burden on the economy is that, unlike any other regulation, it is mandatory for all public companies, uniform throughout the world, and constantly expanding.

Start with *uniformity*: Financial reporting regulations are by and large identical throughout the world. In practically every free-market economy, public companies must periodically disclose to the public balance sheets, income, and often cash flow statements of essentially identical structure, form, and content.[9] Furthermore, the financial statements of all public companies must be audited by external auditors (certified public accountants—CPAs) and are closely monitored by national regulators, like the SEC in the United States. We are not familiar with any other law or regulation that is similarly uniform throughout all free-market economies. Different cultures, economic institutions, and developmental histories exert strong effects on national laws (genetically modified food products are generally banned in Europe but not in the United States; capital punishment is legal in some countries, but not others). Accounting and financial reporting regulations defy diversity.[10]

That's a good thing, you say: The global uniformity of accounting—one business language throughout the world—saves information generation and processing costs to multinational firms, but the unintended consequences of this uniformity are serious. In particular, uniformity deprives accounting of a major force for innovation and rejuvenation—the vital experimentation and evolution that come with diversity. Regulatory development is generally a trial-and-error process, as in the regulations prohibiting tobacco smoking in public places that emerged slowly and sporadically (Minnesota in 1975 was the first US state to ban smoking in most public places), gaining worldwide adoption only after extensive experimentation. Even now, countries differ in the extent of smoking bans. Same with environmental regulations, where cross-country differences are legion. In contrast, the stagnation of the accounting system and the consequent loss of relevance—documented in this book—can be, in part, attributed to the absence of any experimentation with new information structures or modes of disclosure, which comes from diversity of reporting across countries or regions. This is most evident by the fact that accounting regulations keep piling up and ineffective ones are rarely abolished: no trial, no error—just more of the same.

Often, regulatory competition among states in the United States, or stock exchanges around the world, leads to regulatory and institutional improvements (the evolution of gas fracking regulation in the United States, for instance), but there has never been competition on accounting and financial disclosure systems. Even the small differences between certain specific accounting procedures mandated in the United States (GAAP) and those in Europe and certain other countries (IFRS) could soon disappear due to the pressure to converge (harmonize) these systems. Continued fading relevance will be the consequence of such convergence. In contrast, our proposals, set forth in Part III, call for extensive innovation and experimentation in corporate disclosure to investors.

What's also unique about financial reporting regulations is that they keep expanding, constantly increasing the social cost burden. Each wave of corporate scandals and financial failures brings in its wake new accounting and reporting rules aimed at rectifying past failures, and new economic and business developments trigger further changes to accounting regulations. But, old, dysfunctional accounting rules, like the expensing of R&D, rarely die, nor fade away (unlike General MacArthur's memorable old soldiers), they just proliferate. The only regulations that are similar to financial reporting in scope, cost, and constant expansion are environmental laws, with one crucial difference: Environmental regulations are constantly, often heatedly debated and challenged in the public arena. The current controversies in the United States about carbon tax, subsidies for alternative energy sources, and gas fracking, are but a few examples. And not just in the States: In July 2014, Australia scrapped its unpopular national carbon tax, instituted just two years earlier. Such close public scrutiny significantly improves the quality of environmental regulations and mitigates their cost. In contrast, we aren't aware of a serious, change-leading public scrutiny of corporate financial reporting, not even after repeated, demonstrated failures, such as the 2007–2008 financial crisis, which made clear that the financial reports of the troubled institutions—Citibank, AIG, Merrill Lynch, Lehman Bros., Countrywide Financial—didn't alert investors and regulators to the excessive risk-taking and the poor quality of bank assets that caused the failures.[11]

The absence of experimentation and serious public scrutiny, and the constantly rising social costs of accounting regulations set the stage for a comprehensive examination of mission accomplished: the usefulness of corporate financial information to investors, on which we embark in this book.

ABOUT US AND OUR APPROACH

We, the writers of this book, are veteran accounting and finance researchers and educators, and one of us has extensive experience in public accounting, business, and consulting. For years we have documented in academic journals the failure of the accounting and financial reporting system to adjust to the revolutionary changes in the business models of modern corporations, from the traditional industrial, heavy asset-based model to information-intensive, intangibles-based business processes underlying modern companies, as well as documenting other accounting shortcomings. While not alone in this endeavor, our impact on accounting and financial reporting regulations has regrettably been so far very limited. But we now sense an opportunity for a significant change, motivating this book. The deterioration in the usefulness of financial information has been so marked, that it can no longer be glossed over. Corporate managers, realizing the diminished usefulness of financial information, respond by continuously expanding the voluntary disclosure to investors of non-GAAP (accounting) information. Thus, for example, the frequency of releasing proforma (non-GAAP) earnings doubled from 2003 to 2013, standing now at over 40 percent.[12] Researchers, too, sense a serious problem: A recent study by leading accounting researchers examined the impact on investors of all the accounting and reporting rules and standards issued by the Financial Accounting Standards Board (FASB) from its inception (1973) through 2009—a staggering number of 147 standards—and found that 75 percent of these complex and costly rules didn't have any effect on the shareholders of the impacted companies (improved information generally enhances shareholder value), and, hard to believe, 13 percent of the standards actually *detracted* from shareholder value. Only 12 percent of the standards benefited investors. Thus, 35 years of accounting regulation came to naught.[13] The SEC is concerned, too:

Consider, for example, the current initiative of the US Securities and Exchange Commission (SEC)—Disclosure Effectiveness—aimed at " ... considering ways to improve the disclosure regime for the benefit of both companies and investors."[14] The SEC invited input and comments to this initiative, and indeed, a Google search reveals scores of mostly extensive comments and submissions by business institutions, accounting firms, and individuals. Reviewing some of these submissions, we are struck by the following common threads, which sadly remind us of previous futile attempts to enhance financial reporting effectiveness: Commentators generally *presume* to know what information investors need without articulating how they gained this knowledge (research, surveys), and proceed with improvement recommendations that often boil down to generalities, like reduce information overload, focus on material information, or streamline and increase reliability of information, without identifying how exactly this should be done.[15] The exceptions are suggestions with a specific agenda, calling for environmental, social, or sustainability disclosures that are bound, we suspect, to antagonize most information suppliers (i.e., corporate managers).[16] Finally, most suggestions cut across all industries—a straightjacket approach, typical to current financial disclosure. Thus, despite the good intentions, we are skeptical that the current SEC's effort will fare better than its predecessors' in leading to real improvements in disclosure effectiveness, bringing to mind the famous remark: "Everybody complains about the weather, but nobody does anything about it."[17]

We approached our mission in this book—to alert investors to the information they should seek and use for successful investment and lending decisions, and in the process enhance disclosure effectiveness and improve capital markets efficiency—differently:

- First, rather than *assume* that financial disclosure lost its effectiveness, we document comprehensively, on large samples of companies, the fast diminishing relevance of this information to investors, and proceed to identify, again, evidence-based, the major reasons for this information fade (Parts I and II). This identification of failure drivers guided our choice of the information modes that will improve investors' decisions.
- Second, rather than *presume* to know what information investors need, we conducted a detailed examination of hundreds of quarterly earnings conference calls and investor meetings in four major economic sectors, distilling from analysts' questions the specific information items crucial for investment decisions. This, we backed up with lessons from economic theory to construct new *industry-specific* information paradigms—the Strategic Resources & Consequences Reports— proposed in Part III.
- Third, again, in the tradition of research, we don't just *claim* that our proposed information is required by investors—we prove it. We show that selected nonaccounting information items we propose, like insurance companies' data on the frequency and severity of claims, are correlated with companies' stock prices and future earnings, hence their relevance to investors.
- Last, our only book agenda is to outline to investors and lenders the information needed for assessing the performance and potential of

twenty-first-century business enterprises, thereby improving investment decisions and enhancing the functioning of capital markets. Corporate financial reporting will benefit, too.

Enough said.

NOTES

1. The Financial Accounting Standards Board (FASB) issued this new standard on "revenue recognition" in May 2014, classified as ASC 606.
2. See Jacob Soll, *The Reckoning* (New York: Basic Books, 2014), for a historical perspective of the centrality of accounting to economies and nations.
3. Abundant economic research substantiates the crucial role of capital markets in fostering corporate and national growth. For example, Anne Krueger, "Financial Markets and Economic Growth," International Monetary Fund, 2006.
4. If you are of the post-Enron and WorldCom generation, here are more recent accounting scandals, courtesy Japan: Olympus's (cameras, optics) multibillion-dollar accounting scandal concealed investment losses and missing assets, revealed in 2011, and Toshiba's (computers, machinery) also multibillion-dollar accounting scandal, disclosed in 2015.
5. At the very early stage of such enterprises, capital is usually provided by venture capitalists who rarely rely on financial reports. Subsequent to IPO, though, most early investors cash out, and the company is left to raise funds from regular investors whose decisions are often based on financial information, such as earnings and asset values, and on intermediaries (financial analysts), who also rely on financial report information.
6. See John Asker, Joan Farre-Mensa, and Alexander Ljungqvist, "Corporate Investment and Stock Market Listing: A Puzzle?" *Review of Financial Studies*, 28(2) (2015): 342–390.
7. Evidence that decreased transparency increases companies' cost of capital is provided in, for example, Mary Barth, Yaniv Konchitchki, and Wayne Landsman, "Cost of Capital and Earnings Transparency," *Journal of Accounting and Economics*, 55 (2013): 206–224.
8. Deviations from accounting principles (GAAP) lead auditors to qualify their audit report, and often trigger SEC actions and shareholders' lawsuits against managers and directors.
9. There are, of course, certain differences in reporting regulations across countries, but they are few and relate to details, like R&D, which has to be expensed in the United States vs. partially capitalized under strict circumstances in countries—mainly European—following the international accounting rules (IFRS). But these are details. The general structure and content of accounting and financial reporting is practically uniform throughout free-market economies.

10. For systematic, cross-country differences in regulatory approaches, see David Vogel, Michael Toffel, Diahanna Post, and Nazli Uludere Aragon, "Environmental Federalism in the European Union and the United States," in *A Handbook of Globalization and Environmental Policy*, F. Wijen, K. Zoeteman, J. Pieters, and P. Seters, eds. (Cheltenham, UK: Edward Elgar, 2005).

11. A study on the recent financial crisis concluded that: "However, transparency of information associated with measurement and recognition of accounting amounts...were insufficient for investors to assess properly the values and riskiness of the affected bank assets and liabilities." Mary Barth and Wayne Landsman, "How did financial reporting contribute to the financial crisis?" working paper (Stanford University, 2010), 3.

12. See Jeremiah Bentley, Theodore Christensen, Kurt Gee, and Benjamine Whipple, *Who Makes the non-GAAP Kool-Aid? How Do Managers and Analysts Influence non-GAAP Reporting Policy?* working paper (Salt Lake City: Marriott School of Management, Brigham Young University, 2014).

13. Urooj Khan, Bin Li, Shivaram Rajgopal, and Mohan Venkatachalam, *Do the FASB Standards Add (Shareholder) Value?* working paper (New York: Columbia University Business School, 2015).

14. US Securities and Exchange Commission, *Disclosure Effectiveness*, 2015.

15. Here and there, we found exceptions. For example, the accounting firm Ernst & Young proposes a report on critical estimates underlying financial information and their realizations. We also advance this important suggestion in Chapter 17.

16. We don't mean to denigrate agenda proposals. In fact, there are several research studies documenting an association between sustainability policies and improved corporate performance. For example Robert Eccles, Ioannis Ioannou, and George Serafeim, "The Impact of Corporate Sustainability on Organizational Process and Performance," *Management Science*, 60 (11) (2014): 2835–2857.

17. Generally attributed to Mark Twain, although some claim it originated with Charles Dudley Warner (1829-1900), an author and a friend of Twain.

Prologue

This book is loaded with surprises, not the least of which is that, in recent decades, corporate financial reports—the backbone of investors' information—lost most of their usefulness to investors, despite efforts by worldwide regulators to improve this information. But before delving into the evidence of accounting's relevance lost and what investors should do about it, we wish to share with you, as a preamble, two important findings that surprised even us. These will help to ease your way into the rest of the book:

- First, while accounting and financial reporting appear to be constantly changing to keep up with the times, you will be surprised to learn that the fundamental structure of corporate reporting to shareholders—balance sheets, income and cash flow statements, as well as their specific line items—is, in fact, frozen in time, having stagnated over the past 110 years. Would you believe that?
- Second, in recent years, basing investment decisions on the prediction of corporate earning—a time-honored and lucrative practice by analysts and investors—lost its edge over simpler investment techniques. It is time to look for new approaches to investment analysis.

The reason we open the book with these intriguing, yet fascinating findings is that they chart the path for the rest of the book: an unconventional and uncompromising look at the current state of investors' information, and an innovative approach at providing the information investors really need.

CHAPTER 1

Corporate Reporting Then and Now: A Century of "Progress"

In which we show, using US Steel's financial reports from 1902 (yes, 1902) and 2012, that the structure and content of corporate financial reports—balance sheets, income and cash flow statements—haven't changed over the past 110 years, despite dramatic increases in investors' sophistication, information processing ability, and complexity of business operation. Surprised? We don't blame you.

SPOT THE DIFFERENCES

The year is 1903. Theodore Roosevelt is in his third year of presidency, the Ford Motor Co. produces its first car—the Model A (available, as Henry Ford said, in any color as long as it's black)—and the first World Series is played: Boston Americans (soon the Boston Red Sox) versus the Pittsburgh Pirates. No surprise, Boston wins with Cy Young pitching. Alas, there is no television to watch the game, nor is there air transportation, or shopping malls. Not even the Internet—no Facebook or Twitter. But steel is produced, and the largest steel producer in the world—United States Steel Corporation (US Steel)—publishes its first annual report to shareholders. The main components of this report, the balance sheet and the income (profit or loss) statement for the previous year, 1902, are recast below, alongside with—fast-forward 110 years—their 2012 counterparts. (The original 1902 US Steel statements are reproduced in the Appendix.)

Recall your early childhood when you likely played the popular game Spot the Differences. Examining two seemingly identical pictures, you were challenged to identify minute, hidden differences. We challenge you to do the same with the two US Steel balance sheets and income statements, spanning 110 years, displayed below and in the next page. The purpose of the exercise: a first glimpse at the progress, or rather, lack thereof, of accounting and financial reporting over the past century plus decade.

Amazingly, you'll find that there are absolutely no differences in the structure and information items provided to investors by the two financial reports. Same layout of the income statement (Table 1.1) and balance sheet (Table 1.2), and identical information items disclosed in the two reports: assets, liabilities and equity in the balance sheet; and revenues minus an array of expenses in the income statement—as if investors' information needs and tools of financial analysis and securities valuation were frozen over the past 110 years, and no advances had been made in information processing and data display. Imagine if the report that people get today following a comprehensive physical checkup were identical to what patients received from their doctors 110 years ago. Yet, the corporate annual checkup report is frozen in time. Don't be misled by the "low" sales in 1902—$560 million. Converting this 1902 figure to 2012 values with the help of the Consumer Price Index (CPI) yields $16,324 million, pretty close to the actual 2012 sales of $19,328 million. So, US Steel was already a sizable enterprise 110 years ago, worthy of comparison with today's company.

There is an important difference, however, between the 1902 and 2012 US Steels: While the company generated in 1902 a healthy profit of $133.3 million (equivalent to $3.9 billion in 2012 dollars)—amounting

TABLE 1.1   United States Steel Corporation Consolidated Income Statement

	(in $ Millions)	
	Year 1902	**Year 2012**
Sales	$ 560	$19,328
Cost of sales	(411)	(18,291)
Gross profit	149	1,037
Minus Expenses:		
Selling & general expenses	(13)	(654)
Other gains/(losses)	5	(136)
Interest income	3	7
Interest expense	(9)	(247)
Income tax	(2)	(131)
Net income (loss)	133	(124)

TABLE 1.2　United States Steel Corporation Consolidated Balance Sheet

	(in $ Millions)	
	Year 1902	Year 2012
Assets		
Current Assets		
Cash & equivalents	$56	$570
Net receivables	49	2,090
Inventories	104	2,503
Other current assets	5	211
Total *current assets*	214	5,374
Investments	4	609
Property, Plant & Equipment	1,325	6,408
Intangibles	—	253
Goodwill	—	1,822
Other noncurrent assets	4	751
Total *assets*	$1,547	$15,217
Liabilities		
Current Liabilities		
Accounts payable	$19	$1,800
Payroll payable	4	977
Accrued taxes	1	146
Other current liabilities	26	67
Total *current liabilities*	50	2,990
Long-term debt	371	3,936
Employee benefits	—	4,416
Other noncurrent liabilities	30	397
Total *liabilities*	451	11,739
Stockholders' Equity		
Common stock	1,018	3,282
Retained earnings	78	196
Total *shareholders' equity*	1,096	3,478
Total *Liabilities and Equity*	$1,547	$15,217

to a 13 percent return-on-equity (ROE)—US Steel's operations in 2012 resulted in a loss of $124 million.[1] Many things have changed, of course, over the years, but perhaps a clue to the stark difference in operations lies in the board of directors. In 1902, US Steel had on its board the likes of John D. Rockefeller, J. Pierpont Morgan, Charles M. Schwab (also president of the company), Marshall Field, and Henry C. Frick (of the New York museum fame), among other business titans. Who says directors don't matter?

Seriously, a struggling enterprise, like the 2012 US Steel, providing the same information as the booming 1902 company? Shouldn't today's investors be told what aspects of the business model failed in 2012 or before? Informed about manufacturing setbacks? Specific marketing challenges? And told, backed by data, about the remedial steps taken by management? Shouldn't a twenty-first-century corporation reporting about its operations and economic condition systematically convey such strategic information, rather than report what it paid years ago for buildings and machinery or questionable assets like goodwill? And not just investors, whose money is at stake, should be better informed. The public at large, asked frequently by steel companies to support protective measures against foreign producers, should fully understand the challenges faced by the current US Steel. Really informative financial reports, rather than those frozen in time, are essential to investors and the public at large.

DIFFERENCES SPOTTED

Examining the US Steel financial reports line by line, it is evident that the two income statements are identical in terms of the items presented: sales, cost of sales, income tax expense, and so on. Thus, the 1902 and 2012 investors, different folks to be sure—the latter, with vastly more powerful analyzing capabilities, access to alternative investments and investment tools (multiple hedging mechanisms, short sales, programmed trading)—received similar information from the two profit and loss statements. As for the balance sheets, the only items on the 2012 report absent in 1902 are goodwill and intangibles, the result of certain mergers and acquisitions conducted by the "modern" US Steel. The company founders apparently believed that growth should be internally generated by innovation and investment, rather than acquired externally by hunting for bargains. Recent research, showing that most mergers and acquisitions disappoint due to overpayment and/or acquiring strategic misfits, proves the founders right.[2] Thus, with the exception of goodwill, readers of the two balance sheets were also equally informed. Finally, while in 1902, a cash flow statement—the third major component of a financial report—was not mandatory as it is now, US Steel provided one anyway (see Appendix).

But, you surely say, there is more to an annual report than an income statement, a balance sheet, and a cash flow statement. Today's supplementary information is much more extensive than a century ago. True. The sheer sizes of the two reports attest to this: The 1902 US Steel report is a slim 40-page document, whereas its 2012 counterpart is, in the best accounting tradition of mounting complexity and obfuscation, a hefty 174-page tome. A real forest killer.

But what does the latter report have on the former in terms of useful information? In 2012 there are, of course, the obligatory glossy pictures of smiling employees, executives, and customers, all absent in 1902. Come to think of it, we don't recall ever seeing smiling pictures of J. P. Morgan or J. D. Rockefeller. Those poor chaps really worked for a living; today, it's all about having fun. Lots of colorful graphs and exhibits of financial data adorn the 2012 report, as well as the soup du jour—a lengthy discussion of environmental issues. And not to be ignored—the 2012 report has a 12-page (!) boiler plate list of risk factors facing US Steel and its shareholders. Who would have guessed, for example, that the steel industry is cyclical, that steel production involves environmental compliance risk, that raw materials prices may fluctuate, or that an employer of some 45,000 workers faces litigation exposure? The 2012 risk factors statement tells you all this and more. Seriously, we have yet to meet a financial analyst or investor who learned anything valuable from, or based a decision on, the risk-factors boilerplate or the glossy graphs in financial reports. These are widely ignored, as are the smiling pictures.

In contrast, the 1902 report's discussion of risk, litigation, and environmental issues is much briefer, since legal and regulatory issues were not on top of managers' minds during those happy days. Back then, managers could focus on the business, rather than spend so much valuable time with lawyers and lobbyists; yet another reason for the vastly different 1902 versus 2012 operating performance of US Steel.[3]

REAL IMPROVEMENTS SPOTTED?

Potentially more informative is the 2012 Management Discussion and Analysis (MD&A) section, mandated by the SEC in the early 1990s, in which managers discuss the main factors affecting the most recent financial results and economic situation of the company, compared with the previous two years. Such a managerial discussion was not required in 1902, and is in any case beyond the confines of the accounting system on which we focus.

In terms of accounting, the main difference between the 1902 and 2012 reports is in the footnotes (explanations) to the financial reports. There are only a few footnotes to the 1902 report, whereas in the 2012 report there are no less than 54 pages of explanations and details of accounting matters. Exciting reading, to be sure. Some footnotes just rehash accounting principles known to anyone who took and still remembers Accounting 101 (and a complete mystery to those who didn't), such as that the consolidated reports include US Steel and its subsidiaries, that much of the information reported is based on managerial estimates, that property, plant & equipment is reported at original cost, or that pension costs are also based on estimates. All rather innocuous information.

Potentially more informative is the segment (lines of business) report, classifying certain items by type of product, but much of this was also reported in 1902. Four pages of footnotes discuss stock options awarded to managers and employees in 2012. One wonders how the early US Steel managers produced such remarkable results without the generous stock options incentives and motivation that current managers demand.[4] The 2012 footnotes include 12 pages on various pensions' issues and 4 more pages on environmental matters. Finally, full 6 pages of footnotes recast five years of historical financial data of US Steel—completely redundant these days, since all those data, and much more, are readily available on the Web.

The voluminous footnote disclosure in current financial reports reflects, of course, the surge in accounting regulation. The Financial Accounting Standards Board (FASB)—the accounting rule-making body in the United States—keeps churning new accounting and reporting rules at a breathtaking pace. In its 40-year existence (founded in 1973), the FASB has issued over 250 rules and regulations (standards and updates), some running, with interpretations, hundreds of pages long. This regulatory avalanche, on which we will have more to say later on, requires strict compliance by companies and attention by auditors and results in ever-more-lengthy explanations in financial report footnotes. Just the 2012 US Steel footnote on "Significant Accounting Policies" is 7 pages long. Overall, it's doubtful that the 174-page 2012 report provides substantially more relevant information than the 40 pages released in 1902, but we will hold final judgment until we complete our comprehensive evaluation of empirical evidence.

Still, we find striking that the far-reaching changes in corporate strategy and business organization over the past century didn't have any effect on the structure of corporate financial reports—especially considering that there was, for example, no outsourcing in 1902, currently rendering physical assets in many companies (e.g., Cisco) immaterial; nor was information technology a leading asset early in the twentieth century; alliances and joint ventures were rare; and just-in-time strategy didn't reduce the importance of inventory. Similarly, the profound changes over the past 110 years in the demand for financial information have not been met with commensurate improvements in the financial reports released by public companies to their shareholders.[5] This is the case, despite investors' sophistication (primarily hedge funds and private equity, in recent decades), vast improvement in communication technologies (XBRL, Internet chat rooms), increases in the extent of competition among investors, and in the number of alternative investments available to them worldwide. The consequence of this disclosure ossification, as we will demonstrate empirically in the following chapters, is the inevitably fast and continuous deterioration in the usefulness of financial information to investors.

A DEVIL'S ADVOCATE

Perhaps, you may say, this is inevitable. Corporate financial reporting reached its technological apogee 110 years ago, as did double-entry bookkeeping 550 years ago, and cannot be further improved, like the QWERTY keyboard layout introduced in 1878 in the Remington No. 2 typewriter and still on keyboards today. Absurd as this sounds, it would have made some sense if suggestions for accounting change were seriously tried and found to fail. But there wasn't any serious trial and error in accounting structure over the past century. Even worthwhile suggestions for structural change, like the one by a leading accounting thinker, Yuji Ijiri, a now retired Carnegie Mellon professor, who proposed in 1989 the *triple entry bookkeeping*, which, to the best of our knowledge, was never seriously discussed by accounting regulators.[6] In essence, Ijiri suggested that, in addition to the balance sheet (a static report of assets and liabilities), and the income statement (a report on the "distance" the firm traveled from beginning to end of period), there should be a third report, akin to *acceleration* or *momentum* of operations, informing on the pace of change over the period in sales, expenses, and earnings. Two companies may have identical *total sales* in a quarter, but one firm's sales have been increasing (positive momentum), while the other's sales have been declining toward quarter's end. Wouldn't investors be highly interested in the different paces of change? Of course they would. Such a report would substantially enhance investors' ability to predict future corporate performance. But despite the fact that Ijiri proposed a detailed accounting procedure to measure and report business momentum, the triple accounting idea didn't gain any traction.

To be fair, while the structure of financial reports is frozen in time, the meaning and reliability of the data conveyed may have improved. After all, new accounting procedures related to the measurement and reporting of specific assets, liabilities, revenues, and expenses have proliferated over the years, particularly in the past two-to-three decades. This substantial regulatory growth reflects a genuine attempt by accounting rule makers all over the world to improve the information conveyed by public firms to investors and other stakeholders. But the downside of this regulatory surge is a constantly increasing complexity of financial information and an ever-larger reliance on subjective managerial estimates and projections. On balance, only a thorough empirical analysis can weigh the pros and cons of accounting regulations, and on such an analysis we embark thus.

TAKEAWAY

Surprisingly, with all the advances in information technology, communication, and investment analysis affecting capital markets, as well as the substantial changes affecting the strategies and operations of businesses, the structure and content of corporate financial reports to investors didn't change during the past century. Investors, 110 years ago, received similar balance sheets and income statements as do their present counterparts. This would suggest a constant decrease in the role of financial information in investors' decisions, a phenomenon we document empirically in the following chapters.

APPENDIX 1.1

1. A profit and loss statement

UNITED STATES STEEL CORPORATION AND SUBSIDIARY COMPANIES.

GENERAL PROFIT AND LOSS ACCOUNT

Year Ending December 31, 1902.

GROSS RECEIPTS.		
Gross Sales and Earnings...		$560,510,479.39
MANUFACTURING AND OPERATING EXPENSES.		
Manufacturing and Producing Cost and Operating Expenses...		411,408,818.36*
Balance		$149,101,661.03
Miscellaneous Manufacturing and Operating Gains		
and Losses (Net)..	$2,654,189.22	
Rentals received...	474,781.49	
		3,128,970.71
Total Net Manufacturing, Producing and Operating Income..		$152,230,631.74
OTHER INCOME.		
Proportion of Net Profits of properties owned but whose operations		
(gross revenue, cost of product, expenses, etc.) are not included		
in this statement...	$1,972,31645	
Interest and Dividends on Investments and on Deposits, etc..............	3,454,135.50	
		5,426,451.95
Total Income...		$157,657,083.69
GENERAL EXPENSES.		
Administrative, Selling and General Expenses (not including		
General Expenses of Transportation Companies).....................	$13,202,398.89	
Taxes	2,391,465.74	
Commercial Discounts and Interest..	1,908,027.90	
		17,501,892.53
Balance of Income...		$140,155,191.16
INTEREST CHARGES, ETC.		
Interest on Bonds and Mortgages of the Subsidiary Companies.........	$3,879,439.91	
Interest on Bills Payable and Purchase Money Obligations of		
Subsidiary Companies and Miscellaneous Interest.....................	2,234,144.43	
Rentals paid...	732,843.10	
		6,846,427.44
Net Earnings for the Year, see page 5..		$133,308,763.72

FIGURE A1.1a   The Original 1902 US Steel Financial Report: A Profit and Loss Statement

2. A balance sheet

CONDENSED GENERAL BALANCE

ASSETS.

PROPERTY ACCOUNT:

Properties owned and operated by the several companies........... $1,453,635,551.37
  Less Surplus of Subsidiary Companies at date of
  acquirement of their Stocks by U. S. Steel Cor-
  poration, April 1, 1901................................ $116,356,111.41
  Charged off to Depreciation and Extinguish-
  ment Funds.. 12,011,856.53
                                                                          128,367,967.94

$1,325,267,583.43

DEFERRED CHARGES TO OPERATIONS:

Expenditures for Improvements. Explorations, Stripping and Development at Mines,
  and for Advanced Mining Royalties, chargeable to future operations of the
  properties.. 3,178,759.67

TRUSTEES OF SINKING FUNDS:

Cash held by Trustees on account of Bond Sinking Funds.................................... 459,246.14
  ($4,022,000 par value of Redeemed bonds held by Trustees not treated as an asset.)

INVESTMENTS:

Outside Real Estate and Other Property....................................... $1,874,872.39
Insurance Fund Assets 929,615.84
                                                                                      2,804,488.23

CURRENT ASSETS:

Inventories $104,390,844.74
Accounts Receivable.. 48,944,189.68
Bills Receivable... 4,153,291.13
Agents' Balances... 1,091,318.99
Sundry Marketable Stocks and Bonds....................................... 6,091,340.16
Cash 50,163,172.48
                                                                                      214,834,157.18

$1,546,544,234.65

FIGURE A1.1b   The Original 1902 US Steel Financial Report: A Balance Sheet

SHEET, DECEMBER 31, 1902

LIABILITIES

CAPITAL STOCK OF U. S. STEEL CORPORATION:
Common	$508,302,500.00	
Preferred	510,281,100.00	**$1,018,583,600.00**

CAPITAL STOCKS OF SUBSIDIARY COMPANIES NOT HELD BY
U. S. STEEL CORPORATION (*Par Value*):
Common Stocks...	$44,400.00	
Preferred Stocks..	72,800.00	
Lake Superior Consolidated Iron Mines, Subsidiary Companies..	98,714.38	**215,914.38**

BONDED AND DEBENTURE DEBT:
United States Steel Corporation Bonds....................................	$303,757,000.00	
Less, Redeemed and held by Trustee of Sinking Fund............	2,698,000.00	
Balance held by the Public...	$301,059,000.00	
Subsidiary Companies' Bonds..........................$60,978,900.75		
Less, Redeemed and held by Trustees of Sinking Funds..1,324,000.00		
Balance held by the Public...	59,654,900.75	
Debenture Scrip, Illinois Steel Company....................................	40,426.02	**360,754,326.77**

MORTGAGES AND PURCHASE MONEY OBLIGATIONS OF
SUBSIDIARY COMPANIES:
Mortgages	$2,901,132.07	
Purchase Money Obligations..	6,689,418.53	**9,590,550.60**

CURRENT LIABILITIES:
Current Accounts Payable and Pay Rolls..................................	$18,675,080.13	
Bills and Loans Payable..	6,202,502.44	
Special Deposits due Employes and others..............................	4,485,546.58	
Accrued Taxes not yet due..	1,051,605.42	
Accrued Interest and Unpresented Coupons..............................	5,398,572.96	
Preferred Stock Dividend No. 7, payable February 16, 1903..	8,929,919.25	
Common Stock Dividend No. 7, payable March 30, 1903.............	5,083,025.00	**49,826,251.78**
Total Capital and Current Liabilities..		**$1,438,970,643.53**

SINKING AND RESERVE FUNDS:
Sinking Fund on U. S. Steel Corporation Bonds.........................	$1,773,333.33	
Sinking Funds on Bonds of Subsidiary Companies......................	217,344.36	
Depreciation and Extinguishment Funds....................................	1,707,610.59	
Improvement and Replacement Funds.......................................	16,566,190.90	
Contingent and Miscellaneous Operating Funds........................	3,413,783.50	
Insurance Fund..	1,539,485.25	**25,217,747.93**

BOND SINKING FUNDS WITH ACCRETIONS...		**4,481,246.14**
Represented by Cash, and by redeemed bonds not treated as assets (see contra).		

UNDIVIDED SURPLUS OF U. S. STEEL CORPORATION
AND SUBSIDIARY COMPANIES:
Capital Surplus provided in organization of U. S. Steel Corporation...	$25,000,000.00	
Surplus accumulated by all companies since organization of U. S. Steel Corporation	52,874,597.05	**77,874,597.05***
		$1,546,544,234.65

FIGURE A1.1b   (*Continued*)

3. Summary of financial operations (akin to a cash flow statement)

UNITED STATES STEEL CORPORATION AND SUBSIDIARY COMPANIES.

SUMMARY OF FINANCIAL OPERATIONS OF ALL PROPERTIES.

Year Ending December 31, 1902.

Showing the Net Resources for the Year and Disposition Thereof.

RESOURCES.

Profit and Loss Surplus for the year, per Income Account, page 6.................................		$34,253,656.75
Net Receipts appropriated from Earnings for Bond Sinking, Depreciation and Improvement Funds (See Income Account, page 8)..	$27,814,389.47	
Less, Payments therefrom to Trustees of Bond Sinking Funds...$3,604,064.43		
Expended for Extraordinary Replacements... 7,926,792.60	11,530,857.03	
	$16,283,532.44	
Net Receipts account Insurance and Contingent Funds during the year..	804,319.35	
Balance of Receipts for Year included in Fund accounts	17,087,851.79	
Bonds and Mortgages issued..	2,370,338.35	
Sundry Miscellaneous Receipts..	5,920.98	
Total Net Resources..	$53,717,767.87	

PAYMENTS MADE FROM ABOVE.

Expended for Additional Property and Construction, per page 15.........	$16,586,531.77	
Bonds and Mortgages paid (not including bonds redeemed with sinking funds)..	1,697,577.33	
Purchase Money Obligations, Bills Payable and Special Deposits paid off...	13,652,367.94	31,936,477.04
Balance of Net Resources for the year, accounted for as below..........................		$21,781,290.83

INCREASE IN CURRENT ASSETS, VIZ.:

In Sundry Securities and Investments...	$3,193,604.83	
In Accounts and Bills Receivable in excess of increase in Accounts Payable..	9,595,635.15	
In Inventories and Miscellaneous Accounts................................	12,625,946.02	
	$25,415,186.00	
Less, Decrease in Cash on hand December 31, 1902, as compared with preceding year...	3,633,895.17	
Balance as above..	$21,781,290.83	

FIGURE A1.1c   The Original 1902 US Steel Financial Report: Summary of Financial Operations

NOTES

1. The company continued to struggle since 2012 with low imported steel prices and high pension costs: While it now employs 45,000 workers, it pays pensions to 142,000 employees. To be fair, US Steel was virtually a monopoly in 1902, whereas in 2012 it is one of many fiercely competing steel producers. There is, however, a ray of hope. On August 24, 2015, Barron's article *U.S. Steel Shares Look Like a Steal*, on US Steel opened with: "The worst could be over for U.S. Steel, which has been hit hard by cheap Chinese imports and slumping demand from the oil industry . . . [share prices] could climb more than 60%, to $28 per share, by the end of 2016, as cheap imports wane, steel prices firm, and CEO Mario Longhi's restructuring begins to pay off" (p. 23).
2. See Feng Gu and Baruch Lev, "Overpriced Shares, Ill-Advised Acquisitions, and Goodwill Impairment," *The Accounting Review* 86 (2011): 1995–2022.
3. This brings to mind the great economist ("creative destruction") Joseph Schumpeter: "Success in conducting a business enterprise depends under present conditions much more on the ability to deal with labor leaders, politicians and public officials than it does on business ability . . . Hence, except in the biggest concerns [companies] that can afford to employ specialists of all kinds, leading positions tend to be filled by "fixers" and "trouble shooters" rather than by "production men." In Joseph Schumpeter, *Capitalism, Socialism, and Democracy,* 3rd ed. (New York: HarperPerennial, 1950), 386.
4. Interestingly, the 1902 report informs about an employee's subscription plan to purchase the preferred stock of the company to participate in the future profits of US Steel. The initial plan was very successful—oversubscribed by 100 percent.
5. What, of course, did change is the legal requirement of public companies, established by the 1933–1934 Securities Laws, to file periodic financial reports with the SEC. What also changed, and not for the better, is the auditor's report. Price, Waterhouse & Co.'s 1903 report said simply and clearly: "And we certify that in our opinion the Balance Sheet is properly drawn so as to show the *true* financial position of the Corporation . . . and the Income Account is a *fair* and *correct* statement of the net earnings. . . ." (emphasis is ours). Today's auditors (PricewaterhouseCoopers for US Steel; same auditor for 110 years!) avoid straightforward and clear terms like *true and correct reports*. Rather, they hide behind the statement that the financial reports "conform with accounting principles generally accepted in the United States of America." No longer *true*, just *conform* with a largely obscure set of accounting rules. Interestingly, after the Enron debacle, the *Economist* remarked that the real Enron scandal is that so much of what Enron did conformed with generally accepted accounting principles. So much for those principles.
6. Yuji Ijiri, *Momentum Accounting and Triple Entry Bookkeeping* (Sarasota, FL: American Accounting Association, 1989).

CHAPTER 2

And You Thought Earnings Are the Bottom Line

In which we burst the myth that "earnings move markets" by showing that the time-honored ritual of financial analysts and investment managers of predicting companies' earnings and basing investment decisions and recommendations—buy, sell securities—on these predictions, can be bested by simpler investment routines. Further, we show that the specter of companies missing the dreaded consensus earnings estimate has lost much of its relevance to investors. This is your first exposure to the fast-diminishing usefulness to investors of financial information—a major topic of this book.

THE LUCRATIVE EARNINGS PREDICTION

Forecasting corporate earnings (income) is a major endeavor of financial analysts, whether working for investment banks and independent outfits (sell-side analysts) or hedge funds and private equity firms (buy-side analysts). Financial (accounting) information is, of course, an important input into the earnings forecast models. Analysts use these forecasted earnings to form their stock recommendations to clients[1] and these forecasts also serve as the main benchmark—the *consensus estimate*—to evaluate corporate performance. Analysts' earnings forecasts (estimates), therefore, exert both direct and indirect effects on the equity investment decisions of most investors.

Many corporate managers play an active role in analysts' earnings forecasts by assisting (guiding) analysts in the prediction of sales and earnings. Such input to earnings prediction models is eagerly sought by analysts. Here is, for example, Frank D'Amelio, the CFO of pharmaceutical giant Pfizer Inc., guiding analysts in the company's third-quarter 2013 earnings conference call (October 29, 2013) about the expected financials for the full year 2013:

> *We are narrowing the [guided] reported revenue range to $50.8 billion to $51.8 billion.... Furthermore, these royalty payments [from the Enbrel collaboration with Amgen] will be much less than our current level of Enbrel profits.... Moving onto adjusted cost of goods sold as a percentage of revenue, we are narrowing this range to 18% to 18.5%. We are narrowing our adjusted SG&A expense range to $14.2 billion to $14.7 billion.... We are narrowing and lowering the reported diluted EPS range to $3.05 to $3.15.*[2]

Undoubtedly, the prediction of corporate earnings by elaborate models and multiple inputs is a pervasive and influential investment mechanism.

And indeed, there are very good reasons for analysts and investors to engage in earnings prediction. As Figure 2.1 shows, if you predict the annual earnings of companies in each industry and buy shares of the five highest earners ahead of their respective earnings release dates, while selling short the five lowest earnings companies, you would have beaten the market handily practically every year during the past quarter century.[3] In the post-crash

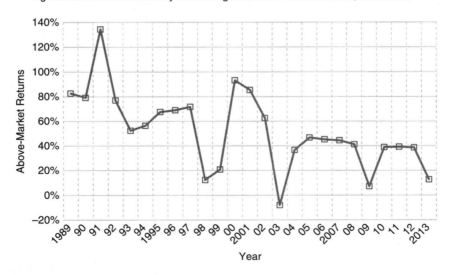

Yearly average above market returns from buying ahead of time the shares of the 5 highest earners in the industry and selling short the 5 lowest earners, 1989-2013

FIGURE 2.1 Predicting Companies' Earnings—A "Winning" Strategy

years, 2009–2013, you would have gained a cool, above-market, 27.3 percent per year, on average (see Appendix for details of our computation).[4] Hedge fund managers would kill for half the return. And not only they. Who wouldn't engage, or engage others (financial analysts, investment advisors) in predicting corporate earnings for such a bounty?[5] Not for nothing Wall Street's mantra is, "Earnings move markets." So, corporate reported earnings seem to matter a lot, and with them the entire massive corporate accounting and reporting systems whose bottom line is earnings. So why are we talking about accounting's relevance lost? Bashing accountants?

CURB YOUR ENTHUSIASM

Now that we have captured your attention with an over 25 percent investment yield, we have a surprise for you. If you substitute cash flows for earnings, namely, buy the shares of the five companies with the highest cash flows in the industry ahead of the cash flows release, and sell short the five companies with the lowest cash flows accordingly, you would have done *even better* than with earnings during 2009–2013—an annual, above-market, return of 35.4 percent.[6] Thus, predicting companies' cash flows would have yielded an 8 percent higher return annually than predicting earnings over 2009–2013. And, as we show in the Appendix to this chapter, predicting cash flows is easier (more accurate) than predicting earnings. A win-win situation.

So, all this massive time and effort spent by analysts in building and constantly updating earnings prediction models—analyzing quarterly corporate financial reports, grilling managers about key income statement items, predicting earnings components—could have been spared. Predicting cash flows is more straightforward and considerably less time-consuming than predicting earnings, because you don't have to forecast the numerous noncash items (accruals) that affect earnings, such as the bad-debt provision, pension and stock options expenses, and depreciation.

Please note that we aren't just substituting one accounting item (cash flows) for another (earnings). Cash flows are inherently different from earnings. They simply are the difference between cash received during the period from customers and paid to suppliers of services: vendors, employees, utilities, and more. Cash flow is a much simpler metric, more straightforward and easier to compute than earnings. It is, in essence, a "lemonade stand" measure: By the end of the day, your profit is total receipts from thirsty drinkers minus the cost of concentrates, ice, and assistants' (often below minimum wage) pay.

In contrast, the modern machinery of accounting, with its numerous noncash revenues and expenses and the marking of assets and liabilities to market (fair values)—which constitutes most of the extensive, worldwide accounting rules and regulations—was intended to *improve upon* the "primitive" concept of cash flows. This was made clear by the Financial Accounting Standards Board (FASB), the exclusive accounting rule-making body in the United States in its original conceptual framework:

> *Information about enterprise earnings based on accrual [noncash] accounting generally provides a better indication of an enterprise's present and continuing ability to generate favorable cash flows than information limited to the financial effects of cash receipts and payments.*[7]

Obviously, as our research shows, reported earnings, the end product of accounting measurement and valuation procedures, do not outperform cash flows, at least for their predicted values to generate investment returns.

Let's be clear: The focus of this book is not on cash flows. It's far more ambitious than that. We just wanted to demonstrate to investors that even the simplest of operating measures, a "lemonade stand" profit concept, beats the much-ballyhooed "bottom line" in terms of investor usefulness. We use cash flows here as a convenient benchmark to advance our message that the universally used corporate accounting and financial reporting system has outlived much of its usefulness and is badly in need of rejuvenation.

Frankly, we expect a certain reader skepticism at this stage. If earnings are beaten by cash flows, how come you didn't hear about this earlier? Why are all those smart and experienced financial analysts still forecasting quarterly and annual (and even three- to five-years-ahead) *earnings* when their usefulness has diminished so dramatically? The answer: because the deterioration in reported earnings'—and, by implication, accounting's— usefulness is a relatively recent phenomenon that very few realize, as we will demonstrate.

EARNINGS HAD ITS DAYS OF GLORY

Figure 2.2 traces the annual gains over the past quarter century from following each of the earnings and cash flow investment strategies. That is, investing ahead of the annual financial report release in the shares of the five companies with the highest earnings (or cash flows) in their industry, and selling short the five companies with the lowest earnings (cash flows) in the industry. As in Figure 2.1, this analysis is performed over all major US industries.[8]

Note that in the first nine years of the past quarter century, 1989–1997, earnings easily dominated cash flows in yielding investment returns. In some years (e.g., 1991 and 1995), the earnings strategy yielded more than twice the cash flow strategy. This was apparently the raisón d'etŕe for analysts' complex spreadsheets designed to predict earnings. Things, however, changed around the turn of the twenty-first century—and Part II of the book will pinpoint the reasons—as the edge of the earnings over the cash-flow strategy narrowed significantly, and commencing with the post-financial crisis, 2009, the edge of earnings over cash flows evaporated.[9] You've surely heard it before—"Nothing lasts forever." But this apparently flew under analysts' radar. They kept their allegiance to earnings.

Earnings no longer move markets as they used to, but you were not told about that. Don't be hard on yourself; you were still smarting from the financial crisis, and your mind was on other things. But now, it's important to recognize the message in Figure 2.2: Over the recent decades, there was a continuous erosion in the usefulness of reported earnings, relative to other information, a symptom of the decline of much of the usefulness of accounting information.[10] In Part I of the book, we provide comprehensive evidence supporting this usefulness fade.

Yearly average above market returns from buying ahead of time the shares of the 5 firms with the highest earnings (or cash flows) in the industry and selling short the shares of the 5 firms with the lowest earnings (or cash flows), 1989-2013

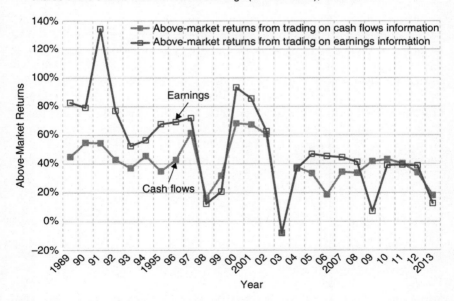

FIGURE 2.2 Pitting Earnings Against Cash Flow Strategies

BUT WAIT, WHAT ABOUT THE EARNINGS CONSENSUS?

You surely ask: How could reported earnings matter so little if we read every day in the financial media about companies releasing earnings that miss the dreaded analysts' consensus estimate, and the dire consequences of such misses? Didn't IBM's shares drop 7 percent on Monday, October 20, 2014, upon announcement of quarterly earnings that missed the consensus? Earnings don't matter?

Upon a closer consideration of the IBM case, though, the earnings miss was the least of the bad news causing the sharp share price drop. For starters, the more important "top line" news was worse: quarterly sales dropped 4 percent from the same quarter a year earlier ($22.4B vs. $23.3B), continuing a pattern of 10 quarters of flat or declining sales. The dream of IBM as a growth company vanished before our own eyes. Weighing even heavier on investors' mind was the announcement that "The Armonk, N.Y., technology giant said it no longer expects to earn at least $20 a share next year, a forecast it has maintained for five years and under two chief executives."[11] The bleak forecast, without releasing a revised one, was undoubtedly a major contributor to IBM's 7 percent share price drop. Thus, in the big scheme of things, particularly IBM's worn-out business model in urgent need of reinventing, the earnings consensus miss pales.

Short of such all-around mishaps, regular misses of the earnings consensus are, as Figure 2.3 shows, a minor event. For the 1,000 largest public companies having analysts quarterly earnings forecasts, this figure traces the share price consequences of missing the earnings-per-share (EPS) consensus by one-to-three cents, beating (surpassing) it by one-to-three cents, and exactly meeting the consensus.[12] The data, for the years 2011–2013, trace the average stock price movements (net of the overall market change) over a 75-day period starting with the quarterly earnings announcement day. The bottom curve is truly surprising: It shows that the "dire" consensus miss isn't so dire after all: On average, a missing company loses 1.5 percent of share price in the first week, barely a blip on stock screens (the average price drops to 2 percent by the end of the month, but by the second month recovers half of the loss, for an average decline of 1 percent). Beating the consensus by one-to-three pennies—a highly coveted outcome, which some executives will even "manage earnings" to achieve—will get you half a percentage point, inching up later to 1 percent. And meeting the consensus—the middle curve—causes investors a big yawn. You haven't heard this too before, because this is a new phenomenon: earnings surprises, relative to analysts' estimates, were much more consequential in previous periods, mainly because reported earnings reflected more of the real changes in business fundamentals, and less of transitory, one-time items.

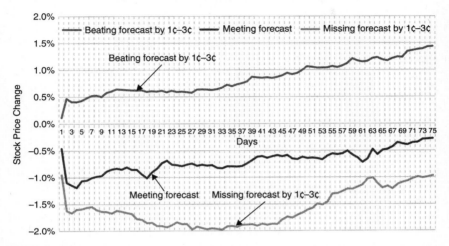

FIGURE 2.3 The Consequences of Missing or Beating the Consensus Earnings Estimate

Nowadays, for reasons we will make clear later on, reported earnings are largely detached from reality and don't really matter much. It is hard to argue with the evidence.

Memo to investors: Don't take it seriously when companies occasionally miss or beat the earnings consensus. Much more consequential are changes in the business fundamentals, like decreases in new customers or in policy renewals at insurance companies, same-store-sales changes, or the size of nonperforming bank loans. More on this is in Part III of the book.

TAKEAWAY

We examined in this chapter the two most prevalent uses of reported corporate earnings: generating earnings forecasts to guide investment decisions and assessing corporate performance by earnings surprises (relative to analysts' consensus estimates). In both cases, we found that the relevance of reported earnings to investors faded. In generating investment returns, earnings are surpassed by cash flows, and in assessing corporate performance, investors' feeble reaction to earnings surprises casts serious doubt on the economic meaning of reported earnings. Since earnings are the main outcome of the elaborate accounting measurement and valuation system, these findings are an early indication of things to come: comprehensive evidence of the diminished usefulness of accounting information to investors.

APPENDIX 2.1: COMPUTATION OF TRADING STRATEGY FOR FIGURES 2.1 AND 2.2

The yearly average above-market returns depicted in Figure 2.1 are measured as follows: First, we compute the above-market (abnormal) returns for each firm-year, 1989–2013, by subtracting the benchmark return on the Standard & Poor's 500 Index from the firm's return over a 12-month period that starts three months after the beginning of the fiscal year and ends three months after fiscal year-end.[13] Because firms' annual financial results are usually reported within three months after the end of the fiscal year, this return period ensures that firms' abnormal returns reflect the financial results from the most recent fiscal year. Second, for each industry in each year, we select the five companies with the highest accounting return on equity (ROE) and the five companies with the lowest ROE. We define an industry using the Fama–French 48-industry classification.[14] Third, we compute the yearly average above-market returns from buying at the beginning of the return accumulation period, the shares of the five most profitable (ROE) firms and selling short at the same time the shares of the five least profitable firms, across all industries in each year (known as a hedge portfolio return). The yearly sum of the average returns of the two groups is depicted in Figure 2.1, as the average annual yield from a perfect forecast of corporate earnings.

Figure 2.2 retains the yearly average above-market returns depicted in Figure 2.1 and adds the yearly average above-market returns obtained from buying, one year ahead of report release, the shares of the five companies with the highest cash flows from operating activities (divided by average total assets) in each industry and selling short ahead of report release the shares of the five firms with the lowest cash flows from operating activities in each industry. The procedure for computing the average above-market cash-flow returns to be earned is identical to that used for computing the yearly average earnings returns depicted in Figure 2.1.

APPENDIX 2.2: CASH FLOWS ARE EASIER TO PREDICT THAN EARNINGS

We compare the prediction error (accuracy) of earnings and cash flows from operations by performing two tests. First, we compute for each company the predicted value of earnings (cash flows) for next year as the previous

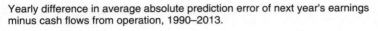

Yearly difference in average absolute prediction error of next year's earnings minus cash flows from operation, 1990–2013.

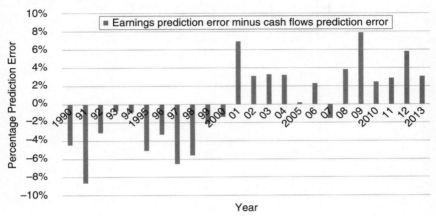

FIGURE 2A.1 Cash Flows Are Increasingly More Accurate to Predict than Earnings

year's earnings (cash flows) plus the average growth rate of earnings (cash flows) over the previous three years (an extrapolative prediction model). We then compute the *prediction error* of earnings (cash flows) as the absolute difference between the reported and predicted values of earnings (cash flows) as a percentage of the former.

Figure 2A.1 above depicts the yearly difference in average prediction errors, across all companies, between earnings and cash flows from 1990 to 2013. It shows that, from 1990 to 2000, earnings consistently had *smaller* mean prediction errors than cash flows (negative bars indicate earnings prediction errors smaller than cash flows' prediction errors). The opposite, however, was true for the later period of 2001–2013: For all but one year, earnings predictions were less accurate than cash flow predictions. This reversal indicates that over time, it has become easier (more accurate) to predict cash flows than earnings.

Our second test of prediction accuracy relies on analysts' forecasts. We compare analyst forecast errors for earnings per share (EPS) versus cash flows per share (CPS). We compute analyst forecast error for EPS as the absolute difference between consensus forecast of EPS and reported EPS, as a percentage of reported EPS. Analyst forecast error for CPS is similarly computed. Analyst forecasts of future EPS and CPS are obtained from I/B/E/S. All other data are obtained from COMPUSTAT and CRSP databases. Figure 2A.2 depicts the yearly difference (outliers removed) in average analyst forecast error for EPS and CPS from 2000 to 2013.[15]

The yearly difference between analysts' prediction errors of earnings and cash flows, 2000–2013

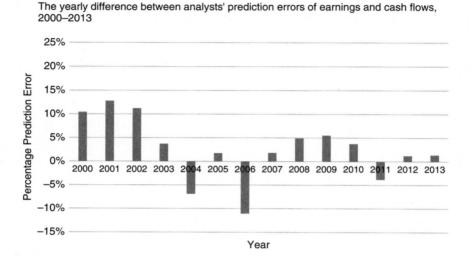

FIGURE 2A.2 Analysts Predict Cash Flows More Accurately than Earnings

It shows that for 11 of the 14 years examined (79 percent), analyst forecasts of cash flows had, on average, smaller forecast errors (positive difference between earnings and cash flows forecast errors), and were thus more accurate than earnings predictions. Thus, analysts were more successful predicting future cash flows than earnings.

NOTES

1. A recent analyst survey found, "More than 70% of analysts indicate that their own earnings forecasts are a very useful input to their stock recommendations. . . ." Lawrence Brown, Andrew Call, Michael Clement, and Nathan Sharp, "Inside the 'Black Box' of Sell-Side Financial Analysts," *Journal of Accounting Research*, 53 (1) (2015): 1–47.
2. And not only Pfizer. Here is, for example, Johnson & Johnson CFO during the company's third-quarter, 2013 conference call with analysts and investors (October 15, 2013): "I'd suggest you consider modeling net interest expense of between $350 and $400 million. . . . We would be comfortable with your models for 2013 reflecting other income and expense at a net gain of $500 to $600 million. . . . We suggest that you model our effective tax rate for the full year 2013 at between 19% and 19.5%. . . . We would be comfortable with

operational sales growth of between 6% and 7%.... We suggest that you consider full year 2013 EPS estimate of between $5.44 and $5.49.... We estimate this headwind [from the Yen devaluation] to negatively impact gross margin in 2014 by approximately 60 basis points."

Or, from the HCA (Hospitals Corporation of America), November 5, 2013, conference call: "We expect this [share] repurchase to be accretive to earnings.... And we would expect margins in that business [the Outsource Group] to ultimately be somewhere in the teens to possibly 20% range...."

3. Selling short is done when one expects a security's price to fall. It involves selling (often a borrowed) stock today and buying it back later on at a lower price, gaining the price differential.

4. Since we are combining companies of vastly different sizes in the analysis, and company size has a strong effect on earnings, we control for size in our analysis by focusing on the return-on-equity (earnings divided by book equity) measure, rather than on the absolute value of earnings. Our analysis is performed over all US public companies having the required data on the Compustat and CRSP databases we use.

5. It is, of course, very difficult, if not impossible, to perfectly predict corporate earnings across industries. Accordingly, Figure 2.1 gives you an upper bound of the gains to be had from earnings prediction. If you predict earnings well, though not perfectly, your gains will be close to those of Figure 2.1.

6. Again, to account for different company sizes, the variable we focus on is cash from operations divided by total assets.

7. Financial Accounting Standards Board, 1978, Statement of Financial Accounting Concepts No. 1: Objectives of Financial Reporting by Business Enterprises (Highlights). This clear statement seems to have been somewhat modified and blurred in subsequent revisions of the conceptual statements.

8. We start with 1989 since this is the first year for which Compustat reports cash flow statement data.

9. The 10-year, 2004–2013, average annual return of the earnings and cash flow strategies were almost identical (35.1% vs. 33.5%), whereas in the last five-year return, cash flows (35.4%) edged earnings (27.3%), particularly due to 2009.

10. Because the stock prices of many banking and other financial service firms experienced highly unusual and large declines during the financial crisis of 2008–2009 and then rebounded in the subsequent period, we have reexamined Figure 2.2 by excluding banking and other financial service firms from our sample. The results for the period prior to 2009 change very little, whereas the results for 2009–2013 show that the returns from trading on cash flows information are higher than those from trading on earnings information in every year.

11. IBM Woes Point to a Fresh Overhaul, *The Wall Street Journal*, October 21, 2014, p. 1.

12. We focus on the 1,000 largest companies, because many smaller companies are not followed by financial analysts, or only by one or two analysts, so that the

consensus forecast isn't meaningful. About half of the consensus EPS misses or beats are in the range of 1-to-3 cents.

13. For example, for a firm with fiscal year-end of December 31, 2012, the 12-month period for computing the return begins on April 1, 2012, and ends on March 31, 2013.

14. To ensure meaningful within-industry ranking and focus on major industries, we retain in our sample industries with more than 20 firms in every year.

15. Beginning in 2000, analyst forecasts of cash flows have become more prevalent.

One

Matter of Fact

In this part of the book, we provide comprehensive, large-sample—but very intuitive—evidence on the fast-diminishing usefulness to investors of accounting and financial report information. This evidence, provided here comprehensively for the first time, spans the past 50 to 60 years and is based on several, complementary research methodologies, employing state-of-the-art statistical techniques. They all point to one conclusion: a continuous and fast deterioration in the usefulness or relevance of corporate financial reports to investors.

Rest assured, this part of the book is not only for statisticians. Although the evidence is thoroughly statistically based, our presentation will be clear to any investor, manager, or accountant. A real page turner. If not, return the book within 30 days.

CHAPTER 3

The Widening Chasm between Financial Information and Stock Prices

If financial information is useful and affects investors' decisions, then key financial indicators such as earnings, sales, and asset values should be associated (correlated) with stock prices—high earnings, high capitalization (think Apple). This indeed is the case, but we show in this chapter that the strength of this association, and by implication, the relevance of financial information to investors, deteriorated markedly over the past half century. Decades ago, financial data determined stock prices; now they lost their edge to more timely and meaningful information sources. This is counterintuitive, given the constant and costly efforts of accounting regulators worldwide to improve the usefulness of financial reports.

HOW TO MEASURE THE USEFULNESS OF FINANCIAL INFORMATION

The information in corporate financial reports has various audiences: third parties contracting with the company (lenders, suppliers), labor unions, government, and regulatory agencies, among others. But capital market investors are undoubtedly the predominant group of financial information users. This is made clear by the 1933–1934 Securities Acts and the many Securities and Exchange Commission (SEC) regulations and enforcement actions that are aimed at ensuring that corporate financial reports both *inform* and *protect* investors. The Financial Accounting Standards Board (FASB)—the US standard-setter of accounting and reporting rules—concurs, stating:

> The objective of general purpose financial reporting is to provide financial information about the reporting entity that is useful to existing and potential investors, lenders, and other creditors in making decisions about providing resources to the entity. Those decisions involve buying, selling, or holding equity and debt instruments. . . .[1]

It can't be clearer than that. It is, therefore, appropriate that our tests of the usefulness of financial information will mainly consider the role of this information in investors' decisions.

How can one measure the usefulness to millions of investors of the information in a 174-page document, like the 2012 US Steel annual report? It sounds daunting, but, in fact, can be done. First, how to measure information usefulness in general? You measure it the same way you assess the usefulness of any product, like a loaf of bread or a box of cereal: by consumers' response to the product. Stale bread or tasteless cereal will stay on the shelf, shunned by consumers. Same with information; stale, uninformative messages will be ignored by investors, whereas relevant and timely information will trigger investors' decisions, which in turn, will impact stock prices and trade volumes. Thus, for example, on July 28, 2015, Twitter saw its stock price plummet 11 percent after hours, in response to a quarterly report that showed a weak sales growth and almost no growth in core users. Twitter's quarterly sales information was obviously highly relevant to investors, leading many to sell the stock, ultimately reflected in the sharp price drop.[2]

Stock prices thus reflect the aggregate reaction of investors to the information conveyed to them. Relating stock prices to financial information is, therefore, a straightforward way of assessing the relevance of this information to investors.[3] It also allows the *ranking* of alternative information sources. For example, is operating income a better performance measure than net income? Rather than engage in a futile debate about the merits of each indicator, or conduct a survey, one can examine the differential reaction of investors to reported operating and net income. The indicator that triggers the strongest reaction, measured either by the stock price change (stock return) or by the trading volume change, is more consistently reflected in share prices, and therefore is more useful to investors, simply because it was actually *used more extensively* by them.

Or, take another example: Until a few years ago, when a company's earnings beat (surpassed) the consensus analysts' estimate, investors reacted enthusiastically to the good news and the beater's stock price rose substantially. In recent years, however, investors wised up to the fact that many of those "consensus beats" are achieved either by manipulating the consensus forecast ("walking analysts' consensus down" by low managerial guidance) or by "managing" reported earnings. How else can one explain the fact that roughly 70 percent of public companies beat the quarterly earnings consensus,[4] a feat even more logic-defying than Don Johnson's winning $15 million in 2011 playing blackjack in Atlantic City casinos? The consensus beat (reported earnings exceeding the consensus) thus became largely irrelevant information to investors, and indeed, in recent years, it hardly triggers a stock price reaction (see Chapter 2, Figure 2.3). Relating stock prices to financial information is thus an objective and powerful gauge of the relevance or usefulness of accounting information to investors.

HONEY, I SHRUNK ACCOUNTING

To avoid undue suspense, we will tell you our findings up front, made clear by Figure 3.1. The steady decline of the graph, from over 90 percent in the 1950s (see horizontal scale, spanning the past 60 years) to around 50 percent currently—a fall of almost half—tells vividly the story of the decline in the relevance of corporate financial information to investors. That's quite a

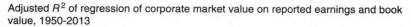

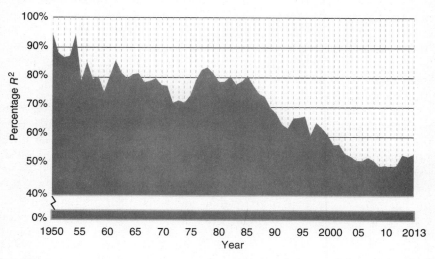

Adjusted R^2 of regression of corporate market value on reported earnings and book value, 1950-2013

FIGURE 3.1 Share of Corporate Market Value Attributed to Earnings and Book Value

fall from grace of the ubiquitous investors' information source—accounting and financial reporting.[5] You surely wonder: How did we achieve such an accurate measurement of decline in information usefulness? How can information relevance be measured so precisely? Please keep reading. It will be worth your while.

SOME USEFUL DETAILS

First, how do we capture the information content of corporate financial reports extending over 150 to 200 pages? We have to be highly selective, of course. Much of the "information" in these reports, like the pictures of the ever-smiling executives, employees, and customers, or the long discourses on the company's products and its many do-goodings, is either outright useless for investment decisions or readily available on the Web. Ditto the extended discussion of risk factors and historical stock price data. But then there are scores of seemingly relevant financial items, like revenues, accounts receivable, cost of sales, and earnings. Obviously, not all of them can be captured in a statistical study. And they don't have to be, if one wisely chooses a few *summary measures*, reflecting the essence of the financial report.

We chose for our initial study the two most widely used indicators of a company's operations and economic condition: earnings (net income) and book value, or equity (balance sheet assets minus liabilities). The former reflects the enterprise's performance during the period—revenues minus all expenses—whereas the latter (net assets) captures its economic position, or net worth at the end of the period: reflecting the company's underlying external *sources of funds* (borrowed money and other indebtedness) vis-à-vis the *uses of fund* (the various assets employed by the enterprise).[6] In earnings and book value, we thus have a parsimonious yet representative set of key financial information items, which uniformly ranks at the top of investors' decision determinants.

Turning to investors' use of earnings and book values, we focus on companies' stock prices three months after fiscal-year-end (during which time the annual reports have to be publicly released) to assure that these stock prices impound the most recent information contained in the two financial items we examine. We then statistically relate for each year, over the past 60 years, the market values (the product of stock price and the number of shares outstanding) of all US public companies with the required data to their recent respective earnings and book value (see the Appendix for a more formal discussion of this analysis). Market values (capitalization) of companies reflect, of course, multiple sources of information, such as interest rates, industry conditions (e.g., depressed real estate in the financial crisis), and monetary policy (the Fed's "quantitative easing"), in addition to companies' earnings and book values. Accordingly, our statistical methodology (a regression analysis) enables us to answer the following question: Of all the information items reflected in companies' market values (stock prices), how much is attributed to corporate earnings and book values? This is the message of Figure 3.1: roughly 80 to 90 percent in the 1950s and 1960s versus 50 percent today.

AND NOW FOR SOME INTUITION

To fully appreciate the meaning of the drop to 50 percent in Figure 3.1, one has to intuitively grasp the derivation of these numbers. We mentioned that we applied a regression analysis. But, what is this creature? A regression is a statistical technique, akin to a correlation, relating one variable, or indicator (dependent variable), to a set of other variables (explanatory variables), intended to answer the following question: How much of the variation in the former (different market values of companies in our case) is explained by, or can be attributed to, the set of explanatory variables? In our case, to what extent do companies' earnings and book values explain their different market values? This question is answered by the regression's adjusted coefficient of variation, or R^2 (henceforth R^2), which is depicted on the vertical axis of Figure 3.1. If differences among companies' market values are mainly attributable to their performance (earnings) and financial situation (book value), then the R^2 will be high (close to 100 percent), whereas if other factors are dominant in setting stock prices, the R^2 will be low. What Figure 3.1 tells us is that in the 1950s, 1960s, and even 1970s, the key financial report variables, earnings and book values, were critical to investors' valuation of companies, whereas the usefulness or relevance of these two variables to investors has diminished considerably since then.[7]

A brief example of a regression analysis in a widely familiar context will solidify your understanding: Suppose medical researchers wish to ascertain the main causes of the different cholesterol levels of people (to understand why yours is so high). They suspect that age, weight, and education level (affecting health awareness) affect cholesterol levels. To determine the impact of these effects quantitatively, the researchers first measure the cholesterol level of members of a sample of, say, 500 persons, and then run a regression of the 500 measured cholesterol levels (akin to our companies' market values) on the 500 triple measures of each person's age, weight, and school years (like our earnings and book values). Suppose the measured R^2 of this regression is 35 percent. This means that the *combined* effect of a person's age, weight, and education level accounts for (or explains) about a third of the (squared) differences in people's cholesterol levels, implying that almost two-thirds of the determinants of cholesterol level are still unknown to the researchers. The search for additional cholesterol determinants, like food intake or parents' cholesterol level, should go on. Now you are a statistical maven and appreciate our empirical finding: The role that earnings and book values—the key financial indicators—play in securities valuation dropped by almost 50 percent during the past half century.

WHO'S THE CULPRIT—EARNINGS OR BOOK VALUES?

Figure 3.1 reflects the *joint* relevance-loss of earnings and book values. Since accounting standard setters sometimes change their emphasis from the balance sheet to the income statement (focusing on income measurement as the primary objective of accounting) and vice versa (emphasizing the valuation of assets and liabilities over earnings), it's instructive to examine *separately* the change over time in the relevance of earnings, the all-important "bottom line" of the income statement, and that of the book value, reflecting the balance sheet information concerning the company's assets and liabilities.

Using the same research methodology previously described, Figures 3.2 and 3.3 portray separately the relevance patterns of earnings and book values to investors. It's clear from the figures that the two patterns are similar: relative stability from the 1950s to the early 1980s, at a range of 80 to

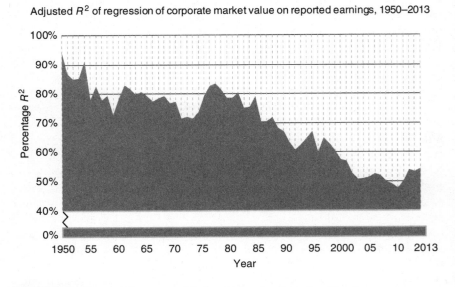

Adjusted R^2 of regression of corporate market value on reported earnings, 1950–2013

FIGURE 3.2   Share of Corporate Market Value Attributed to Earnings

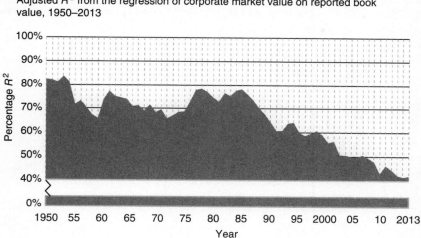

FIGURE 3.3   Share of Corporate Market Value Attributed to Book Value

90 percent for earnings and 70 to 80 percent for book values, and a quick deterioration thereafter. Thus, the causes affecting the deterioration in the relevance of financial information (to be discussed in the concluding section) similarly affect both earnings and book values. Come to think of it, this is not totally surprising: By the structure of accounting procedures, what affects the income statement also affects the balance sheet, and vice versa. The immediate expensing of R&D, for example, depresses earnings (income statement) as well as assets and equity values (balance sheet). For better or worse, accounting is a closed system.

ARE WE FAIR TO ACCOUNTING?

Not really. We draw a rather strong conclusion—accounting information has lost much of its relevance to investors—from examining the association of only two financial information items with stock prices. Isn't it too hasty to base a conclusion on just two, albeit key, financial items? And as one of our colleagues reminded us, one of the indicators—corporate earnings—is very volatile, and therefore, hardly a reliable measure value. Perhaps a consideration of a larger number of financial indicators, including more stable measures, like sales (revenue), will change our view of the usefulness lost? We agree, and therefore depict a reanalysis with triple the number of indicators.

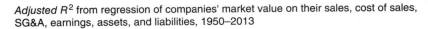

Adjusted R^2 from regression of companies' market value on their sales, cost of sales, SG&A, earnings, assets, and liabilities, 1950–2013

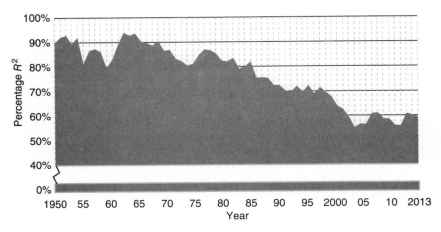

FIGURE 3.4   Share of Corporate Market Value Attributed to Multiple Financial Indicators

Figure 3.4 portrays the association for all US companies with the required data between market values (capitalization) of companies and *six* key financial indicators: sales, cost of sales,[8] SG&A (sales, general, and administrative expenses), earnings, total assets, and total liabilities. Undoubtedly, this is a comprehensive list of key performance and financial condition indicators. But, lo and behold, Figure 3.4's pattern is awfully similar to that of Figure 3.1. As in Figure 3.1, the curve reflecting the explanatory power of the larger set of indicators in Figure 3.4 starts in the 1950s from over 90 percent of R^2, and portrays the familiar continuous deterioration to roughly 50 to 60 percent recently. Thus, with tripling the number of financial indicators and essentially getting the same result, it's highly unlikely that piling on additional items from the financial report will yield a different pattern. We seem to have discovered a general phenomenon: a continuous deterioration over the past half century, accelerated since the late 1980s, in the association between companies' capital market values and their recently reported financial (accounting) information.

An important note: It may be argued that the continuous decrease in the relevance of financial data is driven by the recent entrance to the market of new, small companies. To dispel this notion, we replicated the analysis in Figures 3.1 and 3.4 on the 1,000 largest companies, most operating over long periods of time. Rest assured: This analysis (starting in 1965) yields very similar results to those of Figures 3.1 and 3.4: A 90 percent to 50 percent drop.

HOW CAN THIS BE?

We document that the role of *reported* financial information in investors' decisions eroded systematically and quite rapidly over the past half century, despite the unprecedented expansion of the scope of accounting regulation during this period, particularly by the Financial Accounting Standards Board (FASB), which commenced accounting rule making in 1973. What explains this counterintuitive trend of declining usefulness of accounting? While we provide a full evidence-based explanation in the second part of the book, we give you a glimpse below.

A clue to accounting's relevance lost lies in a close inspection of Figure 3.4: While the curve declines slightly from the 1950s to the mid-1970s, the drop really began to pick up steam from the late 1970s. Something started in those years to increasingly distance financial information from reality (stock prices). Any astute economic observer can easily guess the impetus: The 1980s saw the emergence and steep rise in the economic role of intangible (intellectual) assets. Revolutionary changes, shifting economies and business enterprises from the industrial to the information age, started to profoundly affect the business models, operations, and values of companies in the 1980s, yet, amazingly, triggered no change in accounting. Entire industries, which are largely intangible (*conceptual industries,* as Alan Greenspan called them), including software, biotech, and Internet services, came into being during the 1980s and 1990s. And for all other businesses, the major value drivers shifted from property, plant, machinery, and inventories, to patents, brands, information technology, and human resources. The latter set, all missing from companies' balance sheets because accountants treat intangible investments like regular expenses (wages, or interest), thereby distorts *both* the balance sheet and income statement. The constant rise in the importance of intangibles in companies' performance and value creation, yet suppressed by accounting and reporting practices, renders financial information increasingly irrelevant. We will, in fact, prove this to you empirically in Chapter 8.

But the emergence of intangibles is not the only factor adversely affecting accounting usefulness. Successive accounting regulations have increased the role of managerial subjective estimation and forecasting in the calculation of financial items (asset write-offs, fair valuing of assets and liabilities), further diminishing the integrity and reliability of financial information and distancing it from reality. Warren Buffett famously quipped of the requirement to mark to market nontraded assets/liabilities: "This is not marked-to-market, rather marked-to-myth." And if this were not enough, an increasing number of important business events, such as the success/failure of products under development, a significant technological change, or a misfit acquisition, affect share prices immediately (though inaccurately) but impact financial variables only after long delays. These three factors—intangibles, the proliferation of managerial estimates, and delays in recognizing important business events—all on the rise in recent decades, combine to strip currently reported financial information of much of its value, as will be shown in Part II. The terms *earnings, assets,* and *expenses* remain the same as 50 to 60 years ago, but their relevance to investors has been sharply declining.

TAKEAWAY

The usefulness of financial (accounting) information to investors is reflected in the association between key financial variables and companies' stock prices. We have provided in this chapter comprehensive evidence that this association deteriorated markedly over the past half century, a clear sign of the loss of accounting's relevance. As bad as this is, reality is even worse. The straightforward research methodology we use in this chapter—correlating financial information with stock prices—masks a more serious usefulness deterioration documented in the next chapter, which should be skipped by diehard accountants bent on believing that financial information effectiveness is improving.

APPENDIX 3.1

We obtained the yearly adjusted R^2s shown in Figure 3.1 from the annual cross-sectional regressions of sample firms' market value (MV) on their recently reported net income (NI), book value of equity (BV), and the number of shares outstanding (NSH).[9] The regression model is as follows:

$$MV_{it} = a_{1t} + a_{2t}NI_{it} + a_{3t}BV_{it} + a_{4t}NSH_{it} + e_{it},$$

where i and t are firm and year subscripts, respectively. To ensure that market value reflects all the recent information on earnings and book value, we use market value as of three months after the firm's fiscal year-end to which earnings and book value pertain.[10]

Similarly, the yearly adjusted R^2s shown in Figures 3.2 and 3.3 are obtained from the annual regressions of sample firms' market value on their accounting earnings (book value) and the number of shares outstanding. The yearly adjusted R^2s shown in Figure 3.4 are obtained from the annual regression of sample firms' market value on their sales, cost of goods sold, selling, general, and administrative (SG&A) expenses, net earnings, total assets, and total liabilities. The samples for all regressions include all US-listed companies with the required data, as retrieved from the intersection of the Compustat and CRSP databases for 1950 to 2013.

NOTES

1. FASB, 2010, Statement of Financial Accounting Concepts No. 8, Conceptual Framework for Financial Reporting, Chapter 1, Introduction.
2. See Yoree Koh, "Twitter Ad Woes Subside but Growth Stalls," *The Wall Street Journal* (July 29, 2015), B1.
3. Some readers, accustomed to the proliferation of surveys and polls in many walks of life, may wonder why we don't survey investors about the relevance of financial information. First, our main objective is to examine relevance patterns over half a century, which requires consistent surveys from the 1960s, 1970s, and on. Such surveys are obviously unavailable. Second, as the Nobel laureate economist Milton Friedman once remarked in a class one of us took: "When complex decisions are involved [like valuing securities], it's better to observe people's actions, rather than ask them how they reached their decisions." Experience, intuition, and even luck underlie investors' decisions, but these are very difficult to articulate. Observing investors' decisions, as reflected in stock prices, is a more reliable and objective way of assessing information relevance.
4. See Marcus Kirk, David Reppenhagen, and Jennifer Wu Tucker, "Meeting Individual Analysts Expectations," *The Accounting Review*, 89 (2014): 2203–2231.
5. Similar analyses, though on shorter spans of time, were conducted earlier. For example, Baruch Lev and Paul Zarowin, "The Boundaries of Financial Reporting and How to Extend Them," *Journal of Accounting Research*, 37 (1999): 353–385.
6. We aren't the only ones to use book value as a financial health indicator. Warren Buffett, in his celebrated annual reports to shareholders, focuses on changes in Berkshire Hathaway's book value (equity), which he considers a key measure of operating performance. These changes, primarily from retained earnings, reflect the accounting-based growth in shareholder value.
7. The value of 80 to 90 percent of capitalization differences attributed to financial information in the 1960s and 1970s may strike some readers as exceedingly high. We think it is not surprising that back then, differences among companies' market values mainly reflected reported earnings and book values. Many information sources that in recent years affect stock prices, such as analysts' earnings forecasts, managers' guidance, or automatic program trading, didn't exist half a century ago, leaving financial variables such as earnings and book values as the main determinants of capitalization differences.
8. By having sales and cost of sales in the regression, we implicitly also consider the gross margin (sales minus cost of sales), which most financial analysts reckon as one of the most important operating indicators.

9. This approach follows Mary Barth and Sanjay Kallapur, "The Effects of Cross-Sectional Scale Differences on Regression Results," *Contemporary Accounting Research*, 13(2) (1996): 527–567.

10. This regression is run on the *levels* of the variables (market value, earnings, and book value). A *change* regression yields similar results: Anup Srivastava reports for annual regressions of stock returns on levels and changes in earnings that the adjusted R^2 "... of the new-firm segment declines from 20.4% to just 2.6% from the period 1970–1974 to the period 2005–2009 ... the average earnings relevance for seasoned firms declines less dramatically, from 20.1% to 14.4%." See Anup Srivastava, "Why Have Measures of Earnings Quality Changed over Time?" *Journal of Accounting and Economics*, 57(2014): 196–217.

CHAPTER 4

Worse Than at First Sight

In which we apply a more sophisticated research methodology to examine the contribution of financial information to investors, focusing on the decision-relevant element of the information and comparing financial reports to alternative information sources available to investors. This accurate reading of financial information usefulness yields a highly surprising, or depressing, result: corporate quarterly and annual reports currently contribute only 5 to 6 percent (!) of the total information used by investors. What a loss for accounting's relevance.

WHEN IS A MESSAGE INFORMATIVE?

A critic once commented on Richard Wagner's music: "It's not as bad as it sounds." The reverse is true for the degree to which accounting has lost its relevance, as portrayed in Figure 3.1: The deterioration is actually worse than it looks. Figures 3.1 and 3.4 might give the impression that financial reports currently convey about 40 to 50 percent of the information used by investors—less than the 80 to 90 percent of a half century ago, to be sure, but still a respectable contribution. After all, in the 1960s and 1970s, financial reports were the only game in town as far as investors' information was concerned, whereas today, a large number of buy- and sell-side financial analysts and sophisticated online investor services provide substantial information for securities' valuation. Competition in the financial information market is fierce, and providing 40 to 50 percent of investors' needs is very respectable. So, what's our problem? Accounting still seems to be very relevant.

This is an illusion, unfortunately. In fact, the amount of *new* or relevant information conveyed today by corporate financial reports is much less than 40 to 50 percent; it is more like 5 percent. Yes, 5 percent. To see that, we first have to explain our emphasis on "new" information in the previous sentence. Why new? Simply, because as far as information usefulness is concerned, *newness* and *timeliness* are of the essence. This is a subtle issue that requires elaboration.

Pardon the following brief tutorial, aimed at clarifying an important information principle, central to *information (communication) theory*, which was developed in the 1940s by Claude Shannon and Warren Weaver and played an important role in the development of computers and communication systems.[1] The theory provides a measure of the amount of information conveyed by a message. For example: "It will start raining at 3:00 p.m. tomorrow." This measure is based on the extent of *surprise*, or *unexpectedness* of the message to the receiver. If, for example, it is now November in Seattle, and it rained heavily the whole week, a forecast of rain continuation tomorrow isn't that surprising, implying a low information content of the "rain tomorrow" forecast. If, in contrast, the 3:00 p.m. rain forecast is issued in the summer in an arid area, like the Middle East, the same forecast is very surprising and therefore highly informative and useful (the action called for: plant seeds today). Information content is thus a function of the surprise, or newness of the message, to the receiver.[2] End of tutorial.

The fairly simple statistical methodology underlying Figures 3.1 and 3.4 in the preceding chapter cannot determine the extent to which the information in the financial reports was new (surprising) to investors. It only measures to what extent the information examined (sales, earnings, assets, etc.) is *consistent with* the information impounded in stock prices. This is an important distinction. Suppose, for example, that a company's income statement shows that earnings rose 20 percent from last year—a healthy earnings growth. This is definitely important information to investors. But, what if the financial analysts following this company *predicted* (consensus estimate) a 20 percent earnings growth prior to the financial report release, based on industry trends, or the earnings growth of similar companies? Then the just-released income statement is in fact a nonevent to investors. It just confirmed what they had already expected. Remember: no surprise, no information. Research indeed shows (middle curve in Figure 2.3, Chapter 2) that reported earnings which just confirm analysts' expectations don't trigger a significant stock price response, since the stock price already impounded analysts' expectations.[3] Stated differently, the 20 percent reported earnings growth in the previous example was late to the game and therefore largely irrelevant to investors' decisions.

But note, and this is important, the 20 percent reported earnings growth in our example will still be *correlated* with the stock price, despite the fact that it was the earlier analysts' forecast, rather than the earnings report that triggered the price increase. This is akin to the 40 to 50 percent association measure in Figures 3.1 and 3.4 in recent years, which doesn't necessarily indicate that financial reports affected share prices. Thus, Figures 3.1 and 3.4 do not reflect the crucial issue of information timeliness—being first to market. What these figures actually say is that earnings, book values, and other key financial indicators are currently *consistent* with about half of the information reflected by stock prices (down from 80 to 90 percent), but they fail to say to what extent those financial indicators, *when they were publicly disclosed to investors*, were in fact actionable: news capable of moving markets. If they were, for example, preempted by analysts' forecasts, managers' guidance, industry trends, or other information sources, then the financial reports were largely uninformative to investors (except for the small confirmation effect, to which we return later). To recap: Usefulness of financial information depends on its timeliness, or newness, as demonstrated thus.

A PREEMPTED ANNOUNCEMENT

On January 21, 2014, telecommunication giant Verizon reported fourth-quarter 2013 results: a 73.7 percent EPS growth from the year-earlier quarter, and a revenue growth of 3.4 percent year-over-year. Stellar results to be sure. Investors, however, greeted the great news with a big yawn—Verizon's stock price was largely unchanged around the announcement. How can this be? A 73.7 percent EPS growth chump change? No, but investors weren't surprised at all by the fourth-quarter good news. The financial report was completely preempted by the analysts following Verizon, whose consensus earnings estimate preceding the report release fell only one penny short of Verizon's actual EPS. Thus, while the financial report information was indeed stellar, analysts had stolen its thunder. The earnings report was late to the game. Accordingly, to measure the real contribution of financial information to investors, one has to go beyond a mere correlation of accounting information with stock prices—our preceding analysis—and examine the impact of financial report information on investors' decisions *relative to* competing information sources. Such an analysis follows.

MEASURING FINANCIAL REPORT TIMELINESS

To measure the timeliness—or the new information content—of financial reports, we consider the main information sources for investors and focus on *investors' reaction* to these information sources, all dealing with corporate performance and value. Investors' reaction is measured by the stock price change from the day before to the day after the information release.[4] The performance-related information sources we examined are as follows:[5]

1. **Financial reports:** quarterly and annual earnings releases, as well as the filing with the SEC of the 10-Q (quarterly) and 10-K (annual) reports.[6] We thus consider here all the information in financial reports, rather than selected items, as in the preceding chapter.
2. **Other corporate SEC filings:** various (nonaccounting) required company filings, like 4-K, revealing insider trading; and 8-K, announcing new developments (new products, contracts, directors change, etc.), concerning important business events.[7]
3. **Analysts' forecasts:** earnings/sales forecasts and forecast revisions made by financial analysts.
4. **Managers' forecasts:** managers' pre-earnings release forecasts and guidance regarding future firm performance, disclosed separately from financial reports.

These are the four main company-related information sources that affect share prices. Most other effects on share prices are not directly related to the company, like anticipated changes in interest and inflation rates, regulatory changes, or an impending economic slowdown. So, the question we are posing here is: *Relative to* the nonaccounting (beyond financial statement information sources) managers' and analysts' forecasts, and nonaccounting filings with the SEC, what was the unique contribution of financial report (accounting) information to investors' decisions during a year? Thus, for example, if an earnings report is preempted by analysts' forecasts, as in the preceding section case, investors will react to the forecast revision (a significant stock price change around the revision), while the reaction to the subsequent earnings release will be muted (no price change). Accordingly, the information contribution will be credited in our analysis to the analyst forecast (category 3, above), rather than to financial reports (category 1).

We perform this test of unique information contribution over the 21-year period, 1993–2013, since analysts' forecasts were rare before 1993. All publicly traded US companies with the required data are included in our test. To recap, the usefulness of each of the four information sources just mentioned is measured by the three-day stock price change around the information release day. Informative messages will trigger large price changes, whereas uninformative ones will leave the price largely unchanged. These stock price changes, averaged over the sample companies, enable us to measure unique information usefulness, focusing on the timeliness (decision relevance) of the information.

Since we are now asking a deeper question than that raised in the preceding chapter, the statistical methodology required for estimating the *unique contribution* of financial reports, given competing information sources, is more involved and requires a certain statistical knowledge. A technical explanation of the methodology we use is, therefore, provided in the Appendix to this chapter, but rest assured that the following discussion will be clear to the general reader.

ROLL THE TAPE

Figure 4.1 presents the contribution to investors of three of the four information sources described above (managers' forecasts are deleted from the exhibit to avoid cluttering the figure). The percentages you see on the vertical axis of the graph indicate the unique contribution of each information sources to the total information investors used during the year. Thus, for example, on the left side of the graph (the year 1993), the top dot indicates 10 percent, implying that financial report information, source no. 1, uniquely contributed 10 percent of investors' information in that year. This is a relatively high contribution, because the other two sources (analysts' forecasts and SEC nonaccounting filings) were rare in the early years. But the most remarkable finding revealed by Figure 4.1 is that, whereas the information contribution of analysts and SEC nonaccounting filings increased markedly during the past 20 years (in 2013, SEC filings and analysts forecasts contributed 25 percent and 20 percent, respectively, of total information used by investors), the contribution of the financial reports (including earnings announcements and quarterly and annual filings with the SEC) decreased by almost a half (from 10 percent to 5–6 percent).[8] A sad commentary indeed, at least for accountants and accounting educators like us.[9]

Note the increasing usefulness to investors of analysts' forecasts and nonaccounting SEC filings in Figure 4.1, particularly from the early 2000s. Analysts' forecasts gained prominence and ubiquity, mainly due to SEC Regulation Fair Disclosure (adopted in 2000), which provided a wider range of analysts—not just privileged ones—with firsthand company information. This regulation increased the number of analysts and the quality of their information, and consequently investors' reliance on their forecasts, as indicated by Figure 4.1. As to company SEC (nonaccounting) filings, their number and impact, particularly of 4-K and 8-K filings, increased substantially in response to the SEC's expanded requirement for public announcement of important business events (new contracts, director changes, etc.). The upshot: While company-related information increasingly affects the price of securities, financial (accounting) information is losing ground to its more timely and relevant competitors.

Percentage of all information used by investors contributed by financial reports, analysts' forecasts, and nonaccounting events. All firms, years 1993–2013

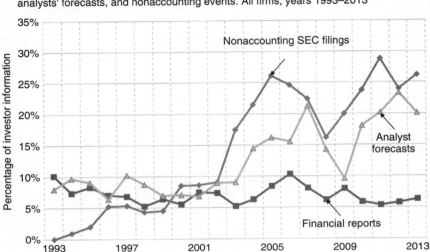

FIGURE 4.1   The Unique Contribution to Investors' Information: Financial Reports, Analysts' Forecasts, and Nonaccounting SEC Filings

AREN'T WE TRIVIALIZING ACCOUNTING'S CONTRIBUTION?

We have documented that analysts' and managers' SEC filings provide considerable information to investors, often preempting the subsequent earnings announcement. This created a pushback from certain early draft readers, arguing that the analysts' message cannot be separated from the subsequent earnings announcement, because the ability to validate the forecast against reported earnings gives the forecast its relevance. Stated differently, without the release of reported earnings, keeping the forecasters honest, analysts' estimates would be largely irrelevant. We beg to differ. The fact that investors react strongly to the *release* of analysts' forecasts and forecast revisions implies that analysts are considered by investors informed experts about companies' future operations. The same holds true with people's response to weather forecasts—evacuate areas threatened by storms—irrespective of whether the storm subsequently materialized or not. Even if quarterly reports were abolished, there surely will be a need for experts (e.g., analysts) to inform investors of companies' operations as the year unfolds; if anything, in the absence of quarterly reports, this need would grow.[10]

The current contribution of the financial report is primarily in *updating* investors' information; that is, highlighting differences between forecasts and actuals. A reported $2.00 EPS relative to a $1.80 consensus estimate informs investors of the need to revise upward their assessment of the company's performance. That's the information contributed by the earnings release. But note, we fully capture this information contribution by measuring the three-day stock price reaction around the surprise in earnings releases, and attribute it in Figure 4.1 to category 1—financial (accounting) information contribution. So we give accounting its due, but not more. What is not captured by our analysis is the somewhat elusive "contextual role" of financial reports. These reports provide a financial history of the company, enabling investors to better interpret other information items (e.g., a new contract). So, the actual contribution of financial (accounting) information may be somewhat higher than 5 percent, but, given the major flaws of this information (Part II of the book), not much higher, we believe.

TAKEAWAY

The research methodology we use in this chapter allows us to focus on the unique information contribution of financial reports—the new, decision-triggering content of their message—relative to competing information sources. The surprising finding is that, whereas information related to corporate operations (SEC filings, etc.) has an increasing impact on investors' decisions, only a small amount of that information is contributed by companies' quarterly and annual reports. An accounting fade, to be sure.

APPENDIX 4.1

For each year, 1993–2013, Figure 4.1 portrays the unique contribution to investors' information of three corporate-related information sources: (1) financial accounting reports (quarterly earnings announcements, 10-K filings, 10-Q filings, and related filings), (2) nonaccounting corporate SEC filings, and (3) analysts' forecasts. Managers' forecasts (management earnings guidance) were included in the analysis but not exhibited in Figure 4.1. The unique contribution of a given information source in a calendar year is measured by the partial R^2 associated with the information source for the year. The procedure for computing the partial R^2s for financial (accounting) reports—source no. 1—is illustrated as follows:

First, for each quarter, the quarterly buy-and-hold abnormal return of a firm's shares (CAR) is regressed on the three-day buy-and-hold abnormal

returns associated with each of the three following types of events (information sources): corporate (nonaccounting) SEC filings (CAR_SEC), analysts'
forecasts (CAR_AF), and managers' forecasts (CAR_MF), that is, the nonaccounting events occurring during the calendar quarter. The cross-sectional
regression model is as follows (pooling across quarters of the year):

$$\text{CAR}_{jt} = a_t + b_t \text{CAR\_SEC}_{jt} + c_t \text{CAR\_AF}_{jt} + d_t \text{CAR\_MF}_{jt} + \varepsilon_{jt}, \qquad (4.1)$$

where j and t are firm and year subscripts, respectively. The residual of this
regression is ε_{jt}.

Second, the three-day buy-and-hold abnormal returns associated with
the firm's financial accounting reports released during the calendar quarter
(CAR_FAR) are regressed on the three-day buy-and-hold abnormal returns
associated with the three nonaccounting events: corporate (nonaccounting)
SEC filings (CAR_SEC), analysts' forecasts (CAR_AF), and managers'
forecasts (CAR_MF). The regression model is as follows (pooling across
quarters):

$$\text{CAR\_FAR}_{jt} = \alpha_t + \beta_t \text{CAR\_SEC}_{jt} + \chi_t \text{CAR\_AF}_{jt} + \delta_t \text{CAR\_MF}_{jt} + \rho_{jt},$$
$$(4.2)$$

The residual of this regression is ρ_{jt}.

Finally, the residuals from the first regression (ε_{jt}) are regressed annually
on the residuals from the second regression (ρ_{jt}):

$$\varepsilon_{jt} = \kappa_t + \gamma_t \rho_{jt} + \theta_{jt}. \qquad (4.3)$$

The R^2 of this regression (equation (4.3)) is the unique contribution
to investors' information of firms' financial reports, in a given year, and is
reported in the bottom line of Figure 4.1. The unique contributions of firms'
other information sources—corporate SEC filings, analysts' forecasts, and
managers' forecasts—are computed similarly, and exhibited in Figure 4.1.[11]

If an information source encompasses multiple events during a calendar
quarter (e.g., more than one earnings guidance is issued by management during the quarter), the abnormal returns for this source are the sum of abnormal returns across all individual events. For a given information source, we
include only events that do not coincide with the events of other information
sources (e.g., we exclude managers' forecasts that occur on the same day as
quarterly earnings are announced). Sample firms included in Figure 4.1 are
all US-listed companies with the required data, obtained from Compustat,
CRSP, I/B/E/S First Call, and the S&P SEC Filings Database.

NOTES

1. Claude Shannon and Warren Weaver, *The Mathematical Theory of Communication* (Champaign–Urbana: University of Illinois Press, 1949).
2. Mathematically, the amount of information conveyed by a message is measured in communication theory by the logarithm of the ratio of the prior (before the message was received) to the posterior (after the message reception) probabilities of the event (e.g., rain at 3:00 pm tomorrow) occurring. Thus, if my probability for rain tomorrow is, say, 30 percent, and after receiving the rain forecast, I revise the probability to 90 percent, then the amount of information of the weather forecast is $\ln(0.9/0.3) = 1.10$. If, for example, I am not confident about the rain forecast and revise my rain probability to 50 percent only, the amount of information in the forecast decreases by over 50 percent to $\ln(0.5/0.3) = 0.51$.
3. Analysts frequently use the expression, "The expectation is baked in the price."
4. This widely used research methodology is known as an "event study," putting a much sharper focus on the impact of information on its receivers, rather than the association analysis performed in the previous chapter.
5. A similar approach was used by Anne Beyer, Daniel Cohen, Thomas Lys, and Beverly Walther, "The Financial Reporting Environment: Review of the Recent Literature," *Journal of Accounting and Economics*, 50 (2010): 296–343. The period covered in this study is 1994–2007, while ours is 1993–2013.
6. Some companies provide a forecast (guidance) of future earnings/sales with the earnings release. These forecasts generally have a significant effect on stock prices, often a larger effect than the earnings release itself. Since we cannot empirically separate the accounting (earnings release) from the nonaccounting (forecast) information, we deleted the earnings releases that were jointly announced with a forecast from this analysis.
7. We made sure to exclude corporate filings with financial report (accounting) information from this category, to distinguish it clearly from category 1.
8. The dip in the top two curves of Figure 4.1 around 2007–2008 is likely due to the financial crisis, when practically all stock prices plummeted, severing their close relation to fundamental information.
9. A similar conclusion was reached by Ray Ball and Shivakumar Lakshmanan, "How Much New Information Is There in Earnings?" *Journal of Accounting Research*, 46 (2008): 975–1016. "We conclude that the average quarterly announcement is associated with approximately 1 percent to 2 percent of total annual [investor] information."
10. Reported earnings are useful in enabling investors to assess the accuracy of individual forecasters.
11. We don't exhibit in the figure the contribution of managers' forecasts to avoid cluttering the exhibit.

CHAPTER 5

Investors' Fault or Accounting's?

In the preceding chapters, we documented the fast-diminishing relevance of financial report information to investors. But why blame accounting for that? Perhaps investors became increasingly less sophisticated or more irrational, subject to fads and hysteria, and therefore shunned the potentially useful accounting information? In this chapter, we accordingly apply a test of accounting usefulness that is detached from investors and capital markets. We put the spotlight on accounting itself. Given that the major use of reported earnings in investment analysis is to predict future company performance, we examine the accuracy of predicting future earnings from those previously reported and find a continuous erosion of accuracy, indicating a marked deterioration in the ability of reported earnings to predict corporate performance. Relevance lost once more.

IRRATIONAL INVESTORS?

The previous chapters' evidence, showed the following: (i) Over the past 60 years, the role of corporate earnings, book values, and other key financial indicators in setting share prices diminished rapidly, and (ii) in terms of information timeliness, or relevance to investors' decisions, financial report information (not just earnings and book values) is increasingly preempted by more prompt and relevant information sources. When the financial reports are publicly released, their thunder is largely stolen.

While solidly based on large-scale empirical data, our conclusions could be challenged on the grounds that they are drawn from two moving parts:

share prices and financial information. What we have essentially shown is that the link between the two has been seriously eroding over the past half century, representing a rapidly widening chasm between accounting information and investors' decisions. We then put the blame squarely on the decrease in usefulness of financial information. But, some colleagues challenged us: What if the culprit is the stock price? What if investors became less rational and sophisticated over time, increasingly affected by, say, psychological factors, moods, or fads? Wasn't the tech bubble of the late 1990s a classic example of such investor irrationality?[1] Hundreds of "dot.com" startups, based on flimsy business models, nevertheless sucked up billions of dollars of investors' money, going down the drain shortly thereafter.[2] These investors, rather than evaluating dot.com prospects on the basis of fundamentals (sales, business model) relied on unproven measures, such as "clicks" and "eyeballs," irrespective of the hard facts showing mounting losses and nonexistent assets. Isn't that evidence of gross irrationality on the part of investors? And what about the hundreds of biotech companies currently burning rapidly through cash and producing deep losses, but nevertheless commanding billions of dollars in market values? If, indeed, investors' valuations are increasingly irrational, erratic or delusional, even the best of information systems will exhibit a deteriorating link with stock prices. Why then pick on accounting?

There is, of course, an obvious flaw in such investor irrationality explanation to our evidence. For investors' irrationality to cause the *deteriorating* link between stock prices and financial information that we document, it's not enough that certain investors are sometimes irrational, or just silly. Some surely are. But for a *deteriorating* link to exist, investors would had to become *increasingly* irrational and less sophisticated over the past half century. More irrational in the 1990s than in the 1950s and 1960s, and less sophisticated in the 2000s than in the 1990s. What's the evidence supporting such a runaway irrationality? There is none. On the contrary, it is well known that every process governed by learning from education and experience—and investing is definitely such a process—leads to improved decision making over time (ascending the learning curve), not deterioration.[3] Indeed, the dot.com craze of the 1990s didn't repeat in the 2000s with, say, social media, or alternative energy companies. Even Facebook's superhyped IPO (2012) was greeted by investors with deep skepticism and sharp price declines. So, it's highly unlikely that financial report information retained its usefulness, while investors' capacity to use this information deteriorated markedly.

Nevertheless, given the importance of the issue, it is incumbent upon us to cover all bases and provide more nuanced evidence on the usefulness of financial information, evidence that is not dependent on a specific group of users. We do this below, focusing on the primary financial information item—earnings (net income).

EYES TO THE FUTURE

Henry Ford, who knew a thing or two about business, famously said: "History is more or less bunk." So, why is anybody interested in corporate financial reports? After all, they are purely historical documents, describing, not very accurately or with great timeliness, the firm's performance (sales, earnings) and financial position (assets, liabilities), as of the prior year or quarter. What relevance can such backward-looking information have for investors' decisions, which are based on prospective outcomes, such as a company's future cash flows, products, or market share? Apple's sharp share price decline during late 2012 and early 2013 (close to 40 percent) wasn't a reaction to a deteriorating past or current performance—which continued to be stellar—rather, the consequence of investors' concerns about the continuation of the revolutionary, Steve Jobs-initiated innovations by Apple and the encroachment of competitors, Samsung in particular, on its turf. Analysts' *forecasts* move markets, not their analysis of past financial reports.

So, why are investors interested in financial reports, as evident, for example, by the reaction of stock prices to disappointing earnings announcements? The answer is that, Henry Ford notwithstanding, people generally believe that financial history tends to repeat itself, to a certain extent.[4] That one can learn from past sales or earnings about future corporate performance. There is certainly some justification for such belief: Many social processes, as well as institutions, like governments and business enterprises, exhibit a certain "path dependence," namely the evolution of the process or institution depends, in part, on its history—where it came from and the impact of changes that have occurred along the way (large acquisitions, say).[5] In other words, a path-dependent process is one where its history affects its future evolution. History matters.

Take the leading oil company Exxon, for example. Its 2012 net income—a staggering $44.9 billion, larger than the 2011 GDP of 114 UN member nations—isn't a fluke. Exxon has been ranked at the top of corporate earners worldwide for many decades. Why? Mainly because of path dependence. Exxon's almost $45 billion income in 2012 is the outcome of the business ingenuity of its founder, John D. Rockefeller, its heavy investment over decades in oil prospecting and explorations, as well as on the careful development of highly skilled personnel, global relationships with governments, satisfied customers, and trusting shareholders. All those past investments in physical and human capital charted an increasing path of development and growth for the company that can be expected to persist for a considerable time. Even major environmental disasters, like the Exxon Valdez spill (March 1989), were, in retrospect, just a hiccup in the relentless growth path of the company.[6]

Given a certain degree of path dependence in the evolution of all business enterprises, historical financial reports presumably provide a basis for predicting their future performance, after allowing, of course, for foreseeable future changes in economic conditions (recessions) and circumstances (major restructuring). Thus, Benjamin Graham, the "father" of systematic investment research, and Warren Buffett's teacher at Columbia University, wrote in his classic book *Security Analysis: Principles and Techniques*: "In the absence of indications to the contrary, we accept the past record [of earnings] as at least the starting basis for judging the future" (1951, p. 425). Warren Buffett refined this approach, suggesting that the long-term average of past earnings is an even better predictor of the future earnings of a business, since it smoothes out transitory fluctuations.

In case you wonder where we are going with all this, rest assured, we are on course: Path dependence—justifying the use of earnings in predicting future corporate performance—provides the basis for our next test of the usefulness of financial information. In what follows, we examine the ability of reported earnings to predict future corporate profitability over the past half century, as an alternative test of accounting information usefulness, independent of investors' rationality and acumen in setting stock prices—a capital markets-free test.

PREDICTING CORPORATE EARNINGS

Suppose it is now early January 2012, and, fulfilling a New Year's resolution, you are reviewing your portfolio and consider particularly your large investment in Exxon. You have read about the recent considerable fluctuations in oil prices, and you are naturally concerned about your exposure to Exxon's future performance. For starters, you would like to get a reasonable estimate of Exxon's 2012 full-year earnings and use it to predict the end-of-year stock price, using Exxon's normal P/E ratio. Following Graham's and Buffett's prescriptions (previous section), a reasonable estimate of Exxon's 2012 earnings will be the most recently reported 2011 earnings of $41.06 billion. But you know you can do better than that. Since Exxon's earnings, along with those of most large public companies, are growing over time, adding to Exxon's 2011 earnings its average earnings growth rate over the prior five years—3.6 percent per year—will provide a better estimate than just last-year's earnings. Thus, you predict Exxon's 2012 earnings to be $42.54 billion: $41.06 billion (2011 earnings) + a 3.6 percent growth.

In fact, Exxon's 2012 earnings came in a bit higher: $44.88 billion. But your prediction of $42.54 billion was prescient: You, in fact, missed the actual earnings by just 5.2 percent ([44.88–42.54]/44.88). Pretty good for a back-of-the-envelope forecast, even compared with the 17 financial analysts following Exxon—all experts on Exxon and the oil and gas industry—which had in January 2012 a mean (consensus) full-year earnings estimate of $46.27 billion, overshooting actual earnings by 3.1 percent. Surprise—you are in the same league as the experts.

One can devise, of course, more sophisticated models to predict earnings than the above: last-year's earnings plus average growth. Taking into account expected events—like the termination of the Fed's "quantitative easing," leading to higher interest rates, or an impending corporate acquisition—will likely improve the accuracy of the forecast. But our aim in this chapter is not to devise the best earnings prediction model, but rather, to focus on the ability or usefulness of reported earnings to predict those in the future. Our test is designed for this specific purpose.[7]

Back to our task of assessing reported earnings' usefulness over time. We use the earnings prediction model described above over a large sample of thousands of US public companies—all listed companies with the required data, spanning the past half century—to determine changes in the usefulness of reported earnings in predicting future earnings, which is, to remind you, the major use of historical earnings by investors. Our focus is on the annual percentage prediction error (reported minus predicted earnings, divided by reported earnings)—like the 5.2 percent in the preceding Exxon example—over the entire sample. Here, one encounters a technical but serious problem: If you compute the average earnings prediction error over, say, 1,000 companies, then positive (undershooting) and negative (overshooting) firm-specific errors will, to a large extent, cancel out each other. Thus, a poor prediction model, generating large positive and large negative errors, will look like a successful one when the company-specific prediction errors are averaged over the sample. It is better to consider the "absolute value" of the error for each company, namely the error without the sign (both +5.2 and −5.2 percent enter the analysis as simply 5.2 percent). Focus on the *magnitude* of the earnings miss, irrespective of its direction, and then average the absolute values of the company-specific forecast errors over the entire sample.[8] That is what we do thus.

AND THE RESULTS ARE...

Figure 5.1 portrays the annual median absolute prediction error of two widely used performance measures: total earnings, and the more meaningful metric of return on equity (ROE); the latter accounts for the widely different sizes of the sample companies. To recap, for each company, next year's earnings (or ROE) are predicted as the prior year's earnings (ROE) plus the mean three-year growth rate. In each year, 1954–2013, the median of the company-specific absolute prediction errors over the entire sample is

Median absolute prediction errors from estimating one-year-ahead earnings (or ROE) from past reported earnings, all firms, 1954–2013

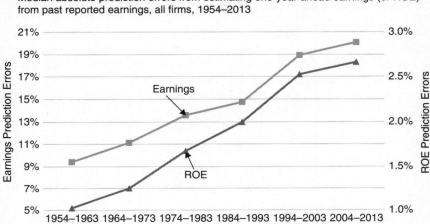

FIGURE 5.1 Declining Ability of Reported Earnings to Predict Future Earnings

computed, to yield a point in Figure 5.1. We replicated Figure 5.1, based on three-year growth rate, with predictions derived from five-year growth rates—there is nothing sacred about the three-year growth—and obtained essentially identical results to those portrayed in Figure 5.1.

The message portrayed by Figure 5.1 is unmistakable: The annual median prediction errors of both earnings and ROE have increased quite steeply and almost continuously over the past half century.[9] Thus, for example, the median prediction error of earnings in Figure 5.1 (left axis) more than doubled, from about 9 percent to 20 percent. Nine percent prediction error (actual earnings minus forecasted earnings, divided by actual earnings) indicates a reasonably good prediction for a 12-month ahead forecast that is solely based on previously reported annual earnings. Twenty percent error renders the prediction, and with it reported earnings, rather unreliable. The ROE predictions (right axis) demonstrate an even larger deterioration of accuracy. Bottom line, no pun intended, is that reported earnings are becoming *less and less useful* in predicting companies' future earnings, the major use of earnings by investors.[10] This evidence of deteriorating usefulness of earnings is obviously consistent with the previous chapters' evidence, but importantly, the prediction-based evidence of this chapter doesn't rely on investors' understanding and correctly using financial information. We have thus reached a similar conclusion about the financial report relevance lost, using three very different research methodologies (two in Chapters 3 and 4 and one here).

REASONS, PLEASE

We know you are dying to comprehend the reasons for the rapidly deteriorating ability of reported earnings to predict company performance. How could the usefulness of the key financial item—earnings—deteriorate in face of all the efforts that accounting regulators invest in improving the quality of earnings to reflect the performance of the enterprise, as well as the enforcement actions of regulators (SEC, PCAOB) to enhance the integrity (honesty) of reported earnings? Ironically, some of these very same efforts are among the main reasons for the decreasing predictive-ability of earnings. Speak about unintended consequences!

While a full explanation for the diminishing usefulness of financial information awaits you in Part II of the book, to satisfy your curiosity, we briefly outline a major reason for the deteriorating predictive ability of earnings—the proliferation of the so called *one-time items*. Those are revenue and, particularly, expense items included in quarterly or annual earnings that do not recur in future periods. Their sporadic and often large impact on reported earnings diminishes the ability of past earnings to predict those in the future. It is as if results of past elections were frequently affected by large population changes or catastrophic events, rendering those election results irrelevant for the prediction of future ones. Consider, for example, United Technologies, the aerospace/defense contractor, which charged (reduced) fourth-quarter 2012 income with $258 million restructuring costs arising from workforce reduction and consolidation of manufacturing operations, all in an effort to improve performance.[11] Fourth-quarter 2012 earnings fell 27 percent relative to the same quarter a year earlier (EPS of $1.05 vs. $1.44), as a result of the restructuring charges. Obviously, these abnormally low earnings are poor indicators of future United Technology earnings, particularly if the restructuring efforts succeed in improving the company's performance.[12]

The proliferation in recent decades of accounting regulations that require companies to include numerous one-time, transitory items in earnings—such as assets and goodwill write-offs, or gains/losses from marking assets and liabilities to market values, all intended to improve the valuation of assets and liabilities on the balance sheet—plays havoc with the ability of reported earnings to reflect enterprise performance and predict future earnings.[13] Like in the United Technologies example, these items increase the volatility of reported earnings, thereby eroding their predictive ability. If you doubt the detrimental potency of "one-time" items, look at Figure 5.2, which traces, for all US public companies with positive earnings, the mean ratio of "special and extraordinary item"—the income statement category that includes most one-time items—over earnings.

Average ratio of "special" and "extraordinary" income statement items to net earnings, 1950–2013

FIGURE 5.2 Increasing Impact on Earnings of Transitory Items

The steeply increasing curve—from less than 2 percent to 17 percent of earnings—demonstrates vividly the continuous increase in the impact of transitory items on reported earnings, diminishing their usefulness as predictors of future operations.[14] One-time items, are, of course, not the only detractors of earnings usefulness, as we will show in Part II, but they do considerable damage.

The implications of this much-diminished usefulness of the bottom line for investors, lenders, and others relying on this seemingly important indicator ("earnings move markets") are obvious.[15]

INVESTORS ALERT: AN ACCOUNTING LOSS ISN'T WHAT IT USED TO BE

"Losses loom larger than gains" famously said Amos Tversky and the Nobel (economics) laureate Daniel Kahneman, meaning that people strongly prefer avoiding losses to acquiring gains.[16] So, reporting a loss is a big deal for a company and its constituents, and it better be a credible signal of a company in distress, not a false alarm. Which brings us to another surprise for you: Many of the losses reported by companies are due to accounting procedures that don't really reflect a permanent deterioration of business fundamentals. This is a false but expensive alarm to investors.

How do we know? For each of the past 50 years, we ranked the 1,000 largest US corporations by their return-on-equity (earnings over book value), and focused on the bottom decile (10 percent), populated by losing or very poorly performing enterprises. You don't want to be there. And here comes the crux of our simple, but cogent test: If poor reported earnings really reflect business fundamentals (failing operations, outdated technology), which usually don't change quickly (think Blackberry, Nokia, or Kodak, which struggled for years before succumbing to reality), then companies ranked in the bottom decile one year will tend to stay in the bottom profitability decile the next year. Real losers remain losers, in life as well as in business. If, in contrast, earnings are largely affected by chance or accounting rules detached from business fundamentals (expensing of intangible investments), then many companies ranked in the bottom decile one year, will escape this inglorious categorization the following year.[17]

Our analysis shows that in the 1950s and 1960s, 60 percent of the companies ranked bottom 10 percent of profitability in a given year remained in the bottom 10 percent in the subsequent year. This retention percentage decreased to 50 percent in the 1970s, and further to 45 percent in the 1980s, currently at 40 percent. So, about 60 percent of the companies currently reporting a loss aren't in fact, real losers, because they recover and report a lower loss or profit in the subsequent year. Accordingly, before you panic and dump the stock when a company you are invested in reports a loss, check carefully the reasons for the loss. Likely they are temporary: a write-off, effect of an accounting change, or simply bad luck.

TAKEAWAY

Corporate earnings garner close investor attention because they are widely believed to be harbingers of future performance. That's the reason earnings are said "to move markets." The tests provided in this chapter lay this belief to rest. Reported earnings no longer provide a reliable basis to predict future corporate performance, mainly due to successive accounting regulations that contaminated those earnings with multiple nonrecurring, transitory items. Sheer noise. Even reported losses aren't what they used to be—reliable indicators of serious operating business problems. The lesson: In evaluating corporate performance and predicting the course of business, investors should use more reliable gauges than earnings, like those proposed in Part III. This lesson is particularly important to individual investors who tend to rely on a few summary measures, primarily earnings and the price-to-earnings ratio, in their investment decisions.

NOTES

1. Robert Shiller, one of the 2013 Nobel winners in economics, was awarded this highest recognition mainly for his research on investors' irrationality. See his book *Irrational Exuberance* (Princeton University Press, 2005).
2. The tech bubble burst in 2000, as NASDAQ lost 50 percent of its value, a slide that continued through 2002.
3. Ample evidence indicates that investors learn from mistakes, thereby increasing the efficiency and rationality of capital markets. For example, it has been shown in the 1990s that investors got overly enthused with companies whose reported earnings outstrip cash flows (high accrual firms). Investors, enamored with the high earnings, invested heavily in such companies, only to see the shares of investee companies decline in the following year or two, when the vulnerability of these earnings (often manipulated, or containing large one-time items) became evident. These prevalent investors' mistakes—dubbed Sloan's "accruals anomaly"—were, however, corrected in the 2000s, as shown by the evidence that large accruals (earnings higher than cash flows) no longer attract investors' funds; see Jeremiah Green, John Hand, and Mark Soliman, "Going, Going, Gone? The Apparent Demise of the Accruals Anomaly," *Management Science,* 57 (2011): 797–816.
4. Someone cynically quipped: History doesn't repeat itself, only historians do.
5. See, for example, Kenneth Arrow, "Path Dependence and Competitive Equilibrium," in *History Matters: Essays on Economic Growth, Technology, and Demographic Change*, ed. William Sundstrom, Timothy Guinnane, and Warren Whatley (Stanford, CA: Stanford University Press, 2003).
6. Even a far larger disaster, British Petroleum's (BP) 2010 oil spill in the Gulf of Mexico, costing the company tens of billions of dollars, didn't dethrone BP from its membership in the group of major international oil companies. The current (2016) oil glut and price drops may prove more consequential to oil companies.
7. As an aside, any prediction model that incorporates other predictions (like the expected rising interest rates post quantitative easing) is subject to additional inaccuracies from the errors of those predictions. So our prediction, based solely on adjusted reported earnings, may perform quite well compared with "more sophisticated" ones. See, for example, Joseph Gerakos and Robert Gramacy, *Regression-Based Earnings Forecasts*, working paper (Chicago: University of Chicago, 2013).
8. An alternative, often used by researchers, is to compute the "root mean-squared error," which is computed by squaring the errors, averaging them, and taking the square root of the average, which also abstracts from the error sign.
9. To smooth out yearly fluctuations of the prediction errors, we averaged them over successive 10-year periods, 1954–1963, 1964–1973, and so on. These are the errors presented in Figure 5.1. To weed out totally unreliable predictions, particularly for young, volatile companies, we restricted the sample to companies with annual growth rates of earnings between +15 percent and −15 percent per year.
10. A comprehensive empirical study surprisingly documented that cash flows predict corporate performance better than accounting earnings, consistent with our findings here. See, Baruch Lev, Siyi Li, and Theodore Sougiannis,

"The Usefulness of Accounting Estimates For Predicting Cash Flows and Earnings," *Review of Accounting Studies*, 15 (2010): 779–807.

11. A restructuring charge is an expense reflecting the costs involved in restructuring operations, such as laying off employees, closing divisions, and selling assets at a loss.

12. Relatedly, a recent study documented that the correlation between accruals (the noncash components of earnings) and cash flows has dramatically diminished over the past half century, and all but disappeared in recent years. As to reasons, the authors say: "We find that increases in one-time and non-operating items... explain about 63% of the decline in the overall correlation between accruals and cash flows." (Introduction). See Robert Bushman, Alina Lerman, and Frank Zhang, *The Changing Landscape of Accrual Accounting,* working paper (Chapel Hill: University of North Carolina, 2015).

13. Much of this "damage" to reported earnings is done by the FASB's so-called "balance sheet approach," adopted in the 1980s, which perceives the prime objective of accounting to value assets and liabilities at fair (current) values. Accordingly, the quarterly/annual adjustments of assets and liabilities to fair values spill over to the income statement in the form of one-time gains or losses, detracting from reported earnings' ability to predict future enterprise performance.

14. A regulator challenged us by saying: "If one-time items decrease the usefulness of earnings, then investors should consider earnings *before* those items. What's all the fuss?" Easier said than done. Many one-time items, or their components, are "buried" in other income statement items, making it impossible for investors to clearly separate all one-time items from earnings. Thus, for example, Gilead Sciences' Q2-2013 report provides guidance for full year 2013, indicating that R&D and SG&A expenses include one-time items, such as acquisition-related expenses and restructuring expenses. Most companies, though, do not disclose one-time components included in income statement items.

15. We aren't the only researchers to observe the deteriorating usefulness of reported earnings. In a thoughtful critique of accounting regulations, Emory University Professor Ilia Dichev wrote: "Earnings is the single most important output of the accounting system. Thus, intuitively, improved financial reporting should lead to improved usefulness of earnings. However, the continual expansion of the balance sheet approach [by the FASB] is gradually destroying the forward-looking usefulness of earnings, mainly through the effect of various asset revaluations, which manifest as noise in the process of generating normal operating earnings." In "On the Balance Sheet-Based Model of Financial Reporting," Occasional Paper Series, Center for Excellence in Accounting and Security Analysis, Columbia Business School, 2007, p. 2.

16. Daniel Kahneman and Amos Tversky, "Prospect Theory: An Analysis of Decisions Under Risk," *Econometrica*, 47 (2) (1979): 263–292.

17. This, of course, is a reflection of the widely known phenomenon—"mean reversion," namely extreme observations in one period, will tend to get closer to the average in subsequent period. The speed of such reversion to the mean indicates the impact of chance, or transitory items on the observation (earnings in our case).

Finally, For the Still Unconvinced

In which we show that measures of financial analysts' uncertainty, or ambiguity about the future prospects of the companies they follow have been trending up during the past three decades. We attribute this intriguing finding, in part, at least, to the deteriorating quality of the main information source analysts rely on — the corporate financial report. This complements our previous evidence on the diminishing usefulness of financial information, showing that it affects even the primary capital market experts — financial analysts.

"BUT ACCOUNTING IS COMPLICATED"

A final objection we have heard to the battery of accounting usefulness tests we reported in the preceding chapters may be summed up in three words: Accounting is complex. Portraying the operations and financial condition of today's companies—global, fiercely competitive, fast changing, and innovative—requires a highly sophisticated, nuanced, and complex information system. For most investors and lenders, this information system may indeed be obscure, even confusing, hence the increasing chasm we documented between stock prices and financial information. By necessity of reflecting business complexity, our critics argued, much of the information in financial reports is targeted at experts. Indeed, who besides an expert can fathom the accounting jargon of fair values of assets and liabilities (what's fair about those?), impairment of goodwill value, off-balance-sheet financing, or special-purpose entities, among other hallmarks of recent financial reports regulations. So, examining the average investor reaction to this complex information misses its real insights, goes the argument.

Since we wish to leave no stone unturned in our quest of accounting's usefulness, we focus in this final relevance test on capital market's prime experts—financial analysts. These professionals were specifically trained in analyzing corporate financial reports and comprehending the intricacies of accounting information. Being industry experts, they also fully grasp the economic context of financial information and are comfortable with prediction methodologies. Most importantly, they have strong incentives to exploit any advantage they can gain from thoroughly dissecting financial reports to benefit their clients, since their bonuses and promotions hang in the balance. And analysts don't shy away from accounting intricacies. When encountering a difficult issue, they have direct access to managers via conference calls or investor relations personnel within the company in question. Rest assured that as long as there are real insights about a company's future performance and economic condition in financial reports, analysts will strive to get them. We, therefore, ask in the following test: Is the work product of financial analysts, who rely on accounting information, improving over time? Improving quality and relevance of underlying information, just as improvements in meteorological data and instrumentation, should be reflected in an increasing quality of analysts' (weather forecasters') work product, and vice versa for deteriorating information quality.

EXPERTS AT WORK

Thousands of sell-side financial analysts employed by financial institutions and independent research outfits follow most US public companies, as well as many companies abroad.[1] Analysts generally specialize in industries and typically track a subgroup of 10 to 15 firms in a sector. They provide periodic industry and company analyses, stock recommendations, and earnings/sales forecasts to specific clients and the investment community at large. These information intermediaries are widely considered experts in the companies they follow; they and their support teams analyze a broad set of information emanating from companies and other sources (industry trends, technological developments), participate in companies' conference calls and investor meetings, and often talk to customers and suppliers of the companies they follow. At the core of the information analysts gather and process are the companies' periodic financial reports.

By participating in post-report conference calls, investors' meetings, and often one-on-one confabs with executives, analysts gain a unique perspective and context to interpret financial information.[2] It can, therefore, be safely assumed that analysts reflect in their work product much of the information in financial reports relevant to securities' valuation, irrespective of complexity and obscurity.

VAGUE INFORMATION AND DISAGREEMENT

Consider a group of investors receiving two messages: The first message states that the number of subscribers to the company's product (entertainment content at Netflix, say) increased 20 percent, while the second message is that the company's earnings rose 10 percent from the prior year. The first states a fact, immune to different interpretations. There will, therefore, be a high degree of *agreement* among investors considering the implications of such a substantial rise in the number of the company's subscribers.[3]

Consider now the 10 percent earnings increase message. A company's earnings are not a fact, like the number of subscribers; rather, they are a complex combination of certain facts (a sales increase), managers' subjective estimates (like the amount of customers' bad debts that will not be paid next year), luck or lack thereof (winning a patent infringement lawsuit), and sometimes even a certain amount of earnings manipulation by management. Accordingly, the message of a 10 percent earnings increase is rather vague regarding its implications for investors: Opinions will differ as to how much of the earnings increase is due to substantive causes that will raise future earnings too, how much is transitory, largely irrelevant for valuation, and how reliable are the many managerial estimates and forecasts underlying earnings. And, of course, there is the question of whether earnings were "managed." It is not surprising, therefore, that there will be considerable *disagreement* among investors about the implications of the reported 10 percent earnings increase for predicting future earnings and making investment decisions. Those who suspect that the earnings increase resulted primarily from transitory factors or manipulation will largely ignore it, whereas others will act on it—buying the stock.

In general, the less precise and variously interpretable is the message—the farther it is from facts—the larger will be the disagreement about its implications. The important takeaway is this: Disagreement is an indicator of message vagueness and imprecision, which, in turn, points to the usefulness or relevance of the message.[4] This is the basis for the following, final test of the usefulness of financial information. (What a relief!)

QUANTIFYING DISAGREEMENT

It was mentioned earlier that most public companies are followed by several financial analysts; large companies are often followed by as many as 20 to 30 analysts or more (Google by 40 analysts, and Exxon by 20; see Yahoo@

Finance, December 31, 2015). The *dispersion,* or variation, of the individual earnings estimates of the analysts following the company is a reliable indicator of the disagreement among analysts about the future performance of the company. Consider, for example, three analysts following Company A, and issuing the following forecasts for its next-quarter EPS: $2.50, $2.60, $2.75. For Company B, in the same industry, the three EPS forecasts are: –$0.75, $2.0, $3.75. Obviously, in the latter case, the forecast dispersion is substantially higher than in the former, one analyst of Company B even predicts a loss.[5] The higher degree of forecast dispersion for Company B clearly indicates a high level of disagreement, uncertainty, and even ambiguity among the analysts concerning future company performance. Comparing the two companies in the same industry (similar risk and economic circumstances), it's clear that the information analysts had about Company A—much of it presumably from its financial reports—was much more precise and unambiguous than the information about Company B. Forecast dispersion is, therefore, an important indicator of information quality. This is the basis for the following usefulness test.

We recorded the dispersion (variation) of analyst forecasts around the consensus earnings estimate for all firms followed by more than two analysts, for each of the past 35 years.[6] The five-year medians of forecast dispersion are depicted in Figure 6.1 (the mean dispersions behave almost identically).

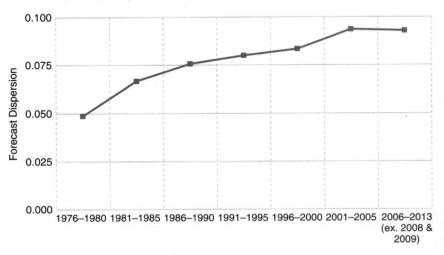

Five-year median analysts' dispersion (standard deviation) around the consensus estimate, 1976–2013 (2008 and 2009 omitted)

FIGURE 6.1   Analysts' Ambiguity on the Rise

If analysts' information had improved over time, you should observe a *decrease* in their uncertainty about the future prospects of the companies they follow. But Figure 6.1 portrays the opposite: a persistent increase over time, implying a continuous rise in financial analysts' disagreement, or uncertainty about the future performance of the companies they follow. Since the next chapter rules out the possibility that the business environment just became much more volatile and difficult to predict (and furthermore, we omitted from Figure 6.1 the difficult to predict financial crisis years 2008–2009), a major reason for the increase in analysts' uncertainty is likely the continuous decrease in the quality (precision, accuracy) of the information available to them, in particular, financial report information.[7] A vague, imprecise message—financial information—inevitably increases analysts' ambiguity.

TAKEAWAY

In this chapter, we presented a unique perspective of the usefulness of financial information to the leading capital market experts, sell-side analysts, who are investors' main opinion makers: information relevance in terms of increasing agreement (consensus) among analysts about firms' future performance. This large-scale test clearly indicates a sustained decrease in the usefulness of financial information.[8] It is hard to argue with facts, particularly when our findings are consistent across all the tests performed in this and the preceding three chapters.

We'll conclude with an important lesson for investors and managers: The increasing analysts' disagreement and bewilderment reflected by Figure 6.1 suggest that you shouldn't take analysts' earnings forecasts too seriously. Missing the consensus estimate isn't the end of the world for managers, and it is far from a sufficient reason for investors to dump the stock. Evaluating a company's performance shouldn't be based on a simplistic consensus miss or beat, but rather, on fundamental considerations of the company's business model and its execution, as we prescribe in Part III of the book.

NOTES

1. It is customary to distinguish between sell-side and buy-side analysts. The former are employed by financial institutions and independent research firms and provide information to these firms' clients and the general investment public, while the latter (buy-side) work for hedge funds, private equity, and money managers. We focus here on sell-side analysts because their work product—earnings forecasts

and stock recommendations—is public and therefore researchable, whereas buy-side analysts' product is proprietary. Importantly, a recent study found that sell-side analysts' research is also very valuable to institutional investors (Lawrence Brown, Andrew Call, Michael Clement, and Nathan Sharp, "Inside the 'Black Box' of Sell-Side Analysts," *Journal of Accounting Research*, 53 (2015): 1–47).

2. See Eugene Soltes, "Private Interaction between Firm Management and Sell-Side Analysts," *Journal of Accounting Research*, 52 (1) (2013): 245–272, on privileged analysts' meetings with corporate executives.

3. Whether the 20 percent subscriber growth is good or bad news depends on investors' prior expectations (it is bad news if they expected 30 percent growth). But whatever the prior expectations, the message and its implications are unambiguous.

4. Disagreement is also affected, of course, by other information (context) had by those who receive the message.

5. The standard deviation, a measure of dispersion, is 0.126 for the three forecasts of Company A, and a much larger 2.268 for Company B's forecasts.

6. Analysts' forecast dispersion for each company is obtained from I/B/E/S. It is the dispersion around the first consensus estimate of the annual earnings forecasts for each company, available in the fourth fiscal month (after the previous year's annual report was published). To control for the different sizes of companies, we divide the standard deviation by the mean of the forecasts for each company (this measure is known as the "coefficient of variation"). We use the absolute mean of the estimates to avoid negative numbers in the denominator. We then compute the five-year medians for these measures across the sample companies. These medians are portrayed by Figure 6.1.

7. There may be other factors affecting forecast dispersion, but the quality of the information underlying the forecasts is undoubtedly a major one.

8. Financial report information isn't the only source used by analysts. A recent study (Lawrence Brown, Andrew Call, Michael Clement, and Nathan Sharp, "Inside the 'Black Box' of Sell-Side Analysts," *Journal of Accounting Research*, 53 (2015): 1–47), for example, found that analysts rank high the information they receive from direct contacts with management. It seems unlikely, though, that managers *increasingly* misinform analysts in their private communication, leaving the diminishing quality of accounting information as an important driver of Figure 6.1.

CHAPTER 7

The Meaning of It All

Having presented in the preceding four chapters comprehensive evidence on the deteriorating relevance of financial
information to investors, and before highlighting the reasons for the deterioration and, importantly, the way forward,
we need to address two pertinent questions: First, should
investors really care about accounting's relevance lost? In
this day and age, aren't there ample substitutes for accounting information? Second, is all our documented relevance
lost due to failures on the part of accounting, or the result of
extraneous factors, like increasing economic volatility, which
will fail any information system? Our evidence-based answers
to these questions will surprise you.

TO RECAP

We have presented in this, the first part of the book, comprehensive evidence
that clearly portrays a continuous and steep deterioration in the usefulness of
financial (accounting) information to investors.[1] The evidence, based on large
samples comprising of most US public companies, spans the past half century,
and examines information usefulness from four different perspectives:

- The role of key financial report indicators—sales, cost of sales, SG&A
  expenses, earnings, assets and liabilities—in investors' equity decisions.
- The timeliness (decision relevance) of financial information released to
  investors.
- A capital market-free test: the ability of reported earnings to predict
  future corporate performance.

- The quality of the financial information underlying financial analysts' work product, as reflected by their uncertainty about future corporate performance.

What is remarkable about our findings is that they are perfectly consistent across the four very different research methodologies, or information usefulness perspectives: They all indicate that corporate financial reports and the accounting information conveyed by them have lost much of their usefulness to their prime users. Investors and lenders no longer find them highly relevant. Undoubtedly, the most "shocking" of our findings is that, currently, these very costly financial reports provide only a tiny amount of the information—roughly 5 percent—used by investors. This is a sad commentary to be sure, particularly in light of the significant worldwide efforts of regulators and accounting standard-setters to enhance the usefulness of financial information.[2] But before we fully comprehend the reasons for the loss of accounting's relevance—a necessary condition for any remedial action—we need to overcome two hurdles: First, the nagging question: So what if financial information lost most of its value? Who besides accountants should be concerned about this? In today's sophisticated capital markets and abundance of information, investors surely have ample alternative information sources. Second, should we consider that perhaps all this loss of information relevance is not the fault of accounting? The turbulent political and business environment, which seems to be on the rise, will detrimentally affect any information system trying to make sense of things.[3] Accountants are doing their best under increasingly difficult circumstances. Let's briefly address each of these intriguing questions that were surely on your mind.

SHOULD INVESTORS REALLY CARE?

So what if financial (accounting) information has lost most of its usefulness to investors? Bread, which used to be the staple food not so long ago, is now a small part of the diet in developed economies. No one complains about that. Similarly with investors: If one source of information—accounting—loses its relevance, there are surely good substitute information sources. So, except for accountants (and accounting educators) why should anybody, and particularly investors, be concerned with our findings?

The short answer is this: If there were good alternatives to financial information, we wouldn't have observed the findings portrayed by Figure 6.1 in the preceding chapter. With more relevant and timely information than that conveyed by corporate financial reports, financial analysts surely wouldn't have exhibited *increasing uncertainty* and ambiguity about these companies' prospects. High-quality substitutes to accounting information would have led to *improved* work product of these experts, not deteriorating output.

But it's not only our research that shows a lack of good alternatives to financial report information. Our findings are neatly corroborated by a recent, comprehensive study on the *informativeness* of share prices, namely the information reflected by stock prices.[4] When investors are amply informed about companies' financial condition and growth prospects, they trade on this information (buy stocks with attractive growth potential and sell "losers"), and through such trade share prices reflect investors' information. Consequently, well-informed share prices will be good predictors of companies' future performance. In contrast, poorly informed share prices (due, say, to investors being misled by corporate misinformation) will inaccurately predict companies' performance. This is the main test that Bai, Philippon, and Savov use to determine the change, since 1960, in the informativeness of US share prices.

The researchers first focus on the nonfinancial S&P 500 companies—roughly 400 large enterprises, widely followed by financial analysts, that constitute less than 10 percent of all US public companies. They report that the share price informativeness of these companies improved over the past half century. It is, of course, hardly surprising that for these leading, highly visible companies, each followed by multiple financial analysts and owned primarily by institutional, sophisticated investors, share price informativeness improved. But the interesting finding lies in the remaining companies—the more-than-90 percent of public companies for which the researchers found that share price informativeness *declined* significantly over the past 50 years, despite revolutionary advances in information processing technology.[5] This suggests that for the vast majority of public companies, the alternative (to accounting) information sources were unable to compensate for the deteriorating informativeness of corporate financial reports that we have documented above. Thus, not only are analysts becoming less informed—as evidenced by Figure 6.1—so too are other investors. And deteriorating information means poor investment decisions and investor losses. So, fellow investor, you should definitely care a lot about our findings.

Why aren't there good alternatives to the relevance-challenged financial (accounting) information? Simply because investment in information alternatives—primarily generated by Wall Street research—is shrinking alarmingly. The *Wall Street Journal* reports that aggregate spending on investment bank research fell from over $8 billion a year during 2007–2009, to slightly over $4 billion in 2014, and is predicted to continue its decline.[6] A 50 percent cut in the search for relevant information sources, coupled with a deterioration in the relevance of financial reports, is sure to lower share price informativeness. The sharp decreases in funds available for investment research primarily affected medium and small companies—the main engine of employment and growth—most of which lost research coverage in recent years since the relatively thin trade in the shares of these companies doesn't compensate banks for the research costs. Consequently, a few well-endowed investors can afford high-quality research, while most investors can't.[7] They rely mostly on corporate financial reports whose diminishing usefulness we have already documented.

Even with ample research funds, reliable corporate financial information will always dominate alternative information sources, because managers will always know more about their companies than outsiders. Moreover, the company speaks with one voice—one report informs all constituents, while alternative information sources on companies, such as information vendors, financial analysts, or online investment services, speak in multiple voices, with all manner of repetition and redundancy. Such information sources are, therefore, more costly and often more confusing than the parsimonious, single corporate financial report, and their credibility (how reliable is your online investment service?) is more difficult and expensive to ascertain than that of an independently audited corporate financial report that comes with a legal liability of executives for its integrity. Thus, relevant and informative financial reports—not those that are released currently—will always dominate alternative information sources, in terms of cost effectiveness and reliability. That's the reason we don't give up on corporate reporting; rather we strive to restructure it, as proposed in Part III.

A LAST-DITCH DEFENSE OF ACCOUNTING

Before we proceed with unlocking the reasons for our findings, we have to lay to rest a final criticism we heard from several colleagues with whom we shared our evidence. Your findings, they said, particularly the decreasing predictive power of earnings and the increasing uncertainty of analysts' forecasts (Chapters 5 and 6), are primarily caused by the rising volatility and uncertainty of the environment within which businesses operate, rather than a deterioration in the usefulness of financial information. It's the fault of the business environment, not of accounting. Frankly, this sounds like the justification you sometimes hear from a weather forecaster who failed to alert you to an oncoming storm: It's not my fault; blame the weather's increasing unpredictability (global warming, of course) for the poor forecast. (Would you keep listening to this weatherperson?) Nevertheless, we'll fully address this criticism. True to our approach in this book, we rely on evidence, and once again, you'll find the evidence highly surprising (it surely surprised us): In fact, despite widely held beliefs, there has been no increase in the volatility of the business environment. The alleged volatility increase, hampering accounting information and analysts' forecasts, is yet another myth.

THE DECREASING VOLATILITY OF BUSINESSES

Occasional financial crises, such as the recent one of 2007–2008—and pundits' hyperventilation around them (each one is "the worst crisis since the Great Depression")—create a perception of constantly rising economic turbulence and volatility. But this perception is outright wrong. Commenting on the October 2014 market volatility (the S&P 500 decreased 6 percent in mid-October 2014, yet ended the month in record high), an opinion piece in the *Wall Street Journal* reminded readers:

> *...the volatility in the macro (real) economy is very low.... [L]ooking back over the entire business cycle, the volatility of GDP growth during the past four years is comparable to the previous two business-cycle expansions.... To describe similar phenomena in the 1990s, about a decade ago economists coined the term the Great Moderation—and its back in use today.*[8]

Thus, we experience a great moderation rather than rising turbulence.

The volatility of the overall economy is, of course, a major determinant of business enterprises' volatility. Economic lurches between boom and bust affect consumers' demand, resource prices, and ultimately companies' operations. So, what is the volatility record of the economy? In a word—it's *declining*. For quite some time, leading economists like Blanchard and Simon (2001), noticed "a long and large decline in US output volatility over the last half century." In particular, economists recorded a shift in the mid-1980s toward stabilization of economic activity: It has been estimated that, since 1984, the variance (a statistical measure of volatility) of GDP growth has declined by an astounding 50 percent. The search for a full understanding of this phenomenon goes on, but stabilizing factors like improved inventory management by companies, better control of firms' operations brought about by information technology, smarter government interventions in crises, and the increased use by companies of stabilizing (risk hedging) financial innovations are among the volatility-reducing factors already identified. And what about the substantial business disruptions caused by the 2007–2008 crisis, you ask? Just a hiccup. A 2014 study by Furman shows that the pre-crisis declining volatility was resumed after the financial crisis (" ... but overall volatility still appears to be at a lower level than in the past.")[9] So, our documented declining usefulness of financial information cannot be blamed on an increasingly turbulent business environment. If anything, this environment is getting more tranquil.

While being a major determinant of companies' volatility, overall economic activity (say, GDP growth) isn't the only factor affecting corporate turmoil. Industry-specific technological disruptions, resource price changes, and abrupt shifts in consumers' demand, among other factors, also contribute to business volatility. Perhaps these micro volatility factors diminish accounting usefulness? To allay this concern, we examine the *micro* volatility of business operations, focusing on companies' sales; significant changes in corporate volatility should be reflected by the "top line"—sales. Accordingly, we measured the volatility of sales for the largest 1,000 US companies over the course of the past 60 years.[10] The results are portrayed by Figure 7.1. Once more, volatility is exonerated (of the accounting demise blame): It is evident that corporate sales volatility has been *on the decline* from 1966 through 2013, mirroring the macro studies mentioned earlier, where the volatility decline accelerated since 1984.[11] The post-1984 deceleration of volatility, indicated by both the macroeconomic studies and our microeconomic study (Figure 7.1), seems to be primarily caused by improved managerial and control systems (better inventory—"just in time"—control systems) brought about mainly by information technology innovations, which accelerated from the mid-1980s.[12]

The bottom line: The last-ditch defense of accounting crumbled. Volatility, or turbulence, either of the economy-at-large or of companies' own operations, has in fact been decreasing and therefore cannot be blamed for the documented fall in financial report usefulness or in the rising uncertainty of analysts. The reasons for the usefulness decline are not to be

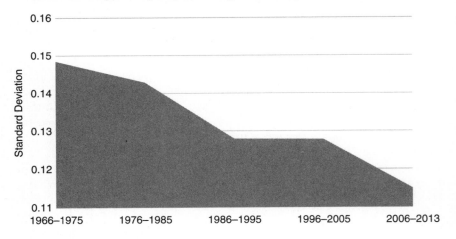

FIGURE 7.1 Decreasing Volatility of Corporate Sales over Time

found outside the accounting system; rather, as we will shortly show, they are deeply embedded in accounting procedures and regulations. Totally self-inflicted wounds.

TAKEAWAY

Two important conclusions: First, accounting's usefulness deterioration cannot be blamed on exogenous factors, such as an alleged increasingly turbulent economy or investors' increased irrationality. The reasons for accounting's relevance lost are endemic to this information system and will be identified thus. Second, investors have no good alternatives to relevant and reliable financial reports information, as evidenced by the deteriorating informativeness of the stock prices of most companies. The solution, therefore, is to fix corporate reporting, not abandon it.

NOTES

1. We aren't the only ones questioning the usefulness of financial information. For example, two senior consultants at the leading consultancy McKinsey wrote the following as a preamble to a proposed improved income statement: "If neither companies nor investors find GAAP reported earnings useful, it's clearly time for a new approach." (Ajay Jagannath and Tim Koller, "Building a Better Income Statement," McKinsey Company, *Corporate Finance,* November 2013.) Similarly, the Institute of Chartered Accountants in England and Wales (ICAEW), with 140,000 members in 160 countries, published an extensive study on the state of corporate reporting and advanced suggestions for change. They open the executive summary of this 80-page report with the following statement: " ... there is a widely-held view that financial reporting disclosures need to be reformed. Views differ on what exactly the problem is, but few people seem to be happy with the current position." ICAEW, Financial reporting disclosures: Market and regulatory failures, 2013. The difference between most criticisms and ours is that we: (i) provide new, comprehensive evidence in support of our claim of accounting's loss of relevance, and (ii) fully explain the reasons for our findings (Part II of this book).
2. Tellingly, we are not familiar with comprehensive research that contradicts ours by showing an *increase* in the usefulness or relevance of financial information to investors. We are aware of a couple of studies showing an increasing reaction of investors to earnings releases, but the major reason for this is not the rising usefulness of earnings, but rather, an increasing number of managers' forecasts (guidance) accompanying quarterly earnings announcements (more than 30 percent now). Managers' guidance triggers, of course, a strong investor reaction.

3. A related version of this defense of accounting is that the loss of financial report relevance is due to the entry to capital markets in recent decades of companies with different business models (intangibles-based). But this is just another way of saying that accounting failed to adjust to the dramatic shift in the business models of most companies (from industrial to knowledge-based). Relevance loss once more.

4. Jennie Bai, Thomas Philippon, and Alexi Savov, *Have Financial Markets Become More Informative?* working paper (Stern School of Business, New York University, 2015).

5. The researchers attribute this decline to the changing composition of firms over time—smaller and more technology-reliant companies entering the market. But this is exactly our point—accounting and financial reporting is wholly inadequate for such twenty-first-century enterprises.

6. Margot Patrick, Juliet Samuel, and Alexandra Scaggs, "Banks Forced to Shake Up Analyst Research Business," *The Wall Street Journal* (February 10, 2015, p. C1). The reason for the research decline is that the securities trading revenues of banks and brokerage houses, which support much of the equity research function, fell precipitously since the 2007–2008 financial crisis. *The Economist* reports that between 2009 and 2013, total stock trading commissions fell in the United States from $13.9 billion to $9.3 billion (33%), and in Europe from €4.2 billion to €3.0 billion (29%). "Analyze This," *The Economist* (September 21, 2013), p. 79.

7. *The Economist* (September 21, 2013, p. 79) provides the following examples of the innovative but very expensive information some hedge funds procure: "Hedge funds now use research dollars to pay for ground surveillance on the progress of mining or oil projects in Africa, in order to value them better. Others take to the sky. RS Metrics, a satellite-intelligence provider, has reported strong demand from the financial sector for its aerial-imaging services. Some funds even hire former intelligence agents . . . to test whether corporate bosses are massaging the truth in investor meetings." Most investors, however, cannot afford such costly research.

8. Jason Cummins, "Wall Street Volatility Doesn't Shake Main Street," *The Wall Street Journal* (December 1, 2014).

9. References for the research mentioned in this paragraph: Olivier Blanchard and Jon Simon, "The Long and Large Decline in U.S. Output Volatility," Brookings Papers on Economic Activity, No. 1, Brookings Institution. Jason Furman, 2014, Whatever happened to the Great Moderation? Remarks at the 23rd annual Hyman P. Minsky Conference, April 10, 2001.

10. Specifically, for each company and year (say 1995), we measure volatility by the standard deviation of its sales-to-total-assets ratio (to account for the different sizes of companies) over the previous five years (1991–1995, in our example). We then average those standard deviations (volatility) over the 1,000 companies in our sample for that year. These annual mean sales volatilities are plotted in

Figure 7.1. To smooth yearly fluctuations, Figure 7.1 shows 10-year averages of volatilities: 1966–1975, 1976–1985, etc. Sales volatility for all companies, not just the largest 1,000, increased from 1966–1975 to 1976–1985, and subsequently decrease up to 2006–2013.

11. We also examined the volatility of the *growth* in companies' sales (year-to-year change) and found a similar pattern to that of Figure 7.1.

12. To be sure, there has been an increase in the volatility of *reported* corporate earnings over the past two decades, but this was mainly due to various accounting regulations, such as assets write-offs and mark-to-market, which increase the frequency of one-time (transitory) items in earnings, as we showed in Chapter 5, rather than a reflection of economic volatility.

TWO

Why Is the Relevance Lost?

"There are three kinds of lies: lies, damned lies, and statistics," said Mark Twain in reference to the use of numbers; that is, drawing on statistical evidence to bolster weak arguments.[1] The extensive statistical evidence on the fast-diminishing relevance of corporate financial (accounting) information we presented in Part I is so counterintuitive and surely disturbing to the multitude of investors using financial information that it may conjure in mind Twain's phrase about misleading with statistics. It is, therefore, incumbent upon us to carefully identify and document the *reasons* for accounting's fall from grace to substantiate and support the statistical evidence and to provide the foundation for the remedial actions we propose in Part III. Numbers without comprehension are just that—numbers. That's what we do in this, Part II, of the book: carefully outline, with full empirical support, the main reasons for the continuous decline in the relevance or usefulness of financial information to investors and other corporate stakeholders. To avoid undue reader suspense, here are, in essence, the three major reasons for accounting's relevance lost:

1. *The inexplicable accounting treatment of intangible assets—the dominant creators of corporate value.* Something remarkable happened to the US economy, and to varying degrees of similarity to other developed countries, in the past four decades: While aggregate US investment in tangible assets (things you can touch, like property,

plant and equipment, inventory, etc.) has *decreased* by over a third, corporate investment in intangible assets (patents and know-how, brands, information and business systems, and human capital) rose by almost 60 percent, from 9 percent to 14 percent of gross value added. Corporate investment in intangible capital now surpasses investment in physical assets by a wide margin, and the gap keeps growing. The reason: During these recent decades, intangible (intellectual) assets have increasingly bolstered corporate value and competitive edge, whereas tangible (physical) assets are essentially "commodities," equally available to all competitors, and therefore unable to create considerable value and confer competitive advantage. The patents of Apple and Pfizer, the brands of Coca-Cola and Amazon, the highly efficient business processes (organizational capital) of Walmart and Southwest Airlines drove these companies' success, rather than their machines, physical premises, or inventory. The increasing dominance of intangibles among corporate assets is widely recognized, with its consequences having become known as the "knowledge economy," except, that is, by accountants, who strangely persist in ignoring the intangibles insurgence.

How ironic that physical and financial investments, unable to create substantial value by themselves, are fully recognized as assets on corporate balance sheets—think about the "contribution" of inventory or short-term investments to the growth prospects of Pfizer—whereas investments in internally generated intangibles, such as patents, brands, or knowhow—powerful value creators—are immediately expensed; that is, treated in the income statement as regular expenses (salaries, rent) without future benefits. Even more inexplicable, if you develop a brand, like Coke did, it's not an asset by GAAP, but if you buy it, it will be proudly displayed on your balance sheet. Just think about the misguided managerial incentive—preferring buying over developing—created by accounting. This inept treatment of intangibles in financial reports adversely affects *both* the balance sheet and the income statement in a rather complex manner, highly confusing to investors: Asset and equity values of intangibles-intensive businesses are seriously understated, but their profitability measures (ROE, ROA) often overstated, while the earnings of firms with increasing investment in intangibles are diminished, due to the full expensing of intangibles. Every aspect of the financial report is adversely affected by this dated, industrial-age treatment of intangible capital. This, as we will show in the next chapter, is a major cause of the deteriorating usefulness of accounting. And given the likely continued rise in the role of intangibles in corporate value creation, the decline in the usefulness of financial reports is all but certain to persist.

2. *Accounting isn't about facts anymore.* This always comes as a surprise to nonaccountants. They have heard or personally experienced that accounting can be rather boring (not when taught by us!), but they are convinced it's at least factual and accurate. After all, doesn't the term accounting come from *counting*, as in counting money, inventory, or product units sold? This is, however, a myth. In fact, accounting isn't about facts anymore, but rather about managers' subjective judgment, estimates, and projections. Almost every income statement item and most balance sheet values are based on estimates: Assets are displayed on the balance sheet net of estimated depreciation and amortization; accounts receivable is presented net of the bad-debt reserve (again, an estimate); employee pensions and stock options expenses are based on multiple estimates, as are the recognized fair values of nontraded assets and liabilities, affecting both the balance sheet and the income statement. Often multiple estimates are stacked on each other to form a financial statement item, like the stock options expense.

There are two major problems with these accounting estimates: (i) All estimates are subject to errors, and the multitude of errors associated with the various revenue and expense estimates ultimately become embedded (accumulate) in earnings, adversely affecting the reliability of this key performance indicator; worse yet, they do so to an unknown extent by both managers and investors. Consider: No one really knows how much of corporate reported earnings are estimates—or sheer guesses—and how much fact. A terrifying thought, and a thought that most investors conveniently ignore. (ii) Accounting estimates are sometimes manipulated by managers to "make the numbers" (beating consensus forecasts, enhancing managers' compensation), since the perpetrators can rarely be pinned down for misestimations. Even if the estimate, say, of delinquent debts, is later found to be far off the mark, managers can always claim that *at the time* they made the estimate it was based on their best information. Good luck disproving this. And since, as we will show in Chapter 9, the prevalence of estimates in accounting is constantly increasing, these two challenges to reliable estimates seriously erode the usefulness of financial reports, distancing the information conveyed by them from reality.

3. *Unrecorded events increasingly affect corporate value.* Accounting records (the "infamous" debits and credits) and the consequent financial reports are mostly triggered by *transactions* with third parties: purchases and sales, salaries and interest payments, stock issues, and buybacks. Those transactions are systematically recorded and reported by the accounting system. Increasingly, however, *nontransactional business events* affect corporate value too: success or failure of drugs or

software products under development in feasibility tests, competitors' new products or strategic moves disrupting incumbents, environmental mishaps, the signing of new contracts or contract cancellations, strategic moves by the firm (restructurings, launches of new products or services), or new regulations affecting the company. These and other major business events substantially affect corporate values and growth, but are not recorded by the accounting system as they occur, or, if recorded, they are often reflected in a biased manner (the costs of restructuring, for example, are fully recorded, but not the expected benefits). The occurrence of such nonaccounting events generally has an immediate and profound impact on stock prices (e.g., a clinical test failure of a drug hits the stock price), while their reflection by the accounting system is delayed, sometimes for years, until they affect sales and earnings. This creates a widening chasm between firms' values, as reflected by share prices, and financial data—a chasm that is partially responsible for the declining association between financial information and share prices, which we have documented in Part I.

The three usefulness-diminishing factors we just outlined are not conjectures; nor are they speculation. In what follows, we will empirically prove, for the first time, that these three factors or causes—intangible assets, accounting estimates, and unrecorded business events—are primarily responsible for the deterioration in the usefulness of financial information. We will also show that the impact of each of the three factors has increased over time, mirroring the documented decrease in the usefulness of financial information. Importantly, overcoming these hindrances provides the basis for the information system we will propose in Part III of the book.

NOTE

1. Mark Twain himself attributed this phrase to the nineteenth-century British prime minister Benjamin Disraeli (1804–1881), although, according to Wikipedia, the phrase isn't found in any of Disraeli's extensive writings, and the earliest appearance of the phrase was years after Disraeli's death.

CHAPTER 8

The Rise of Intangibles and Fall of Accounting

In which we present the first reason for the waning usefulness of financial (accounting) information — the surge of intangible (intellectual) assets (patents, brands, information technology) — to become the prime value creators of businesses. We document empirically that the failure of the accounting system to reflect the value of these assets in financial reports, to properly account for their impact on firms' operations, and to provide investors with information about the exposure of these assets to threats of infringement and disruption, is a major cause of accounting's relevance lost. How ironic (or sad) that largely irrelevant assets to companies' growth and competitive edge — like inventory, accounts receivable, or plant & machinery — remain prominently displayed on corporate balance sheets, whereas patents, brands, IT, or unique business processes are accounting MIAs.

THE INTANGIBLES SURGE

Figure 8.1, which traces the pattern of US corporate investment in tangible (plant, equipment, inventory) and intangible assets over the past 40 years will surely surprise you. What you see is truly a tectonic economic shift:

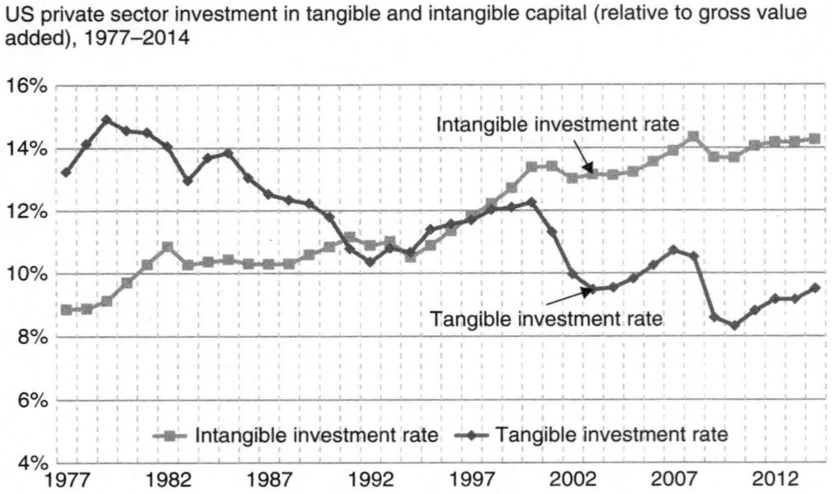

US private sector investment in tangible and intangible capital (relative to gross value added), 1977–2014

FIGURE 8.1   The Intangibles Revolution
Source: We are grateful to Professors Carol Corrado and Charles Hulten for providing us with this figure.

The rate of investment in what many people still think of as the *real assets*—physical capital—fell by 35 percent over the period, whereas the rate of investment in intangibles—what Alan Greenspan called *conceptual assets*—increased by almost 60 percent, and keeps rising. Note, in particular, the continuously widening *gap* between the rising investment in intangibles and the declining spending on tangible assets, starting in the mid-1990s. And not only in America. "While German companies pulled back on machinery investment during the crisis, R&D spending continued to rise."[1] The reason for this dramatic shift in the productive resources of the business sector is compelling: Corporate value and growth are increasingly driven by intangible assets, whereas physical capital (like factories, machines, or inventory) is just an enabler—a commodity—equally available to all competitors and hence a marginal creator of value and competitive advantage. So is, by the way, financial capital: stocks and bonds.[2] Value is created nowadays by ideas and smart implementation.[3] *The Wall Street Journal* reports that six companies: Amazon, Google, Apple, Facebook, Gilead and Walt Disney, " ... account for more than all of the $199 billion in market-capitalization gains in the S&P 500 [so far in 2015]."[4] Guess what's common to these companies: Their business models totally rely on intangible assets (patents, brands, movie rights, etc.).

It is important to realize that intangibles aren't creating value just at high-tech, Internet, or pharmaceutical businesses. Consumer product companies gain competitive edge by developing and using unique brands and trademarks, rather than by operating large manufacturing and distribution facilities. Financial companies thrive on innovation (Allstate's online Esurance) and unique services customized to specific clients' needs, rather than on massive capital, the old value-creating resource. Physical assets-intensive companies, like retailers, gain competitive edge by continuous innovation of business processes, like Walmart's unique supply chains, Federal Express's highly reliable distribution channels, or Amazon's customer recommendations algorithms. Coca-Cola's major asset is its highly valuable brand, and Goldman Sachs' dominance among investment bankers is due to its unique human capital and customer relations. Thus, successful enterprises in any sector are, by definition, intangibles-rich. The dominance of intangibles as a value-creation vehicle and main driver of a competitive edge is the hallmark of all modern economies, not just the United States. Increasing the number of patents granted to local companies has, in recent years, been a declared policy of the Chinese government.[5] So, we deal here with a pervasive and persistent worldwide phenomenon that is sure to continue rising.

One would expect the dramatic rise of intangible capital as the major creator of corporate value to generate a substantial change in accounting and be fully reflected in corporate financial reports. No chance. In fact, despite the shift portrayed by Figure 8.1, no significant changes or modifications were made in the accounting system to accommodate the surging intangibles phenomenon. Thus, an outdated and poorly reasoned accounting standard enacted 40 years ago, before the rise to prominence of the software, biotech, telecommunication, and the Internet sectors—all virtually intangible—still governs the accounting and financial reporting for R&D in the United States.[6] Go figure.

ACCOUNTING FOR INTANGIBLES, INCONSISTENT AND OPAQUE

The US accounting rules are clear: Internally generated intangibles—through R&D (patents and trademarks), marketing (brands, customer relations), development (business processes), or training (human resources)—are treated like regular expenses (charged immediately to income), whereas the same intangibles, if acquired, either directly, like patents or brands, or through corporate acquisitions (R&D-in-process, customers lists), are considered assets and capitalized and, then, some are amortized.[7] Why the difference? Because, accounting standard-setters argue, the values of acquired intangibles are objectively determined in arm's-length transactions with the sellers, while the values of the intangibles generated internally by the company are uncertain—an R&D program can fail—and therefore don't qualify as assets to be reported on the balance sheet.[8]

This distinction and its underlying justification defy logic. First, acquired intangibles, like patents, can fail in the development or marketing stages, just as internally generated intangibles can. In 2011, Hewlett-Packard acquired the UK Company Autonomy for over $10 billion. A large part of this acquisition were Autonomy's intangible cloud software and development programs. A year later, HP wrote off almost 90 percent of the $10 billion acquisition cost as a loss. So much for the "certainty" of acquired intangibles. Second, regarding the "arm's-length" nature of acquired intangibles, the major cost components of internally generated intangibles—scientists' salaries for R&D, or advertising outlays for brands—are also determined in arm's-length transactions with third parties: scientists and advertising agencies. So, what's the difference between acquiring intangibles directly from other companies (capitalized) or acquiring the services of third parties to develop intangibles (expensed)? There is none, of course. In each case, the company transacts with third parties. Thus, the accounting contrast between internally generated versus acquired intangibles is a distinction without a difference. Both internally generated and acquired intangibles create risky assets, but being subject to risk doesn't justify ignoring (i.e., expensing) these assets. The fact that US companies spend over a trillion dollars a year on intangibles (R&D, brands, IT, human resources) attests to the fact that these are real assets generating substantial future benefits and should be treated as such by the accounting system.[9]

WORST YET—MISLEADING INFORMATION

Consider Pfizer, a pharmaceutical giant, which has struggled in recent years with blockbuster drugs (Lipitor) going off patent, with the absence of similarly best-selling drugs coming off the pipeline, and the consequent declining revenues. An investor relying on accounting indicators to analyze Pfizer wouldn't know all this. Pfizer's 2013 return-on-equity (ROE) was a whopping 28 percent. Very few large and successful companies boast such an elevated ROE (Exxon's was 19 percent in 2013 and Walmart's 21 percent). How did the challenged Pfizer manage to rack up a 28 percent ROE? You guessed it, with the "magic" of accounting for intangibles. While the numerator of the ROE (earnings) fully reflects the benefits of past drug development and an efficient sales force, the denominator—net assets (equity)—doesn't reflect the assets (patents, brands) generating those benefits, because the outlays on R&D, brands, and employee training were expensed (charged to income) long ago.[10] Thus, a shrunken denominator does the 28 percent ROE trick.

But note the accounting absurdity: Had Pfizer acquired its drug patents, rather than having developed them, its ROE would have been substantially lower, since its equity (ROE denominator) would have fully reflected the amortized values of the acquired patents. Same company and assets; vastly different reported performance. Obviously, accounting rules make it impossible to compare profitability of companies within a sector having different innovation strategies: developing internally vs. buying intangibles. How many investors and analysts routinely make such comparisons, unaware of the accounting distortions? But wait, the accounting plot gets thicker.

The expensing of intangible investments affects both the numerator (earnings) and denominator (equity, or total assets) of profitability ratios; earnings are reduced by the expensing of, say, R&D, and equity too is understated by the absence of R&D capital. Regrettably for investors, the total effect on profitability ratios is complex and depends on where in its lifecycle the company is. Pfizer is a mature company with *decreasing* R&D.[11] For such companies, the negative impact of intangibles' expensing on the numerator of ROE is *lower* than the denominator effect, hence Pfizer's high ROE ratio. For growth companies like Google, with increasing investment in intangibles, the accounting effect reverses, and the expensing of intangibles understates profitability measures, such as ROE or ROA (return-on-assets).[12] This is very tricky, and, we bet, unknown to most investors and analysts. Since the intangibles' accounting distortions are legion, we can't resist exposing one more.

Consider Boeing and competitor Lockheed Martin, which follow different innovation strategies: Boeing develops most of its technology internally—its 2012 R&D-to-sales ratio was 4 percent and its goodwill-to-assets ratio, reflecting the intensity of technology acquisitions, was 5.7 percent. In contrast, Lockheed Martin relies mainly on technology acquisitions. Its 2012, R&D-to-sales ratio was only 1 percent, but its goodwill-to-assets ratio was 26.8 percent, almost five-times Boeing's. Since Boeing expenses its R&D and other technology outlays immediately—and, unlike Pfizer, these outlays are increasing—Boeing's 2012 ROA is understated and substantially lower than Lockheed Martin's: 4.6 percent vs. 7.2 percent. Is Boeing's *real* profitability so much lower than Lockheed's? Highly unlikely. Various factors affect companies' ROA, of course, but the arbitrary accounting treatment of the different innovation strategies of the companies—internal generation vs. acquisition—had a large effect on the ROA difference, distorting any meaningful comparison of the relative profitability of Boeing and Lockheed Martin, and disabling an evaluation of the different technology development strategies. It is not for nothing we titled this section *Misleading Information.*[13]

As a disturbing aside, think about the distortions in important managerial decisions induced by the accounting for intangibles. For growth companies, for example, acquiring intangibles, rather than developing them internally, will raise reported earnings and asset values (avoiding the expensing of intangibles). A desire to report higher earnings—particularly for early-stage, earnings-challenged companies—will obviously lead managers to prefer acquisitions over the internal generation of intangibles, even if long-term this is the wrong strategy.[14] We apologize, patient reader, for dwelling on accounting matters here, but the intangibles issue is so central, and the resistance of accounting authorities to change so strong, that to be effective, a comprehensive critique is required.

MORE BAD NEWS

As if the accounting rules for recording intangibles aren't bad enough, the opaqueness of financial reports are an even greater hindrance for investors. Except for the total expenditure on R&D, which has to be reported by US companies (but not uniformly throughout the world), financial reports don't provide *any* useful information about investments in intangibles and their outcomes, in footnotes or supplementary data. Which brings to mind a meeting one of us had a few years back with the CFO of a major pharmaceutical company, in which the executive waxed proudly about the hundreds of successful alliances and joint ventures the company has, intended to enhance research, production, and marketing activities. Are these alliances contributing to your revenue stream we asked? Substantially so, was the answer. But your financial reports are mum about alliances, and your income statement doesn't indicate the amount of revenues, and/or cost savings from all these joint ventures, nor does it reveal the costs of this activity, we said. True, said the CFO, but accounting rules don't require such disclosure. Sadly, this is also true. Thus, both the investment and outcomes of a major strategic intangible—alliances and joint ventures—are completely obscured from investors.[15]

A similar "conspiracy of silence" applies to all other intangibles: The reported R&D expense isn't a very meaningful number without the underlying breakdowns, such as how much the company spent on the R (basic research, aimed at developing new technologies) and on the D (development, the tweaking of current technologies). Without such a breakdown, investors remain in the dark about the innovation strategy of the company. Is it primarily an imitator, or a real innovator? But at least *total* R&D is reported,[16] which is not the case for other major investments in intangibles, such as information technology (software, in particular), brands and trademarks, unique business processes, or human resources. None of these value-enhancing expenditures are disclosed separately in the income statement; they are, rather, buried in sales, general and administrative expenses (SG&A), or other accounting "graveyards."[17]

There is no way for investors to know, for example, if the company develops its human capital (invests in employee training) or lets it whither on the vine, or whether it maintains its brands or organization capital or lets them fade away. In the absence of such information, how can investors compare strategies among competing companies? There is also no way for investors to assess the *returns* on those all-important investments in innovation, since no information is disclosed about the *outcomes* of these investments, like revenues from recently introduced products (*innovation revenues*) or from the licensing of patents. A true information blackout. So, even if one accepts accountants' misguided view that intangibles' risk disqualifies them from being recognized as assets on the balance sheet, why not provide illuminating footnote information about these prime value creators? A no brainer, really.

MORE, NOT LESS INFORMATION IS NEEDED

Ironically, rather than having less information about intangibles, both investors and managers should have substantially more information about these critical assets. Why? Along with the considerable value-creation potential of intangibles, there is a dark side to these assets: They are difficult to manage, and their performance and value is particularly hard for investors to assess. Consider the following example.

When investors see $500 million worth of airplanes on American Airlines' (AA) balance sheet, they aren't overly concerned that these airplanes may be whisked away by United, or simply vanish—a ridiculous idea for corporate-owned physical assets. Investors can also ascertain pretty accurately the real (as opposed to the balance sheet) value of AA's airplane fleet from footnote information about the type of planes, their age, and public data on used aircraft prices. Similarly, information about the air fleet capacity utilization (load factor) enables investors to assess the productivity of the fleet and the efficiency of its deployment. In short, the uncertainty about the security, value, and productivity of physical assets, like airplanes or plant and machinery is rather low, and the accuracy with which investors can value tangibles-rich companies is commensurately high.

In contrast, the uniqueness and nontradability of intangibles pose a serious challenge to investors: While most physical and financial assets are traded in transparent markets, allowing investors to assess fairly accurately their value from observed transactions and prices, there are no transparent markets in intangibles. There is a certain trade in patents and even brands, but published details (prices) are scarce. Accordingly, an important source of information for investors—market prices, or prices of similar assets (like houses sold in your neighborhood)—is unavailable for intangibles. Nor can investors learn about intangibles' value from competitors' reports, because intangibles are unique. Pfizer's patents are nothing like Merck's, and Coca-Cola's brands (Nestea) bear no resemblance to Pepsi's (Doritos). Thus, an analyst valuing Pfizer can't learn much about its most important assets from other drug companies. The risks associated with intangibles—infringement, disruption, unlawful imitation (planes aren't stolen but patents often are infringed upon)—also differ from the risks of physical and financial assets, and investor's information about intangibles' risks is scarce.

Given such serious information shortages regarding intangibles, one would expect substantially more information about these key assets disclosed in corporate financial reports, rather than practically none. The consequence, as we now show, is that this information lacuna is a major reason for the fast-diminishing usefulness of the financial report.

INTANGIBLES AND THE ACCOUNTING RELEVANCE LOST

We have discussed so far in this chapter the dramatic rise of intangible capital, which is becoming the leading corporate value creator, and the inexplicable lack of recognition of this development by the accounting and financial reporting systems. We have also alluded to a link between the rise of intangibles and the fall of accounting relevance, but we haven't established this link. Here comes this proof.

The rise of intangibles is a fairly recent phenomenon. Prior to the 1980s, intangible assets were primarily deployed in certain R&D-intensive chemical, pharmaceutical, and electrical/electronics companies, as well as some brand-intensive consumer product businesses (Coca-Cola, Procter & Gamble). The 1980s saw the emergence of entire industries that were virtually intangible, such as software and biotech. The intangibles-intensity trend picked up considerably in the 1990s with the burgeoning of the Internet and telecommunication sectors, and further with healthcare and energy alternatives enterprises in the 2000s (the World Wide Web first went live in 1991). Also, starting in the 1980s, incumbents and new entrants to traditional industries—steel, oil & gas, retailing, finance—realized that a competitive edge can only be gained and secured by unique innovations, such as mini-steel mills, online insurance, gas fracking, and so on. Thus—and this is key—from the late 1970s, successive vintages of new businesses were, generally, more reliant on intangibles than were their predecessors. And if intangible intensity contributes to the deterioration of accounting relevance—and this is the crux of our test—then the relevance of the financial reports of successive vintages of new public companies entering the market in the 1970s, 1980s, 1990s, and so on, *should decrease*. This is a test of causality: from intangibles to accounting usefulness.

We accordingly focus on companies that became public (entered a US stock exchange) in each of the past six decades: the 1950s, 1960s, 1970s, 1980s, 1990s, and 2000s. For the new companies in each decade, we replicate the first accounting relevance test reported for all companies in Chapter 3: relating market value (capitalization) to annual earnings and book values in each year, starting with the first year of the decade (1951, 1961, etc.) and ending in the last year. Figure 8.2 reports the R^2 values of these decade regressions, indicating the relevance of earnings and book values to investors' valuations of companies becoming public in the 1950s, 1960s, 1970s, ..., 2000s.[18] Each decade is represented by a bar in Figure 8.2. The up-sloping curve on top of the bars reflects companies' intangible intensity.

The message of the sharply decreasing bars is unmistakable: As new companies enter the market, generally endowed with more intangible capital than their predecessors (see up-sloping curve), the relevance of their financial information decreases sharply: from R^2 exceeding 80 percent in the 1950s, to roughly 25 percent in the 2000s. In each successive decade, the relevance of the key accounting variables is seen to significantly diminish. Since the main attribute that characterizes these successive vintages of stock market entrants is their increasing intangibles intensity (see the rising R&D + SG&A curve in Figure 8.2; many intangible investments are included in SG&A),

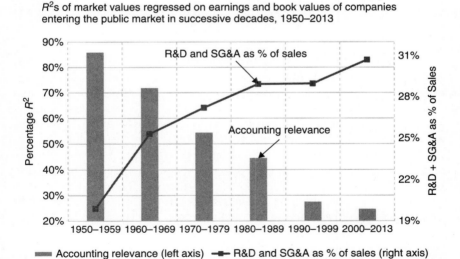

R^2s of market values regressed on earnings and book values of companies entering the public market in successive decades, 1950–2013

FIGURE 8.2 Decreasing Accounting Relevance by Vintage Year of Public Companies

the obvious conclusion is that this intangibles intensity is *a primary cause* of the sharp deterioration in financial information usefulness.[19]

NOT IN THEIR BEST INTEREST

Finally, we know what's on your mind: Given the damage accounting—or rather the nonaccounting—for intangibles causes financial information, why aren't corporate managers, who are primarily responsible for disclosing financial information, or auditors, who attest to the quality and relevance of this information, up in arms about changing the archaic accounting rules concerning intangibles? When it's in their interest, managers and auditors don't shy away from lobbying accounting regulators, and lobbying them hard. Why are managers and auditors so blasé about accounting for intangibles?

The reason lies, we believe, in their incentives: Managers are generally reluctant to present relatively risky assets, such as intangibles, on the balance sheet, since ownership infringement and technological changes (disruptions) may diminish the value of their intangibles (think Blackberry's patents demolished by Apple's iPhone), forcing managers to report the value losses (impairment) and face embarrassing questions by directors and shareholders. Better for managers—but not for investors, of course—to immediately delete such assets from the balance sheet (and investors' memory) by expensing them, than being held responsible for years for their creation or acquisition. Overly cynical? Perhaps, but what else could explain managers' complicity with the demonstrably dated and illogical expensing and opacity of intangibles?[20]

Auditors have different incentives: They are greatly concerned with shareholder lawsuits following large drops in the company's share price, due to unexpected losses or business failure, where plaintiffs allege that the auditors failed to alert investors to the fragility and risk of certain assets on the balance sheet. This litigation risk is mitigated when intangibles aren't reported as assets and auditors don't attest to their value.[21] Thus, the main "influencers" of accounting and reporting rules—managers and auditors—are quite happy with the status quo, despite its glaring deficiencies and damage to investors' information. It seems that only a forceful demand by investors for better information on intangibles could motivate managers and auditors to change their complacency.

TAKEAWAY

Intangibles' rise to prominence among value-creating corporate resources is the most profound business development of the past quarter century.

This change affected every facet of the business world—except accounting. We have argued in this chapter that, due to their unique attributes, intangible assets require *more*, not less disclosure than physical and financial assets, and we proved that intangibles are a major cause of accounting's relevance lost. Obviously, no substantial improvement in financial reporting can ignore intangibles.[22] But intangibles are not the only reason for the accounting fade. Stay with us please.

NOTES

1. Nina Adam, "Business Investment Is Changing Its Stripes," *The Wall Street Journal,* August 17, 2015, p. A2.
2. On the irrelevance of physical and financial capital, see Geoff Colvin, "Heavy Hitters Travel Light," *Fortune*, February 1, 2016, p. 20.
3. The total intangibles value at US public companies in 2011 was estimated as $8.1 trillion, out of $17.4 trillion total market value; see Kevin Hassett and Robert Shapiro, "What Ideas Are Worth: The Value of Intellectual Capital and Intangible Assets in the American Economy," Sonecon.
4. Dan Strumpf, "The Casino's Last Stand—Six Stocks Account for All of S&P Gains This Year," *The Wall Street Journal* (July 27, 2015), p. C1.
5. The policy is indeed successful. Chinese companies currently file twice the number of patents filed by American companies. But doubts regarding the quality of Chinese patents linger, see "Patent Fiction," *The Economist* (December 13, 2014).
6. Financial Accounting Standards Board, ASC 730 (1974). This standard, mandating the immediate expensing of R&D, ranks high among the FASB standards that decreased shareholder value. See Urooj Khan, Bin Li, Shivaram Rajgopal, and Mohan Venkatachalam, *Do the FASB's Standards Add Shareholder Value?* working paper (Columbia Business School, 2014).
7. The accounting distinction between assets (capital) and expenses is clear: Assets, like plant or securities, provide future benefits, whereas expenses, like salaries or rent, are payments for past services without future benefits. Thus, the accounting treatment of intangible investments as expenses absurdly implies that they don't provide reliable future benefits. Tell Microsoft (2015 R&D: $12B), or IBM (2014 R&D: $5.4B) that their R&D efforts have no future benefits. Research refutes this accounting rule by documenting a statistically significant correlation between R&D and stock prices or subsequent sales growth. For example, David Hirshleifer, Po-Hsuan Hsu, and Dongmei Li, "Innovative Efficiency and Stock Returns," *Journal of Financial Economics*, 107 (2013): 632–654. " ... regressions show that a higher IE [innovative efficiency, patents per dollar R&D] measure predicts significantly higher return on assets and cash flows ... and future stock returns ... "
8. The international accounting standard, used in European and some other countries, allows under strict circumstances the capitalization (recognition as assets)

of development costs beyond the initial research phase. However, these circumstances are rather strict and many companies subject to this rule either don't capitalize these costs at all, or they capitalize relatively small amounts. As to the United States, certain software development costs can be capitalized, but relatively few companies do so.

9. For the spending of over $1 trillion a year, see Carol Corrado, Charles Hulten, and Daniel Sichel, in *Measuring Capital in the New Economy*, (Chicago: University of Chicago Press, 2005), pp. 11–45. "... our best guesses suggest that business spending on intangibles was about $1.2 trillion annually in the late 1990s, more than 13 percent of GDP" (p. 30).

10. Since Pfizer's R&D expenses were declining during 2011–2013, the "hit" to current earnings from R&D expensing was lower than in previous years.

11. Pfizer's R&D for the years 2011, 2012, and 2013 was $8.7 billion, $7.5 billion, and $6.7 billion, respectively. Pfizer's sales, general & administrative (SG&A) expenses, which includes many intangibles (IT consultants' fees, for example) also decreased over the three years. Pfizer's 2014 R&D rose to $8.4 billion.

12. See Baruch Lev, Bharat Sarath, and Theodore Sougiannis, "R&D Reporting Biases and Their Consequences," *Contemporary Accounting Research*, 22 (2005): 977–1026, for a comprehensive discussion, supported by evidence, of the distortions of performance measures caused by the inept accounting for intangibles.

13. Interestingly, the governmental accounting of the economy—the National Accounts—is much more advanced than corporate accounting (GAAP) when it comes to intangibles. In the National Accounts, both software and R&D, as well as other intangibles, are capitalized. This accounting change from expensing to capitalization made a big difference: "We find that the inclusion of intangibles [as capital] makes a significant difference in the measured pattern of economic growth: The growth rates of output and output-per-worker are found to increase at a noticeably more rapid rate when intangibles are included ...." From Carol Corrado, Charles Hulten, Daniel Sichel, *Intangible Capital and Economic Growth*, working Paper 11948 (Cambridge, MA: National Bureau of Economic Research, 2006). Obviously, similar information improvements would result from a corporate accounting change related to intangibles.

14. See Lucile Faurel, "Market Valuation of Corporate Investments: Acquisitions Versus R&D and Capital Expenditures," working paper (2013), for the superiority of internally generated investments over acquired ones.

15. Because the inputs (costs) and outputs of corporate "connectivity" (alliances) don't have to be reported externally, they are often not reported internally either, and only a few companies conduct a systematic evaluation of this important corporate activity. This was confirmed by the consulting company McKinsey, reporting that "... very few companies systematically track their [alliances] performance," in James Bamford and David Ernst, "Managing an Alliance Portfolio," *The McKinsey Quarterly*, 3 (2002): 29–39.

16. What's in this item is another question: Some companies, wishing to appear innovative, include in R&D all kinds of "related" expenses, like maintenance or quality control. R&D is ill defined in accounting.

17. Indeed, a recent study shows a constant increase in companies' SG&A expenses, see Anup Srivastava, "Why Have Measures of Earnings Quality Changed over Time?" *Journal of Accounting and Economics*, 57 (2014): 196–217.

18. As in Figure 3.1, in these regressions, we include the number of shares outstanding as a size control. A reminder: The difference between Figures 3.1 and 8.2 is that the former includes in each year *all* the public companies (with required data) trading in that year, new and old, whereas each bar of Figure 8.2 represents companies that *entered* the market during that decade only.

19. For those who are concerned with the changing composition of new companies in every decade, we conducted one more test, focusing on the companies that existed throughout the examined six-decade period. For companies in this sample that increased their R&D-to-sales ratio from the first 30 years to the latter 30 years, the accounting usefulness in the second period decreased sharply relative to the first period. For those that didn't change, or even decreased their R&D, accounting usefulness was stable. Once more, intangibles increase is hazardous to accounting relevance.

20. The comment letters the FASB solicited in the early 1970s, prior to the enactment of the expensing of R&D rule, reveal that many of the responding corporate managers and auditors supported the proposed intangibles expensing rule. While engaging in conspiracy theory, here is an even more outrageous one we heard from no other than the CEO of a large, successful company: When intangibles are expensed, cutting the intangibles outlays, say R&D, increases reported earnings dollar for dollar. When intangibles are capitalized, cutting the outlays will have a much smaller effect on current-year expenses and earnings, since most of the intangibles amortization (replacing the immediate expensing) is determined by past intangibles outlays. Immediate expensing of intangibles thus provides managers with a powerful earnings management tool, said the CEO.

21. There is, perhaps, a glimmer of hope for an accounting change. On December 7, 2013, (page 68), the *Economist* reported on potential changes in the standard and famously bland auditors' report on the financial statements in both America and the European Union: "One aims to make audit reports more useful by requiring a section highlighting 'critical audit matters'—the high-stake judgment calls that keep accountants up at night, such as how the business being audited has valued its intangible assets."

22. The OECD (Organization for Economic Cooperation and Development) concurs. The *Wall Street Journal* reports that following a two-year study, the OECD concluded that "...companies now tend to invest as much or more in knowledge-based capital as they do in physical capital, such as machinery and equipment. That, according to the OECD, is creating new challenges for policy makers, for businesses, and for the ways *in which economic activity is measured*" (emphasis ours). Nina Adam, "Business Investment Is Changing Its Stripes," *The Wall Street Journal* (August 17, 2015), p. A2. This chapter highlighted the challenges for the measurement and reporting of corporate activity by the dated accounting for intangibles.

CHAPTER 9

Accounting: Facts or Fiction?

Accounting information is generally believed to be factual (the company purchased 500 units), but nothing could be further from the truth. Accounting items — like revenues, expenses, and assets — are increasingly based on managers' subjective estimates and projections, which sometimes amount to sheer guesses. We expose in this chapter the detrimental effect of these estimates on the usefulness to investors of financial information, by documenting the steep rise in the frequency of estimates, due to accounting regulations, and linking this rise empirically to the deterioration in accounting's usefulness. We thus identify the second major cause of accounting's relevance lost.

"GE BRINGS GOOD THINGS TO LIFE," BUT NOT TO ACCOUNTING

General Electric's 2013 earnings per share (EPS) from continuing operations came at $1.47, compared with $1.38 and $1.23 for 2012 and 2011, respectively. Don't you marvel at the exactitude of accounting? Computing the earnings of a worldwide company with 307,000 employees and annual revenues of $146 billion *to the last penny?* EPS of $1.47, not $1.46, or $1.48. No uncertainty ("around $1.50"), or range ("between $1.40 and $1.50"). Exact and incontrovertible measurement of business performance. No wonder the accounting system has endured for so long; where in life will you find such resoluteness and reliability?

But scratch the shining surface a bit and you'll find that all this exactitude and definitiveness is a façade; lurking in the background is rampant uncertainty and vagueness. Start with GE's whopping $146 billion revenue in 2013. This is surely a fact, you say, amenable to exact measurement, since it represents sales actually made to customers. Not so fast; a certain part of the $146 billion revenue is, in fact, based on managers' subjective estimates—and quite a few estimates at that. Here are GE's own words, in the 2013 footnote on "Sales of Goods and Services":

> We *estimate* total long-term contract revenue .... For larger oil drilling equipment projects and long-term construction projects, we recognize sales ... in relation to our *estimate* of total expected costs .... We measure sales of commercial aircraft engines by applying our contract-specific *estimated* margin rates to incurred costs .... Significant components of our revenue and cost *estimates* include price concessions and performance-related guarantees.... (italics are ours)

You get the drift: There are multiple estimates—subjective managerial projections—underlying the $146 billion revenue. As for the most important question for investors—How much of total revenue is based on estimates and how much is a fact (5 percent estimates vs. 95 percent regular sales? 30 vs. 70 percent?)—GE doesn't say (it's not required to). So, how certain can one be that GE's 2013 sales were in fact $146 billion and not, say, $135 billion? No one knows.

And this ambiguity relates only to revenue. Continue with GE's income statement and you'll find that many expense items are based on estimates, too: depreciation and amortization, bad-debt reserve, pensions and warranties expenses, employee stock options expense, and so on. So the bottom line of $1.47 EPS for 2013 is anything but an exact number. In fact, it is based on layers over layers of subjective managerial estimates, projections, and sometimes sheer guesses.[1] Not even the company's managers, we venture, know how much of the $1.47 EPS is fact and how much results from estimation. Under slightly different assumptions of the estimates underlying earnings, the $1.47 EPS could easily become $1.30 or $1.55. Amazingly, investors take seriously a one-penny miss of analysts' consensus estimate. TV viewers are warned that polling results are subject to a specific margin of error ($\pm 3\%$), whereas investors are presented with "definite" numbers. It is important to note that estimates are not unique to GE. Managerial subjective judgments are in the nature of accounting and financial reporting, significantly affecting virtually all corporate financial reports.

HOW DID ESTIMATES COME TO DOMINATE ACCOUNTING?

Accounting has come a long way since the late nineteenth century when the limited liability corporation became established as the main form of conducting business. Back then, corporate financial reports to shareholders primarily reflected facts: amounts paid to vendors and received from customers, money raised from investors and lenders and subsequently invested in plant, equipment, corporate acquisitions, or dividends distributed to shareholders. Over the years, accounting authorities enacted an ever-increasing number of rules and standards (accounting and reporting generally accepted principles, or GAAP) calling for the piling on of subjective items in financial reports. Rather than just stating on the balance sheet the factual amount owed by customers (accounts receivable), GAAP imposes the need to subtract from it an estimated loss from expected delinquencies; or, instead of stating the cost of inventories (a fact), one must reduce it to market value (often an estimate), if cost exceeds such value. Other estimates quickly followed: warranties provisions, pension and post-retirement benefits expenses, assets and goodwill write-offs, and, more recently, employee stock options expense, and gains/losses from adjusting assets and liabilities to fair values (quite hairy estimates). Often, multiple estimates and forecasts are layered on in a single expense item: The employee stock option expense, for example, requires three to four different estimates/projections (expected dividend yield, range of interest rates, expected volatilities, expected life), blended into one item.[2] The balance sheet is also replete with items based on managerial estimates: The values of nontraded financial assets and liabilities are adjusted to current (fair) values, but since there are no market prices for these nontraded assets/liabilities, such adjustment is in fact an estimate; and the values of intangibles (goodwill, in-process-R&D) are also estimates derived from the process of determining the fair values of the assets and liabilities obtained through a business acquisition (M&A).

How did accounting get to be so heavily based on managerial subjective estimates, judgments, and projections? Why was the sage opinion of A. C. Littleton, a profound accounting thinker, so totally ignored? He said, "Accounting is concerned only with realities. When accounting is loosed from the anchor of fact, it is afloat upon a sea of psychological estimates which are beyond the power of accounting, as such, to express,"[3] The short—and long—answer: Good intentions run amok.

AWAY WITH HISTORICAL VALUES

A company's assets used to be reported on the balance sheet at original acquisition costs, but as the distance from acquisition date to the present lengthens, those original costs often deviate from current asset values. Is the house you purchased 10 years ago worth the same today? A value updating (mark-to-market) is accordingly called for to retain the relevance of the balance sheet as a realistic report of the values of assets and liabilities. This, of course, makes a lot of sense for assets that are traded in organized and transparent markets, like stocks or bonds, and even for assets whose market value can be reliably ascertained from publicly available prices, like used cars (the famous "Blue Book") and equipment, or from observed comparable transactions, like real estate sales in areas with considerable turnover. However, in their zeal to "fair value" (adjust to current prices) all assets and liabilities, accounting standard-setters mandated the marking-to-market of various assets and liabilities, like financial instruments and other specialized securities that are not traded in organized markets and for which there are no similarly traded securities ("Level 3" assets/liabilities in the accounting jargon). The "values" of such assets/liabilities are not anchored in any reality or fact; they are often derived from complex models with multiple assumptions and projections, prone to error and manipulation. On such *marked-to-market* items, Warren Buffett quipped: "This is not marked-to-market, rather marked-to-myth."

Similarly, standard-setters' drive to enhance the balance sheet's relevance led to the requirement to adjust long-term assets and goodwill values down to fair (market) values, whenever the latter fall below book values. These so called *asset write-offs* are in many cases questionable estimates based on the largely unreliable prediction of elusive long-term future cash flows of assets.[4] Most assets employed by businesses (plant, machinery) operate jointly with other corporate resources, such as information technology, in the production process, and therefore no specific future cash flows can be assigned to such assets. Accordingly, both the "fair" values of these assets and liabilities, and the consequent impairment expenses hitting earnings, are often based on questionable estimates that are hard to audit but easy to manipulate.[5] Are we going too far with this criticism? A colleague justified such estimates by the cliché "better be approximately right than absolutely wrong." But without providing investors with information about the reliability of such estimates (confidence intervals), and their impact on sales and earnings, they just increase information noise.

We aren't rejecting all accounting estimates, since not all estimates are born alike. Some, based on solid past experience, like the bad-debt and warranty expenses, are reasonably reliable, while many others aren't. A vivid example of the latter is found in Pfizer's 2006 annual report, describing the various estimates required to set the balance sheet value of in-process-R&D (IPRD), acquired through M&A:

> ...*the amount and timing of projected future cash flows; the amount and timing of projected costs to develop the IPRD into commercially viable products; the discount rate selected to measure the risks inherent in the future cash flows; and the assessment of the asset's life cycle and the competitive trends impacting the assets*...

And this amalgam of guesses and speculations makes its way to the balance sheet and is supposed to be taken seriously by investors.[6]

Specific suggestions to enhance the reliability of accounting estimates—such as a required periodic report comparing key estimates with subsequent realizations, including managers comments on deviations—were made in the past, yet none were adopted or, to the best of our knowledge, even seriously considered by regulators.[7] Our proposed remedy (Part III of the book) is drastically different. We simply eliminate the need for most estimates from our information paradigm. But, first, true to our approach, we will empirically document that the prevalence of accounting estimates in financial reports is indeed increasing, and that it is a major cause of the deteriorating usefulness of financial information.

ROLL THE TAPE

For accounting estimates to be a major cause of the *deterioration* of financial information usefulness over the past 50 years, they have to increase in frequency and impact. Did they? To check, we have randomly chosen 50 companies of the S&P 500 universe, representing most of the important economic sectors: manufacturing, retail, defense, technology, media & entertainment, financial services, and energy enterprises. We then compiled a "dictionary" of keywords synonymous with the terms estimates and forecasts, such as: expected, estimated, projected, anticipated, likely, assumed, and so on. Finally, we chose five years to detect a recent pattern: 1995, 2000, 2005, 2011, and 2013. For each of the 50 representative companies and each of the five years, we carefully read the footnotes (explanations) to the annual financial reports—these footnotes often stretch over 50 to 60 pages—and counted the number of times the keywords in our "estimate-related dictionary" were mentioned in the footnotes.

Figure 9.1 traces the mean and median of the number of times estimate-related terms were mentioned in the sample firms' annual financial report over the past 20 years. Clearly, both the mean and median frequencies of estimate-related terms in corporate report footnotes sharply increased, from about 30 mentions of estimate expressions, on average, in a 1995 financial report, to around 100 a decade later (2005), growing further to 150 in 2013. A fivefold increase over the period, where the main increase occurring between 2000 and 2011, coincides with major new accounting regulations pertaining to fair value (marked-to-market) accounting. Thus, the increase in the frequency of estimate-related terms in financial reports, suggesting an increase in the actual number of estimates used in the preparation of these reports, correlates nicely with the deterioration in financial information usefulness documented in Part I.

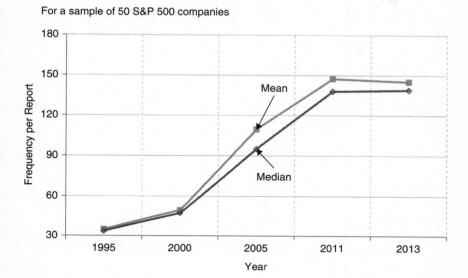

For a sample of 50 S&P 500 companies

FIGURE 9.1 Increasing Frequency of Estimate-related Terms in Financial Reports

Our 50-firm sample evidence is fully corroborated by a recent study, using a similar methodology, but on a much larger sample—4,000 companies (computers came in handy in the assessment).[8] Like us, the authors document a constant increase in the frequency of estimate-related terms over the 1990s and 2000s. Importantly, they also report that the frequency of mentioning estimates is negatively correlated with subsequent stock returns, implying that investors aren't fully aware of the vulnerability of estimation-based financial information to errors and manipulation, only to later on discover that the share prices of companies whose financial reports rely heavily on managerial estimates tend to fall in subsequent periods, likely because the veil of rosy estimates masks underlying operating difficulties. The proliferation of accounting estimates indeed has seriously adverse consequences for investors.

Since readers may doubt whether *speaking* about estimates—our preceding test of counting the frequency of mentioning estimates—is the same as the actual number of estimates, and more important, their impact on financial information, we provide in Figure 9.2 the "real thing." We focus here on the income statement categories known as "extraordinary and special items," along with restructuring charges, which include various substantive accounting estimates (e.g., impairment charges). Figure 9.2 reports for all public companies with positive earnings the mean value

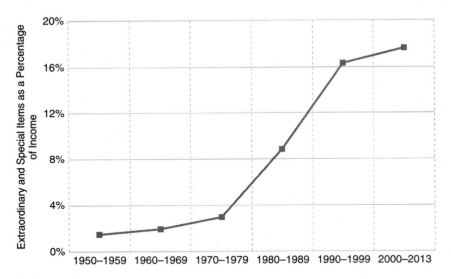

FIGURE 9.2 Increasing Amount of Extraordinary and Special Items Relative to Net Income, All Companies, 1950–2013

of extraordinary and special items (divided by earnings) over the period, 1950–2013, in 10 years aggregates. Once more, it's evident that the impact of accounting special items—multiple estimates—on reported earnings has been continuously on the rise over the past 20 years, reflecting both the sharp increase in the number of estimates used for income determination, as well as their impact on financial information, as measured by the ratio of special items to earnings.

CLINCHING THE DEAL

OK, so there was a substantial increase in the number of accounting estimates and their earnings' impact over the past two to three decades, but can we link this increase directly to the deterioration in the usefulness of financial reports? To address this question we ranked in each of the five years examined (1995, 2000, 2005, 2011, and 2013) the 50 S&P 500 companies for which we documented the increasing frequency of estimate-related terms in financial reports (Figure 9.1), and classified these companies into two equal-sized groups by the frequency of estimation terms: above and below median (midpoint) frequency. We then performed for each company, in each of the five years, the test of earnings usefulness that we introduced in Chapter 5: using current and past earnings (ROE) to predict the following

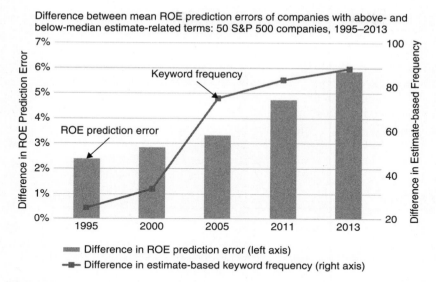

Difference between mean ROE prediction errors of companies with above- and below-median estimate-related terms: 50 S&P 500 companies, 1995–2013

FIGURE 9.3 ROE Prediction Errors Are Higher for Companies with Above-Median Number of Estimates

year's earnings.[9] Finally, we computed the absolute prediction errors of these forecasts (comparing forecasted to actually reported earnings), and averaged them for each of the two above/below median groups classified by the frequency of estimates.

If, as we argue, accounting estimates contribute to the deterioration in earnings' usefulness, then the earnings forecasts of the companies with below-median frequency of estimates (proxied by estimate-related expressions) should be more accurate than the earnings forecasts of the companies with above-median frequency of estimates. More estimates, more forecast inaccuracy and lower earnings usefulness.[10] And that's exactly what we find. Figure 9.3 presents the results of this test: The bars in Figure 9.3 present the difference in mean earnings prediction errors (inaccuracy) between companies with above-median estimate-mentioning frequency and below-median frequency. The fact that all the bars are positive implies that earnings prediction—a major investor activity—is less accurate for companies with multiple accounting estimates, relative to companies with fewer estimates. And the fact that the bars are rising reflects the increasing number and adverse impact of those estimates over time (see also the rising line in the figure showing the difference in estimate-related expressions between the two groups).

TAKEAWAY

We have documented a steep increase during the past two-to-three decades in the number of subjective managerial estimates and projections underlying financial (accounting) information, and directly linked this rise in estimates to the deterioration of financial information usefulness. Sensible suggestions to enhance the reliability of accounting estimates have been proposed (see also Chapter 17),[11] yet, apparently have not been implemented. Our preferred solution—elaborated in Part III of the book—is to dispose of most managerial estimates and primarily rely on facts. It can be done.

NOTES

1. For example, the employee pension expense—a generally large item—requires an estimate of long-term (5–7 years) expected gains on the pension assets (money invested in capital markets by the company to cover employee pension liabilities). No one but accountants can take seriously a prediction of 5–7 years of capital market performance (can you predict tomorrow's market performance?).
2. In its 2011 annual report, valuation of employee stock options footnote, the Cisco company stated: "... in management's opinion the existing valuation models [for employee stock options] may not provide an accurate measure of the fair value ... for the Company's employee stock options." We didn't see this comment in subsequent reports. Did the valuation models improve?
3. A. C. Littleton, "Value and Price in Accounting," *The Accounting Review*, 4 (1929): 147–154.
4. Financial Accounting Standard No. 144 (ASC 360, 2001). The Chairman of the International Accounting Standards Board, Hans Hoogervorst, said in 2012: "Most elements of goodwill are highly uncertain and subjective and they often turn out to be illusory." Available at: http://www.ifrs.org/Alerts/Conference.
5. It has been shown, for example, that managers postpone assets and goodwill write-offs to periods when the consequent expense will not draw investors' attention. See Kevin Li and Richard Sloan, *Has Goodwill Accounting Gone Bad?* working paper (Berkeley: University of California, 2014).
6. Sometimes the projection of future events determines even the classification of an item on the balance sheet, as with convertible debt (SFAS No. 150, 2003). Such debt, which can be at a future date converted to equity, requires managers of the issuing company to predict whether the debt will be converted in the future. Such an opinion/guess determines whether the debt should be included in equity or in liabilities—an important choice that affects the company's leverage (debt/equity ratio). Obviously, whether the debt will be converted or not depends on the future stock prices of the company, something about which neither managers nor the rest of us can have adequate knowledge.

7. Financial reports rarely provide the information needed to match estimates with subsequent realizations. See Chapter 17 for elaboration.
8. Jason Chen and Feng Li, *Estimating the Amount of Estimation in Accruals,* working paper (Ann Arbor: University of Michigan, 2013).
9. Since the 50 companies differ in size, rather than predicting earnings, we predicted the size-adjusted return-on-equity (ROE).
10. There may be, of course, additional factors in play, affecting both the number of estimates and earnings forecast accuracy.
11. See Baruch Lev, Stephen Ryan, and Min Wu, "Rewriting Earnings History," *Review of Accounting Studies,* 13 (2008): 419–451.

CHAPTER 10

Sins of Omission and Commission

Have you had enough already with the reasons for the deteriorating usefulness of financial information? We can't resist one more, since this one flies under the radar of even experts. This is the disturbing fact that despite accounting's aura of exactitude and comprehensiveness, there is an increasing number of important, value-changing business events that escape the accounting net or that are reported in a systematically biased manner. We show in this chapter that this commonplace, yet unadvertised omission is an important contributor to accounting's relevance lost, and should be part of the solution.

THE MISSING ACCOUNTING LINK

On September 20, 2013, the Dutch biotech company Prosensa Holding NV announced that its muscular dystrophy experimental drug Drisapersen failed to help patients more than a placebo. This is the nightmare of every drug and biotech company, and indeed, investors' reaction was swift and harsh: Prosensa's stock plunged 70 percent on the announcement of the trial's failure. It was not a total loss, though, since the stock of Sarepta Therapeutics Inc., a competing biotech firm developing an alternative muscular dystrophy drug increased 18 percent on Prosensa's failure announcement. One company's loss is another's gain. Large drug companies, with diversified portfolios of drugs under development, aren't hit as hard by clinical test failures, but they are hit nevertheless. The large British pharmaceutical company AstraZeneca lost 2.5 percent of its stock price around August 8, 2012, when it announced an unsuccessful Phase IIb test of its treatment for severe sepsis. Lest you wonder: investors react, of course, not only to bad news. On June 24, 2013, Isis (what a choice of name) Pharmaceuticals Inc., saw its stock price rise almost 30 percent after announcing clinical trial results showing that its APOCIII drug successfully raised the "good cholesterol" level in the blood.

The reason we share with you these clinical-test announcements is that they obviously have a significant effect on corporate value (share prices)—signaling, in case of test success, increases in future revenues and earnings, and vice versa for trial failures—but, and this is our point, they have no effect on the accounting system. Similar major business events—like the results of "beta tests" (technological feasibility) for software and technology products, the launch of new products and services, the signing of important contracts, legal or regulatory changes affecting the company's operations, or the resignation of key executives—are also ignored by the accounting system until these events affect revenues, or earnings, which may occur years down the road. In the meantime, a chasm opens between stock prices, reflecting the events as soon as investors learn about them, and corporate financial reports, oblivious to such occurrences. This then is another reason for the increasing disconnect between financial (accounting) information and corporate value, documented in Part I of the book. But why do accountants recognize some business events while ignoring others? Excuse the brief tutorial below.

ACCOUNTING AND NONACCOUNTING EVENTS

With all the shortcomings of the accounting system, and there are quite a few as we point out throughout the book, there is one thing accounting excels in—the meticulous recording of business transactions. In fact, Luca Pacioli (1445–1517), the Renaissance mathematician who formalized and promulgated "double-entry bookkeeping" to the general public in his classic book (1494) *Summa de Arithmetica, Geometria, Proportioni, et Proportionalita*, warned readers that nothing could be omitted from the accounting records and that comprehensive recording of transactions is essential to successful business operations and corporate governance.[1]

But the business events captured so meticulously by the accounting system, and subsequently summarized in corporate financial reports, are primarily *transactions with third parties:* purchases from suppliers and sales to customers; payments of wages, rent, and interest; stocks and bond issues; as well as investments in long-term assets and securities. But many important business events—like the clinical-trial results mentioned in the chapter opening, the signing or cancellation of important contracts, external disruption of the company's technology, or the loss of key talent—aren't recorded in real time because they are not explicit transactions with third parties. Their accounting recognition (recording) is delayed until such

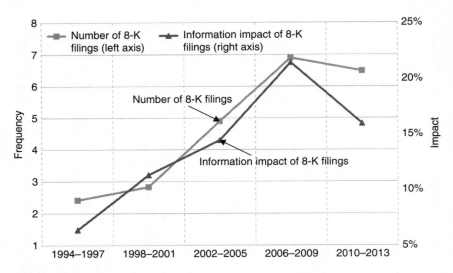

FIGURE 10.1   Increasing Frequency (Left Axis) and Impact (Right Axis) of
Nonaccounting Events in 8-K Filings, 1994–2013

events affect the firm's asset values, revenues or expenses, a delay that is
often considerable. In the meantime, those events are MIA in the financial
reports, while having significant and immediate effect on corporate value
and, if investors learn about them, a big if—on stock prices. Importantly,
as we show in Figure 10.1, the impact of nontransaction events on corporate value is not only substantial, but it has *increased* over time, obviously
contributing to the decrease in financial report usefulness, documented in
Part I. Relevant corporate reports, like those in Part III, should timely alert
investors to the occurrence of such events.

Figure 10.1 spans the past two decades, and portrays for each four-year
period (1994–1997, 1998–2001, ... 2010–2013) the average yearly
number of companies' 8-K filings with the SEC, as well as the economic significance of these filings. The 8-K filings, whose frequency increased in recent
years, report material corporate events (potentially affecting investors' decisions), such as important new contracts, launch of new products, or directors
changes, many affecting corporate value, but not immediately recorded
by the accounting system.[2] Figure 10.1 reflects, for all US companies with
such filings, both the number (average per company and year) of 8-K filings
during the year, and their economic significance, measured by the absolute
abnormal stock price change on the day of the filing (the 8-Ks are made publicly available on the day of the filing).[3] Figure 10.1 shows a sharp increase in
the mean number of filings per company, from around two-three per year
in the 1990s (left vertical scale) to six-seven per company in the 2000s—a
threefold increase in important nonaccounting events. The relevance

(impact) of these events to investors, measured by the absolute stock price reaction to the filings (right vertical scale) is also sharply increasing, from 6 percent (of stock price) in the late 1990s to 15 percent in 2013. (The drop in number and impact of 8-Ks during 2010–2013 in Figure 10.1, reflects a return to normality after the unusual increase in these filings during the financial crisis 2007–2009.)

DID WE FORGET CAUSATION?

Does the increase in unrecognized (by accounting) business events contribute directly to the deteriorating usefulness of financial information? Indeed, it does. To establish this, in each year, 1994–2013, we classified the companies in Figure 10.1 (all US public companies filing 8-Ks) into two classes: companies with above and below median 8-K filings in that year. We then performed the information usefulness test reported in Chapter 5: using current and past reported earnings to predict future earnings on each of the two groups and years. Figure 10.2 shows that, in almost every year, the reported earnings of companies with frequent (above median) 8-K filings led to poorer predictions (larger errors) of future earnings, relative to companies with fewer (below median) 8-K filings. (A positive bar in Figure 10.2 means that the prediction errors of frequent filers are larger than those with

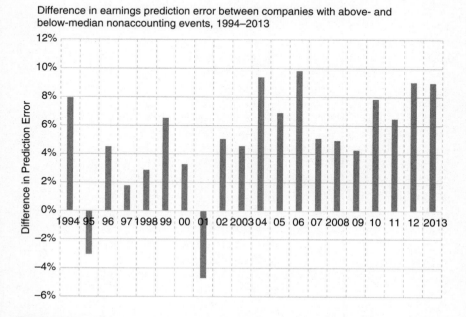

Difference in earnings prediction error between companies with above- and below-median nonaccounting events, 1994–2013

FIGURE 10.2 Nonaccounting Events Leading to Higher Earnings Prediction Error

fewer filings. The only exceptions: 1995 and 2001.) We have thus empirically confirmed that business events that are important, but unrecognized by
accounting, contribute to the deterioration of financial information usefulness (at least, in the predictive power of earnings). Furthermore, the financial
information usefulness test we used in Chapter 3—regressing market values
on reported earnings and book values—confirms the usefulness loss from
nonaccounting events: In every year (1994–2013), the regression's R^2s of
companies with above-median 8-K filings are *lower* (low usefulness of financial information) than the R^2s of companies with below-median filings.[4]

If you thought this delayed or ignored recognition of important business matters is bad enough, there is worse news: There are many events that
are promptly recorded by the accounting system, but in a strangely biased
manner, aggravating financial information usefulness loss. This is the last
self-inflicted (by accounting regulators) detriment to financial information
usefulness we dwell on.

ON CONSERVATIVE ACCOUNTANTS

On February 23, 2012, Royal Bank of Scotland (RBS) announced that
it expected the cost of restructuring its operations to reach a whopping
$1.7 billion. How did investors react to this unexpected expense dragging
down earnings? You probably didn't guess; they rushed to buy RBS stock,
raising its price by 5.4 percent on the announcement day. Moreover, this was
not an aberration. On January 29, 2013, Pfizer announced restructuring
costs of $943 million and saw its stock price rise by 3.2 percent, and
General Electric raised its stock price by 4.6 percent on July 19, 2013, by
announcing restructuring charges of $632 million. What's going on here?
Creating value by hemorrhaging money? A new value-driver?

In a sense, yes. Corporate restructurings are often major events:
Divisions are sold, closed, or significantly trimmed down, product mixes
changed, foreign operations terminated, and almost always employees
are unfortunately laid off. All this mayhem in the service of strategic
changes is aimed to rejuvenate corporate operations and restart growth.
Yes, restructuring is very costly, as you just saw, but investors, as well as
customers and suppliers, often welcome the strategic change, as the opening
examples demonstrate, expecting good things to come. They reckon that
managers finally recognize that something drastic has to be done to change
the company's course and are actually executing a plan.

This is all good and well, but the accounting system, in the name of a
so-called *conservatism principle*, treats restructuring in a totally one-sided
manner: The current and expected costs of restructuring (closing plants,

terminating employees, breaking leases) are recognized in the income statement up front, whereas the expected benefits of restructuring—ending the hemorrhaging from losing operations, or enhancing corporate focus—are ignored, until a future time when revenues and profits finally reflect the restructuring benefits. This biased treatment of an important business event leads to a strange outcome, demonstrated by the opening examples, where a restructuring announcement increases market value while having a significantly negative effect on reported earnings and book (equity) value. Earnings go down; stocks go up—not a relationship you would expect from the prime business performance measure. Furthermore, as you were taught in Accounting 101, a reliable earnings measurement is predicated on a careful *matching* of revenues (gains) with all the expenses incurred in the generation of these revenues. Conservatism defeats such matching and therefore, it adversely affects the ability of reported earnings to predict future performance (as shown in Chapter 5): Current earnings are depressed by the restructuring charges, but if the restructuring plan succeeds, future earnings will rise. A Bizzaro World.

We wouldn't have bothered you with all of this if corporate restructuring were the only case of a conservatism bias in accounting. In fact, accounting is replete with cases where the adverse (cost) consequences of a business decision or economic event are recorded up front, whereas the expected benefits are deferred, sometimes far into the future. The immediate expensing (charge to income) of R&D, along with all other investments in intangibles (brands, business processes), while deferring the recognition of their benefits into the future, is another, prevalent manifestation of the conservatism bias. So, too, is the writing down of assets, including goodwill, for value losses (impairment), while gains on asset values are ignored, or the accounting for employee stock options as an immediate expense, whereas the incentive benefits of granting employees and executives a share in the company are delayed to future periods. Conservatism is endemic to accounting, and so is its detrimental effect on earnings measurement and asset values. True, conservatism is sometimes hailed as a countermeasure to managers' penchant to inflate earnings. But, as with so many other things in accounting, this too defies logic. First, accountants ignore or aren't aware that what's conservative today is aggressive (income inflating) tomorrow, as the benefits of restructuring or R&D expensing are recorded in subsequent periods without the related costs, yielding *overstated* earnings in those periods—an important insight you weren't told of in business school. Second, if managers really want to inflate earnings, there are many earnings-management tools in their shed to easily neutralize conservatism.

The downside of accounting conservatism was noted by others as well. A recent survey of empirical studies concluded that " ... accounting conservatism results in noisy, biased, and inefficient earnings forecasts [by financial analysts]."[5] It has also been shown that accounting conservatism impedes corporate innovation by enhancing managers' short-termism.[6] We wonder, how can anyone expect positive outcomes from a totally biased measurement procedure?[7]

TAKEAWAY

Catch your breath and consider what we have shown so far: Having provided in Part I of the book comprehensive evidence on the fast-deteriorating usefulness of financial information to investors, we turned in Part II to investigate the main causes of this highly disturbing finding. We identified three major causes: a wholly deficient accounting treatment of intangible assets—the increasingly dominant creators of corporate value; the growing prevalence of subjective managerial estimates and projections underlying financial information that decrease its reliability; and, in this chapter, the delayed, or biased recognition of important business events. For each of these three causes we provided evidence on (i) the increasing impact of the cause, over the past decades, on financial information, and (ii) a direct empirical link between each of the causes and the deteriorating usefulness of financial information.

This identification of culprits is important because it makes clear that accounting's road to usefulness recovery isn't going to be easy. Each of the three causes is endemic to accounting procedures, impacting multiple financial indicators, and their adverse effect on the usefulness of financial information keeps increasing. The incremental approach, traditionally followed by accounting standard-setters (FASB, IASB) and regulators (SEC), like the current FASB attempts to tinker with "materiality," is totally ineffective in dealing with fundamental, structural adverse causes, such as the three we identified. This ineffective gradualism of accounting regulators explains their failure to halt the deterioration in financial information usefulness, demonstrated so vividly in Part I of the book. It's time to take a different approach to financial reporting improvement, which we present in the following, Part III of the book.

NOTES

1. Jacob Soll, *The Reckoning* (New York: Basic Books, 2014), Chapter 4.
2. The SEC website reports that 8-K filings deal with the following matters: registrant's business and operations (e.g., entry into, or termination of material agreements), securities markets (e.g., delisting, sale of securities), corporate

governance (e.g., directors' change), and "other events." Since we focus here on nonaccounting information, we excluded from Figure 10.1 filings with accounting or financial report information, such as Regulation FD disclosures and financial statement exhibits.

3. We consider the absolute stock price change, irrespective of whether it was an increase or decrease, since some of the filings have positive implications (a new contract), while others have negative implications (contract cancellation). We subtract from this price change the average change in the price of all stocks during the same day, to focus on investors' reaction to the filing. Finally, we sum for each year the company-specific, one-day absolute price changes and average over all companies. This average reaction to 8-K filings during the year thus reflects the frequency of filings as well as their importance (market impact). This joint message is portrayed in Figure 10.1.

4. We mention once more the potential of intervening factors, affecting both filing frequency and information usefulness, to affect our findings. There may be, of course, additional factors in play, affecting both the number of estimates and earnings forecast accuracy.

5. George Ruch and Gary Taylor, *The Effects of Accounting Conservatism on Financial Statements and Financial Statement Users: A Review of the Literature*, working paper, (University of Alabama, 2014), p. 19.

6. See Xin Chang, Gilles Hilary, Jun-Koo Kang, and Wenrui Zhang, *Does Accounting Impede Corporate Innovation?* working paper (INSEAD, 2013).

7. Some claim that conservatism leads to improved managerial decisions, but even this is largely unsupported; see, for example, Matthew Cedergren, Baruch Lev, and Paul Zarowin, *SFAS 142, Conditional Conservatism, and Acquisition Profitability and Risk*, working paper (New York University, 2015).

Three

So, What's to Be Done?

There is no shortage of criticism of the accounting model and the financial information derived from it, and a whole host of proposed remedies: disclosure of nonfinancial variables (key performance indicators, or KPIs); reporting on the impact of firms' operations on people and the planet, in addition to profits (the "triple bottom line, or the three Ps"); or reporting on the intellectual capital of companies (intellectual capital reports), to name a few. While gathering a limited following, none of these criticisms and proposals had a noticeable effect on corporate reporting worldwide, and definitely not in the United States. The fact is, as shown vividly in Chapter 1, corporate reports today are practically identical to those published a century ago, mirroring the 600-year survival of double-entry bookkeeping. Accounting seems resistant to change.

The reason for the limited success of previous reform proposals is not lack of effort (some change proposals are vigorously pushed by worldwide organizations) or the absence of good ideas—there are definitely some useful suggestions in these proposals. It's, we believe, the lack of a compelling case for change, and the scarcity of workable change proposals that satisfy investors' needs. The extant change proposals generally start from the *premise* that accounting is deficient and proceed with a suggested remedy—to many: a remedy in search of a problem. But unless investors, managers, and policy makers are convinced that the financial reporting system is seriously deficient—and many aren't—the case for reform is not compelling. Furthermore, the proposed remedies are rarely comprehensive, workable solutions that convincingly satisfy investors' information needs. Consider, for example, the various suggestions to report a company's human and environmental impact, in addition to its business performance. Can a company's impact on people and the planet (externalities) even be measured in a reliable and uniform manner across peer companies as, say, revenues are? Just think about the raging controversies about the extent of climate change and the widely different methods to measure the climate (surface temperature, sea level, glacier volume, etc.), and imagine reflecting all this in corporate reports.[1] Furthermore, will managers be willing to report such information that likely exposes them to endless harassment and litigation? And how will investors factor such information into their valuation models? What's the impact of 1 percent increase in the company's greenhouse gas emissions on future sales? The unworkable nature of many of these reform proposals likely explains their limited following.

Our approach in this book is different. First, we empirically and comprehensively substantiate our claim that financial information use-fulness to investors is fast fading. We thus validate the *need for change*. We then identify—again, using empirical evidence—the main reasons for accounting's relevance lost, thereby laying the groundwork for the proposed remedy, which we also develop in a different way from our predecessors. Rather than *claiming* that our proposal is workable and superior to others', we identify investors' information needs by following two approaches: First, we use economic theory to derive a paradigm of investors' needs in twenty-first-century capital markets. Second, we carefully study the questions that financial analysts and institutional investors raise in a wide cross-section of quarterly earnings conference calls with corporate managers to solidify our understanding of the information relevant to investment decisions. Since our approach of actually *listening* to what investors ask for differs from others', we provide two brief examples below before presenting our first approach—learning from economics—in the upcoming chapter.

ANALYSTS' QUESTIONS FOR NETFLIX

Quarterly earnings conference calls—a routine event for most public companies—provide a rare opportunity to identify investors' information needs. The Q&A section of the calls, usually the longest and most relevant, is devoted to managers answering questions posed by financial analysts and investors after they have read the recently released quarterly report and supporting documents and have listened to the presentation with which managers began the call. Analysts' conference call questions are therefore those of well-informed experts, reliably reflecting the information needs of investors. We have carefully read the transcripts of a large number of conference calls in various key sectors to form the basis of our change proposals.[2] An example follows.

Consider Netflix, the leading provider of video and streaming services: In its third-quarter 2012 call (October 23, 2012), the company dispensed with the usual preamble of management presentation and moved directly to analysts' questions. First question was as follows: "Your original thesis was three years of full brand recovery. Is this still the case?"[3] The second question was about Netflix missing its earlier guidance for domestic streaming hours, followed by a question about the dampening effect of the London Olympics (Summer 2012) on subscriber additions and a question on the customer churn rate (subscriber cancellation). Next up was a question about Netflix's negotiations with vendors for content (programs)—movies versus TV shows. Analysts' questions then moved to Netflix's original content (e.g., the series *House of Cards*), followed by questions about its international business. The remaining questions in the call followed a similar pattern.

What's remarkable about these questions is that they hardly touched on traditional accounting measures: earnings, sales, tangible assets or liabilities, pensions and receivables. Clearly, what interests investors most are the *strategic assets* of Netflix—brands, customers, content, and agreements with vendors—all the assets that are sadly missing, courtesy GAAP, from Netflix's balance sheet. In particular, investors care about how efficiently management operates these assets: How quickly will the brand recover from the strategic misstep, or what is the monthly depletion (churn) rate of the customer franchise? That's what investors want to know: the state of the company's strategic (value-creating) assets and their deployment record. In essence, the value creation model of the company. Accounting-based financial reports barely shed light on these issues. But, perhaps this analysts' focus is unique to Internet-based, young companies, like Netflix? Could it be that investors in mature, traditional sectors have different information needs and instead focus on accounting items in the financial reports? Let's have a look at Exxon, the oil giant, a most mature and traditional company.

QUESTIONS THEY ASKED EXXON

Exxon's third-quarter 2012 conference call, conducted November 1, 2012, opened with a brief management presentation. The first question came from a Bank of America analyst who asked about a decrease in the production rate of the firm's oil and gas assets, followed by a question about the strategy underlying the Celtic (a Canadian exploration company) acquisition in the quarter—whether this portends a strategic shift for Exxon. The third question was about other North American acquisitions of oil and gas properties and Exxon's overall M&A strategy. Fourth came a question about recent global trends in customer demand, followed by more M&A questions.

Several questions were then asked about rig counts and drilling prospects. Analysts also wanted to know about applications for new drilling rights in the Gulf Coast, Alaska, and Western Canada. Questions about Exxon's apparent pullback from gas drilling followed, and the rest was more of the same.

Does this sound familiar? Exxon's analysts' questions are very similar to Netflix's, focused on the strategic assets of the company—oil and gas properties and corporate acquisitions for Exxon; brands, content, and customers for Netflix—and the efficiency of deploying these assets. Importantly, our broader examination of over 200 conference calls in various industries confirms that this is a general phenomenon. Here and there are, of course, a few questions about earnings and sales, particularly when the firm in question badly missed targets (consensus estimate, managers' guidance), but investors clearly don't focus on historical financial results (which brings to mind Henry Ford's statement, "History is more or less bunk"), rather they zoom in on the value creation (business model) process: the positioning of the company's strategic assets and the efficiency of their operations. Reassuringly, as you'll see in the next chapter, this is exactly what economic theory asserts are the crucial issues facing a business coping with competition and survival. Accordingly, following the next chapter—"What Really Matters to Investors (and Managers)"—we present in depth four industry cases that demonstrate our proposed disclosure: the Strategic Resources & Consequences Report. You'll clearly see the new information modes we propose investors seek and learn how to perform an insightful assessment of business performance and value creation based on this information.

But, first, here's another memo to investors:

FORGET THE BOTTOM LINE

Imagine facing your doctor at the conclusion of a thorough annual checkup, and hearing: "Your total cholesterol level is 195; you are okay. Next patient." You'll obviously be perplexed and disappointed. What about all the other tests you took (EKG, blood pressure, extensive blood and urine work, bone density, etc.), and all the concerns you shared with the doctor? And where are the recommendations for lifestyle changes? You are, of course, justified to be disappointed, but realize that your doctor's fixation with the 195 cholesterol level is exactly what many investors do when they focus on accounting's "bottom line"—reported earnings, or the "all-important" consensus miss. This, too, is a single indicator presumably telling you all you need to know about the condition and performance of a complex business organization—which is obviously absurd. And, yet, many investors do just that: pay undue attention to one or perhaps two (earnings and sales) performance measures. How do we know? Because numerous studies have documented a stock price reaction, albeit declining, to the release of earnings and sales information. Mind you, at least in the cholesterol level case, the measurement is (hopefully) reliable, and no one tries to trick you with inflated numbers, which can't be always said about earnings.

So, the first premise of our proposed reporting and analysis system is that there is no single magic number, no "bottom line," or even triple bottom line (profit, people, planet).[4] Analyzing a complex, often global business organization, subject to competition and fast-changing technologies, requires a comprehensive *system* of well-integrated indicators and contextual information. It's a mosaic; no shortcuts. And that's what we develop and present in this part of the book.

NOTES

1. The *Wall Street Journal* (March 31, 2015), p. R2 reported on a survey of institutional investors concerning sustainability reporting, a popular reform proposal, by companies. Seventy-nine percent of respondents were dissatisfied with the comparability of sustainability reporting between companies in the same industry, and 74 percent were dissatisfied with the relevance and implications of sustainability risks.
2. Our approach also differs from the frequent surveys of investors and questionnaire studies, which often ask questions that respondents have no way to accurately answer (e.g., What is the quality of financial reports? Should GAAP be based on rules or principles?), or questions that invite a certain answer (Are you interested in the firm's impact on the planet? Who would say no?). Conference call questions, in contrast, are very focused and well chosen (analysts get to ask no more than one or two questions), reflecting the genuine information needs of investors.
3. In mid 2011, Netflix changed its pricing structure, significantly increasing the rates for DVD rental, in order to motivate customers to switch to video streaming. Customers reacted harshly to this change with massive cancellations. The company subsequently reversed the rate increase and predicted a three-year period of brand recovery from the debacle.
4. Professor William Vatter (Chicago, Berkeley), an early leading accounting thinker, wrote about investors' over-reliance on earnings: "Far too frequently the layman [nonaccountant] will assume that the accountant has done his work for him and

that the final [income] figure is the important one for his purposes, when the chances are good that nothing could be farther from the truth ... the easiest and most effective way to do this [avoid user earnings fixation] is to abandon entirely the notion of a 'general purpose' income statement ... abstaining from any reference or suggestion of an income computation in overt form." (*The Fund Theory of Accounting and Its Implications for Financial Reports* (Chicago: University of Chicago Press, 1947), pp. 75–76.) A bit extreme, but definitely in the right direction, and as often happens to good ideas in accounting—totally ignored.

CHAPTER 11

What Really Matters to Investors (and Managers)

We present in this chapter our proposed information system—the Strategic Resources & Consequences Report, intended to complement and partially supplement accounting-based financial statements. We use economic theory to derive five criteria for information usefulness that, with inferences from our detailed examination of questions raised by analysts and investors in earnings conference calls, form the basis of the proposed Resources & Consequences Report.

THE CORPORATE MISSION

Economic theory, particularly the branches known as the "theory of the firm" and "industrial organization," define succinctly the major objective of a business enterprise as striving to gain *sustained competitive advantage*.[1] Such competitive advantage over rivals assures adequate return to owners (investors), workforce employment, and long-term survival of the enterprise for customers' benefit. Focusing on sustained competitive advantage precludes, of course, myopic managerial gimmicks, like corporate acquisitions aimed at boosting short-term reported sales and earnings, share buybacks designed to enhance quarterly earnings-per-share, or earnings manipulations intended to misinform investors. Achieving sustained competitive advantage is thus the fundamental, long-term objective of a business enterprise, and what really matters to its owners. This implies that corporate information released to investors, such as the accounting-based financial reports, should inform investors and other corporate constituents (lenders, suppliers, customers, government agencies) about the extent to which sustained competitive advantage has been achieved, and if not, how successful are managers' strategies in pursuing competitive advantage. That's what the questions posed by Netflix's and Exxon's analysts were all about.

An indication of how important is a company's strategy and organization to investors follows: On August 10, 2015, Google changed its name to Alphabet and announced a significant reorganization, separating search functions from other activities, thereby enhancing its *strategic transparency*. Google's stock price increased the following day 4.3 percent ($21 billion shareholder gain), vis a vis an overall Nasdaq loss of 1.3 percent in the day.

DIGGING A BIT DEEPER

How, then, to achieve sustained competitive advantage? The essence is to create sustained *economic profits*, namely, the residual that remains after subtracting from revenues all operating and financial costs, including cost of equity capital.[2] This is, of course, a far cry from the routinely reported quarterly accounting earnings, which are subject to myriad biases (recall conservatism, discussed in Chapter 10), mix expenses with investments (R&D, brands), mismatch costs with revenues (restructuring charges), and ignore altogether the company's cost of equity capital, that is, the alternative return shareholders could have gained on the funds, including retained earnings, they invested in the company. Accounting earnings are relatively easy for managers to "achieve"; economic profit is a challenge. Enterprises that consistently create value by generating long-term economic profit obviously distinguish themselves from the competition, since not all competitors can achieve such a demanding standard, thereby securing "sustained competitive advantage." With this specification of long-term economic profit, how can a company achieve it?

By efficiently operating the resources/assets of the company. But not just any resources; office buildings, production machinery, airplanes, inventory, or drilling equipment—all those assets that populate corporate balance sheets—cannot create competitive advantage. They are just "commodities," available to all competitors, and, therefore, their use cannot distinguish the user from its rivals. Pfizer cannot rise above competitors by its laboratory equipment, since similar equipment is used by all pharmaceutical companies. The resources (input factors) enabling value creation, henceforth *strategic resources*, are different from accounting-recognized assets. They share the following three attributes:

1. *They are valuable.* They create or contribute to the creation of a stream of benefits, exceeding costs, such as the patents underlying profitable products or services.
2. *They are rare.* A limited amount of these assets is generally available, like wireless spectrum or airlines' landing rights.
3. *They are difficult to imitate.* Competitors cannot easily acquire or produce these resources; quickly mimicking valuable brands (Google) is practically impossible.

Enterprises owning and operating efficiently such strategic assets are able to consistently implement value-creating strategies that their present or potential competitors cannot put into effect and thereby gain a sustained competitive advantage.[3] End of theory.

STRATEGIC RESOURCES

The focus of the economic theory of the firm, particularly the offshoot known as *resource-based theory,* is thus on the strategic resources of the enterprise, like patents, brands, landing rights, extractive properties, loyal customers, or unique business processes—such as Netflix's customer recommendation algorithms—that create sustainable competitive advantage.[4] Ironically, most of those strategic resources are not reported by the accounting system, since the investments made to create the resources are immediately expensed, such that financial reports don't provide any useful information about them.[5] This, then, leads to the first desirable attribute of our proposed information system—the Strategic Resources & Consequences Report—intended to provide investors' needs:

■ *Usefulness attribute no. 1*: Inform investors about the strategic resources (assets) of the enterprise, their characteristics, value, and related attributes (such as number of patents in the company's portfolio, patents supporting products/services, number of patents licensed out, patent quality, protection mechanisms against infringement, etc.).[6]

MAPPING INVESTMENTS TO RESOURCES

Unlike the biblical manna, which descended from heaven on the Israelites crossing the Sinai desert, strategic resources aren't free. Instead, they are generated by targeted corporate investments, such as R&D, brand enhancement, or acquired technology. Accordingly, the mapping of investments to resources is a crucial link in the value-creation strategy of the firm.[7] There are always choices of strategic alternatives to resource development. For instance, a pharmaceutical company could spend considerable R&D funds in quest of a drug, or alternatively, acquire a small biotech company that is already developing that drug—different mappings of investments to resources. The two routes to the drug will obviously have different costs and time-to-market. Or a telecommunication company could develop its customer base internally or acquire a competitor with an established base. The resource development process can also be wasteful. Lou Gerstner, who performed a uniquely successful turnaround at IBM in the 1990s, cut IBM's R&D budget by 30 percent in his early years at the helm. Critics claimed that Gerstner sacrificed IBM's future for a short-term earnings boost, but the successful turnaround proved that some of IBM's vaunted R&D wasn't really productive.

Accordingly, the efficiency of the firm's investment in creating and acquiring strategic assets is obviously a major concern to managers and investors. It affects the speed of resource development, determining the crucial time-to-market of new products and services, as well as the cost of resources and ultimately the value created by them. Thus, the second attribute of our proposed information system is comprehensive disclosure about the mapping of investments (outlays) to resources (assets):

- *Usefulness attribute no. 2:* Inform investors with specificity about the investments (expenditures) made in the process of building the enterprise's strategic assets (customer acquisition costs for telecom and internet companies, for example).

One such investment, R&D, is currently reported in the income statement, whereas most other investments—brand creation and maintenance, technology acquisitions, employee training, consultants' work on business processes, media content creation, IT support of business processes, and like investments—are lumped in the income statement with regular expense items, generally in SG&A, and hence are obscured from investors. We challenge anyone to explain the logic underlying the current practice of separately reporting in the income statement innocuous expenses, such as interest, but not, say, the generally larger and much more consequential information systems expenditures. Even the currently reported R&D expense isn't particularly meaningful without breakdowns to, for example, the "R"—research, mainly aimed at developing new technologies—and the "D"—development, the tweaking of current technologies.[8] Expenditures on basic research are riskier than those on development, but generally generate higher benefits, hence the importance to investors of distinguishing between the two R&D strategies. The mapping of investments to resources is thus a crucial element of investors' needs and, therefore, prominently featured in our proposed information system. Changes in the types and amounts of investments, as well as deviations from peer companies, provide early signs of subsequent shifts in resource values and productivities, obviously of considerable consequence to investors.

PRESERVING AND RENEWING THE STRATEGIC RESOURCES

In countries subject to the rule of law and having an effective police force, there is negligible risk of infringement on corporate physical and financial assets. Stealing accounts receivable or vanishing land aren't common occurrences. Owners of most strategic assets, however, are—or should be—deeply concerned about competitors infringing on their assets. The thousands of patents and trademark infringement lawsuits filed every year in the United States attest to the vulnerability of many strategic assets, even those with legal protection (intellectual property), to appropriation by rivals.[9] But infringement on the firm's strategic resources by rivals isn't the only concern.

Disruption—the term used for an innovation that significantly diminishes or replaces altogether a widely used technology (personal computers disrupted work stations; ultrasound, X-ray imaging; digital photography, chemical photography; Wikipedia, traditional encyclopedias)—is an even greater threat to owners of strategic assets than rivals' infringement.[10] The corporate graveyard is strewn with enterprises whose major technology was disrupted by others: Kodak, Atari, Western Union, untold number of mom and pop retail stores disrupted by Walmart, or travel agencies by online travel booking. Smart companies are constantly on the lookout for possible disruption, and once a threat is detected, take defensive measures.

Given the serious and continuous threats of infringement and disruption of strategic assets, and consequently the harm to the enterprise's business model, investors and other constituents should be regularly informed of those threats and the measures taken by the enterprise to safeguard and preserve its strategic assets. Such measures should, but rarely do, fall under the risk management function of the company, which is a major component of its internal controls.[11] Gross inadequacies of internal controls came to light in the spate of the corporate scandals of the early 2000 (Enron, WorldCom, etc.), and internal control is now required to be audited by the firm's external auditors by the Sarbanes–Oxley Act of 2002. Firms should, therefore, articulate to investors the measures they take to identify and assess the risks of resource infringement and disruption, and the actions they take to manage such risks. We emphasize *articulate* to distinguish our proposal from the current risk boilerplate provided in financial reports, including gems like "estimates underlying financial data are subject to error." Really? And who reads those boilerplates? Meaningful risk assessment, for example, is now enabled by commercial systems that allow companies to systematically track patent applications and grants to competitors that then can be used to identify potential infringement and disruption threats.[12]

Included in the preservation of strategic assets are efforts to slow down the obsolescence of these assets. Brands decay (lose their price advantage) without continuous maintenance by advertising and promotion; customers drift away absent company attention and communication; media content, like TV series, wither without sequels; and certain patent lives can be extended by modification of the invention. In general, as the firm's products or services are widely marketed, competitors reverse-engineer them, gradually eroding their competitive edge. In a sense, the competitive success of an enterprise sows the seeds of its destruction. The battle against resource obsolescence should be a continuous and integral part of the business model of the enterprise; as such, its essentials should be shared with investors.

Finally, business enterprises accumulate considerable organizational knowledge through learning and experience. Essentially, they figure out how to do things, big and small, in the most efficient way. Most of this knowledge is tacit, residing with employees. Some companies attempt to make such tacit knowledge explicit with formal "knowledge management systems." For example, consulting firms formally debrief managers at the end of consulting engagements to preserve the main lessons drawn from the engagement. The fight against organizational amnesia should therefore be an important element of the resource preservation efforts of the company.[13] This all leads us to the third usefulness attribute of the proposed information system:

- *Usefulness attribute no. 3*: Articulate the major risks to the company's strategic assets from infringement by competitors, disruptions by new technologies, and regulatory moves, as well as the measures taken by management to mitigate these risks.

STRATEGIC ASSET DEPLOYMENT AND OPERATION

Deployment of strategic assets represents the first facet of the Resources & Consequences Report that actually tracks corporate value. Patents can just lie dormant, or they can be developed into profitable products and services, or alternatively, licensed out. Broadband capacity may be fully utilized or only partially used. "Big data" on the firm's customers can be extensively mined to enhance sales, or this resource can waste away on the firm's servers. R&D can be conducted solely by the company, or in alliance with other companies to share risks and expenses. Oil and gas rights can be fully explored, or left for future use. Alternative uses of strategic assets abound.

The specific deployment of strategic assets will determine the firm's performance. Accounting-based financial reports provide information only on the *final outcomes* of asset deployment: revenues and earnings. The reports are totally silent on the paths to these outcomes: patents developed or licensed out, insurance sold through agents or online, radio spectrum used or rented to other entities, DVD rented to customers or content streamed online. Each of these alternative paths to revenues has different competitive challenges and varying sustainability (DVD is waning whereas video streaming is flourishing). But no systematic information is currently available to investors on the specific strategies leading to the value creation, unless managers choose to reveal some of this information in, say, conference calls. Understanding the paths to revenues and earnings enables investors to evaluate the company's strategies and their execution, and improves prediction of future corporate performance. For example, whether revenues were derived from licensing (generally long-term) or selling intellectual property has different implications regarding the duration of those revenues. Whether an annual sales increase is a result of a new market penetration or a local price increase has entirely different implications concerning future sales growth. Moreover, multiple factors affect reported earnings and revenues. Since some are beyond managers' control (regulatory changes, competitors' actions, etc.), managers and the board cannot be judged solely on the basis of final outcomes reported in the income statement. A comprehensive enterprise performance evaluation, therefore, requires information on both the company's strategies (asset deployment) and their outcomes, accordingly:

- *Usefulness attribute no. 4*: Outline the specific deployment (uses) of the firms' strategic assets—the strategies to extract value from the assets.

MEASURING THE VALUE CREATED

Managers' strategies for transforming investments into strategic resources, preserving (protecting) these resources from infringement and decay, and deploying them individually (licensing patents), or more commonly in combinations, in production and marketing are all aimed at creating value that enables companies to compete and maintain the supply of investment funds. The value created from the chain of resource creation–preservation–deployment is the fifth and last building block of our proposed information system. Accordingly:

- *Usefulness attribute no. 5*: Quantify and report the consequences—value creation—of managers' activities in creating, preserving, and deploying strategic assets.

This last usefulness attribute seems to be fulfilled by the accounting system, which reports the consequences of managers' activities in the form of revenues, costs, and earnings. Accounting, however, takes a very partial and narrow view of recording and reporting consequences. It ignores major cost items—in particular, the cost of equity capital. (Does anyone, except accountants, believe that the $59.7 billion of Cisco's stockholder equity on July 25, 2015, is free money?) On the other hand, it records as income-reducing expenses various major investments, such as R&D and brand creation. It ignores the value changes during the period of major strategic assets, such as increases in proved oil and gas reserves, or customer franchise. These and other accounting distortions render its measure of value creation (earnings) of limited use, as we have demonstrated in Part I of the book.

We measure value created differently: We focus on cash flows to abstract from the numerous managerial estimates and projections embedded in reported earnings, many of which enhance information noise (recall Chapter 9). For cash flows, we use reported "cash from operating activities." We then *add* to cash flows investments in strategic resources (e.g., customer acquisition costs), which were subtracted in the income statement (and implicitly reduce cash from operations). Next, we *subtract* from cash flows capital expenditures (averaged over three-five years), to compensate for depreciation and amortization eliminated in the cash flow computation. Finally, we *subtract* from cash flows a charge for the use of equity capital. This is our value-creation measure, shown empirically in Chapter 18 to outperform both earnings and cash from operations, and numerically demonstrated in the next chapter. To the extent it can be reliably measured, we add to the value created the changes during the period in the values of major strategic assets (e.g., present value of cash flows from proved reserves of oil and gas companies).

THE PROPOSED STRATEGIC RESOURCES & CONSEQUENCES REPORT

The five investors' information usefulness attributes that we derived from economic theory focus on the enterprise's strategic assets; their creation, preservation, and deployment to create corporate value. These usefulness attributes are brought together in the following Resources & Consequences Report, which summarizes our proposed information paradigm. The following report is a *generic* one, aimed at providing the reader with a general idea of what the proposed Resources & Consequences Report looks like, with examples from various industries to facilitate intuition. In subsequent chapters, we provide detailed cases, applying the proposed report to four leading industries, with real-life numbers and analyses. Figure 11.1 is an outline of the report (boxes convey quantitative data, while circles denote narrative explanation).

The Report's columns pertain to the five information attributes presented above, each crucial to the assessment of the enterprise's ability to achieve sustained competitive advantage: from left to right, details are provided on the investment (quarterly, annual) in strategic resources, information on the stocks and attributes of these resources, the preservation and maintenance of strategic resources, their specific deployment to create value, and finally the benefits from (productivity of) the enterprise's deployment of the strategic resources, encapsulated in the total value created. Much of the information in the report is monetary (denoted by $), some is quantitative (like the number of new customers or patents granted), and some qualitative, or narrative (information on the patent infringement detection programs), denoted by a circle around the item's description. Importantly, only few of the information items in the Resources & Consequences Report are currently required to be reported in accounting-based corporate financial statements.[14] It's mostly new information, and as we have previously outlined, it is critical for the assessment of an enterprise's ultimate objective: achieving and maintaining sustained competitive advantage. That's essentially the information financial analysts and informed investors seek to obtain from managers in conference calls and investors meetings. Note, also, that in contrast with accounting-based financial reports, the proposed information items (customer additions, market share) are mostly *factual*—no managerial estimates, projections, or guesses.

Also important to note: We do not propose here yet another *list* of performance indicators, often referred to as KPIs (key performance indicators), which are frequently advanced by accounting reformers. These indicators are often unrelated to each other (workforce diversity, customer satisfaction, greenhouse gas emissions), and their impact on value creation is rarely substantiated (to what extent does workforce diversity affect corporate value?). We, in contrast, propose an *integrated system* of efforts and achievements, providing a holistic picture of the enterprise's strategies, actions, and consequences, hitherto unavailable to investors and

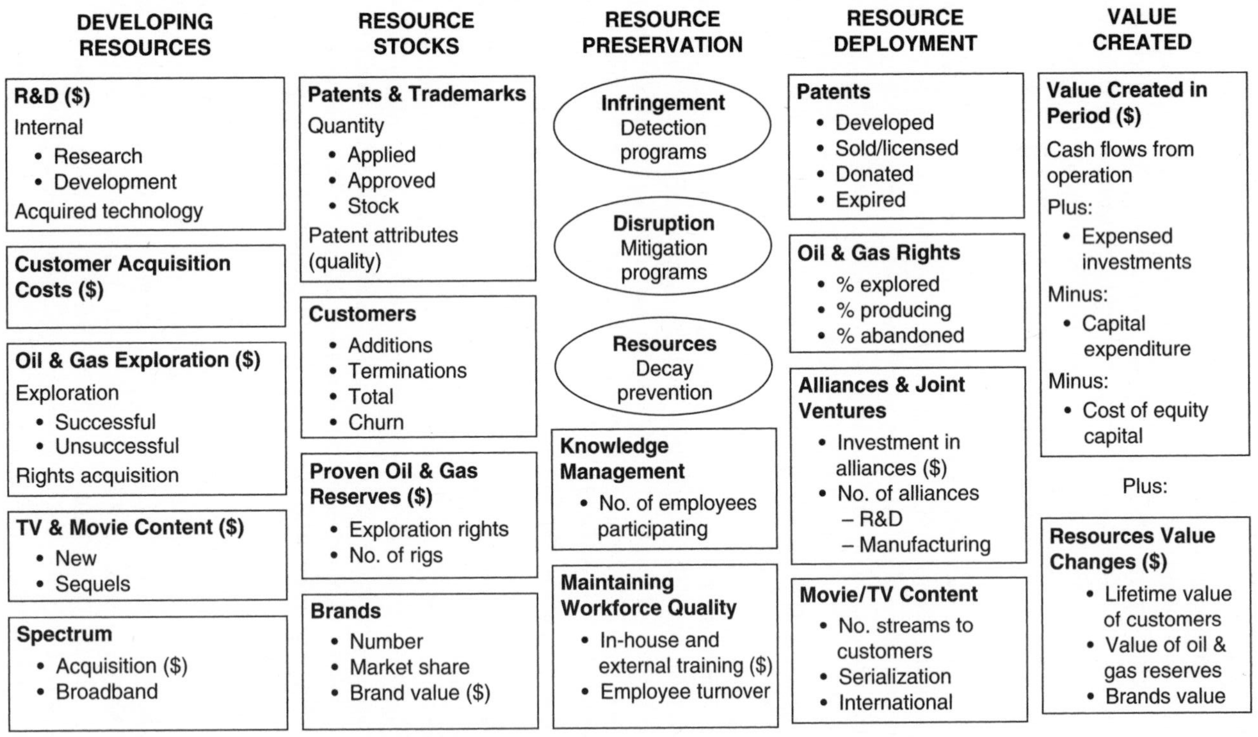

DEVELOPING RESOURCES

R&D ($)
Internal
- Research
- Development
Acquired technology

Customer Acquisition Costs ($)

Oil & Gas Exploration ($)
Exploration
- Successful
- Unsuccessful
Rights acquisition

TV & Movie Content ($)
- New
- Sequels

Spectrum
- Acquisition ($)
- Broadband

RESOURCE STOCKS

Patents & Trademarks
Quantity
- Applied
- Approved
- Stock
Patent attributes (quality)

Customers
- Additions
- Terminations
- Total
- Churn

Proven Oil & Gas Reserves ($)
- Exploration rights
- No. of rigs

Brands
- Number
- Market share
- Brand value ($)

RESOURCE PRESERVATION

(**Infringement**
Detection programs)

(**Disruption**
Mitigation programs)

(**Resources**
Decay prevention)

Knowledge Management
- No. of employees participating

Maintaining Workforce Quality
- In-house and external training ($)
- Employee turnover

RESOURCE DEPLOYMENT

Patents
- Developed
- Sold/licensed
- Donated
- Expired

Oil & Gas Rights
- % explored
- % producing
- % abandoned

Alliances & Joint Ventures
- Investment in alliances ($)
- No. of alliances
  - R&D
  - Manufacturing

Movie/TV Content
- No. streams to customers
- Serialization
- International

VALUE CREATED

Value Created in Period ($)
Cash flows from operation
Plus:
- Expensed investments
Minus:
- Capital expenditure
Minus:
- Cost of equity capital

Plus:

Resources Value Changes ($)
- Lifetime value of customers
- Value of oil & gas reserves
- Brands value

Note: The information in squares is quantitative ($ denotes monetary values), and in circles is qualitative (narrative).

FIGURE 11.1 The Strategic Resources & Consequences Report

other corporate constituents. As our following case studies will show, the integrated nature of the Report allows for cost–benefits analyses: What was the return (ROI) on customer acquisitions costs? Or, on content creation? Disparate lists of KPIs, for example, don't enable such an integrated analysis. The comprehensiveness of our proposed system, encompassing all the strategic stages, from resource development to their ultimate value creation, is a unique feature of the Resources & Consequences Report. You get, in one statement, an exhaustive description of the company's strategy (business model) and its execution.

By definition, a report on the creation, deployment, and value added by strategic resources is *industry specific*. Given the fundamental strategic and business model differences across industries (insurance, retailing, health care, telecommunication), forcing companies in different industries to report uniformly, as current accounting rules do, is a straightjacket that leads to a substantial loss of information. How can the same balance sheet effectively inform on the assets of a bank, hospital, and telecom company, or the same income statement fit an oil and gas, biotech, and insurance enterprise? Obviously, they can't. Thus, any meaningful business reporting system must be industry-specific. The industry cases presented in the following chapters demonstrate how different is the information required for an insightful analysis of enterprise performance and value creation across different sectors.[15]

Finally, we are well aware of managers' competitive concerns in disclosing strategic information. Obviously, we aren't advocating compromising proprietary information and plans. The following case studies will demonstrate that practically all the items in the Resources & Consequences Report are currently disclosed voluntarily by certain companies, albeit in a haphazard, not uniform, and inconsistent manner, rendering them of little use to investors. The proposed Report, in contrast, organizes the information logically (from investments to resources, their deployment and created value), and assures consistency and comparability. We are also aware of the onerous burden of current disclosure requirements on corporate executives. The fact that these disclosures, as we have demonstrated, are of marginal value to investors, doesn't lighten their administrative burden on managers; if anything, it increases the burden, forcing managers to respond to bewildered investors. Given that the Resources & Consequences Report we propose is a substantial endeavor, requiring a considerable effort by the company (mostly, though, in its initial setup), it calls for a certain relief from current disclosure requirements to secure managers' cooperation in the Report's disclosure. Accordingly, we will suggest in Chapter 16 (Implementation) various ways to lighten the current disclosure burden.

TAKEAWAY

The Strategic Resources & Consequences Report proposed in this chapter aims to provide the essential information investors need to evaluate the strategies (business model) of businesses and the extent of their execution by management, to assure the company is on a course of sustained competitive advantage. It is important to note that the information we propose in the Report overcomes the three causes we identified in Part II for the loss of accounting's relevance: The Report highlights the intangible assets of the company (most strategic resources are intangible), it is essentially factual (customer's churn, frequency and severity of auto insurance claims, income from licensing patents—are all facts) and thus avoids the harms of subjective managerial estimates and projections proliferating in financial reports, and the Report does not distinguish, like accounting records, between transactions with third parties and other value-changing business events. That is, essentially, how our proposal overcomes the numerous shortcomings of the accounting system.

NOTES

1. For elaboration, see Harold Demsetz, "Industrial Structure, Market Rivalry, and Public Policy," *Journal of Law and Economics*, 16 (1973): 1–10. Michael Porter, "The Contribution of Industrial Organization to Strategic Management," *Academy of Management Review*, 6 (1981): 609–620. The introduction to this chapter draws on Nicolaï Foss and Nils Stieglitz, "Modern Resource-Based Theory(ies)," in *Handbook on the Economics and Theory of the Firm*, Michael Dietrich and Jackie Kraft, eds. (Edward Elgar, 2011).
2. Economic profit is the revenue of the enterprise minus the current (not historical) cost of all the resources consumed in the process of generating these revenues, including the cost of equity capital. Asset depreciation, for example, is measured by accountants on the basis of the historical (purchase price) value of the assets. Economic depreciation will account for the technological obsolescence of the assets. For an example of certain adjustments made to measure economic profit, see the modifications to inventory and depreciation made in the measurement of corporate profits in the national accounts. For details, see www .bea.gov/national/pdf/chapter13.pdf. Obviously, measuring perfectly economic profit is very difficult, if not impossible.
3. For elaboration, Jay Barney, "Firm Resources and Sustained Competitive Advantage," *Journal of Management*, 17 (1991): 99–120. Note that most accounting-recognized assets, like property, plant, or equipment, lack two of the three above-mentioned attributes: They are not rare, and they are easy to acquire or imitate by competitors.

4. In a recent conference call, Netflix's CEO noted that three-quarters of its streaming views were generated by the recommendation algorithms.

5. The accounting system records certain *acquired* strategic resources as assets (patents, customer lists), whether acquired directly or through mergers and acquisitions.

6. A number of indicators have been developed and validated empirically to quantify patent quality. Arguably, the most indicative measure of quality is the number of "forward citations"; that is, the number of citations (references) to a given patent in the grant applications of subsequent patents. A large number of forward citations indicates that a patent was influential in the development of science and technology. It has been shown that companies whose patents are frequently cited enjoy above-normal sales and stock price growth. See Dirk Czarnitzki, Katrin Hussinger, and Bart Leten, *The Market Value of Blocking Patent Citations,* working paper (Leuven: Katholieke University, 2011).

7. Important to note that resources/assets, as valuable and unique as they may be, don't create any value by themselves. Even the most promising patent has to be developed into a product and then marketed smartly. Value creation, therefore, requires an *organization* around the strategic assets: a managerial team to devise and implement strategies to create the resources, and that preserves and deploys them successfully to gain an edge over competitors. Our Resources & Consequences Report conveys the effectiveness of this capability, often called *organization capital.*

8. Some claim that making a distinction between the R (basic research) and D (development) isn't practicable. Not so. All respondents to the annual "Business R&D and Innovation Survey," conducted by the National Science Foundation with the Census Bureau—essentially all US companies conducting R&D—routinely report this classification, along with other important details related to R&D. But you won't find this important information in financial reports.

9. In 2013, almost 6,500 patent infringement lawsuits were filed in the United States (PricewaterhouseCoopers, 2014 Patent Litigation Study, at www.pwc.com).

10. The classic on disruption: Clayton Christensen, *The Innovator's Dilemma: When New Technologies Cause Great Firms to Fail* (Boston: Harvard Business School Press, 1997).

11. See Internal Control—Integrated Framework, Committee of Sponsoring Organizations of the Treadway Commission, December 2011, at www.ic.coso.org ("Risk assessment also requires management to consider the impact of possible changes in the external environment..." p. 51).

12. We recognize, of course, that certain protective measures against infringement are proprietary and should not be publicly disclosed in detail.

13. Key-employee retirement is a serious cause of organizational amnesia. Retirees leave with considerable knowledge. Xerox Corp., for example, used to conduct formal debriefings of equipment maintenance personnel who, over long years of

work, developed more efficient methods of diagnosing equipment problems and fixing them than those specified by their manuals. The manuals were constantly updated with such employee process innovations.

14. Certain elements of the proposed Report are sometimes provided in the management discussion & analysis (MD&A) section of the annual report required by the SEC, but not in the succinct, comprehensive, and integrated manner of the proposed Resources & Consequences Report. Many MD&As stretch over scores of pages, making it difficult to discern the relevant bits of information.

15. Even the current accounting and reporting system recognizes the need for certain industry-specific regulations and disclosure, mandating different disclosures for insurance companies, movie producers, software, media, oil and gas, and so on.

CHAPTER 12

Strategic Resources & Consequences Report: Case No. I—Media and Entertainment

Customers are the most important strategic asset of media and entertainment companies, particularly because in most subsectors, the customers' identity is known to the provider of services, enabling active management of the customer franchise. Achieving sustained competitive advantage in media and entertainment is a major challenge due to fierce competition and low entry barriers. Accordingly, detailed information on companies' strategic resources, their vulnerabilities, deployment, and productivity is essential for investors and lenders to make successful investment decisions and monitor managers. In this chapter, the proposed Strategic Resources & Consequences report will first be demonstrated on a specific company—Sirius XM—to highlight the unique investor insights offered by our proposal, followed by the outline of a general resources & consequences report for media and entertainment companies. The chapter provides a new indicator: an estimate of the lifetime value of the subscriber franchise, the main strategic asset of the company.

This is the first of four detailed case studies, each for a major economic sector, intended to demonstrate with specificity our proposal for the new information disclosure: the Strategic Resources & Consequences Report. We open our case studies with a large, vibrant, and very innovative sector—media and entertainment.

SECTOR SYNOPSIS

Media and entertainment is a ubiquitous and fast-growing sector that includes many companies in various subsectors, such as cable and radio, telecommunication, movies and TV, Internet services providers, and, of course, print newspapers and magazines. The main characteristics of this sector are a high rate of innovation (wireless technology, social media), frequent technological disruptions (online information services rattling print media), low barriers to entry, and relatively easy penetration of foreign markets, all enhancing cut-throat competition within the subsectors. Customers are the most important strategic asset of media and entertainment companies, particularly because in most subsectors, the customers' identity is known to the provider of services (Internet service providers; cable, satellite radio, and telecom companies; newspaper and magazine publishers; etc.), enabling active management of the customer franchise. Indeed, customer management is a prime driver of competitive advantage in this sector. Other strategic assets are legal rights and licenses (cellular spectrum, TV licenses), content (movies, TV serials), and unique business processes (e.g., Netflix's and Amazon's customer recommendation algorithms).

Achieving sustained competitive advantage in media and entertainment is a major challenge due to fierce competition and low entry barriers. Accordingly, detailed information on companies' strategic resources, their vulnerabilities, deployment, and productivity is essential for investors and lenders to make successful investment decisions and monitor managers. That's indeed the gist of most analysts' questions in the sector's many conference calls that we examined. Conventional accounting and financial reports in this sector are particularly deficient, since most investments in strategic resources are immediately expensed (brand creation, customer acquisition costs, business processes) and, therefore, absent from the balance sheet, while other assets (cellular spectrum) are presented at historical, mostly outdated values. And, of course, given the integrated structure of financial reports, when the balance sheet is flawed, so too is the income statement. For example, the reported earnings of growing media and entertainment companies are seriously understated due to the expensing of large investments in strategic assets (customer acquisition costs, brand creation). Overall, the usefulness of accounting-based financial reports in this dynamic, fast-changing sector is marginal, as clearly evidenced by the limited attention of analysts in conference calls to the companies' reported assets, earnings and other accounting performance indicators.

Enter the proposed Strategic Resources & Consequences Report. For clarity, this Report will first be demonstrated on a specific company—Sirius XM—to highlight the unique investor insights offered by our proposal, followed by the outline of a general Resources & Consequences Report for media and entertainment companies.[1]

SIRIUS XM: RESOURCES & CONSEQUENCES REPORT

Sirius XM is the major provider of satellite radio services in North America—more than 20 percent of all cars in the United States carry Sirius's services. The company creates and broadcasts commercial-free music, comedies, talk and sports shows, as well as some live events. It also provides GPS and weather information. Recently, Sirius started providing Internet radio for connected devices, and telematic, two-way services for connected vehicles, for security (accident reporting) and convenience (restaurant location) purposes. Sirius satellite radios are primarily distributed through car makers and dealers. The company, which was founded in 1990, had about 21 million paying subscribers in 2014, and among its main draws is the notorious Howard Stern show with its endearing call-in number: 1–888–9ASSHOLE.

Sirius's income statement for the second quarter ending June 30, 2013, tells a solid, but somewhat uninspiring story: Total revenues grew 4.8 percent from the earlier quarter ($940 million vs. $897 million), while net income inched up a mere 1.5 percent. How, then, to explain the CEO's ecstatic opening of the quarter's conference call with investors: "Sirius XM turned in an extraordinary second quarter that was marked by a number of new records and milestones"? A 1.5 percent earnings increase being called a "milestone"? Is this just hype? Or, perhaps, as we argue all along, accounting numbers don't tell the real story.

SUBSCRIBERS GROWTH

Let's examine Sirius's Resources & Consequences Report in Figure 12.1. This report was not, of course, produced by Sirius. It's a demonstration of our proposed Resources & Consequences Report based primarily on nonaccounting data disclosed voluntarily by Sirius in its earnings presentations, answers to analysts' questions, and other sources. Sirius's main strategic resource is its customers, or subscribers, see the SUBSCRIBERS box in the Strategic Resources column (second from left). The data inform that Sirius managed to acquire 2.7 million new customers in the quarter—a record—amounting to an 8 percent increase from the previous quarter.[2] Customer termination, 1.9 million, while substantial, was lower than in the earlier quarter (2.1 million customers). The net customer gain—over 700,000 subscribers—was also a record. The icing on the cake: The churn rate (monthly rate of cancellations) decreased nicely to 1.7 percent from

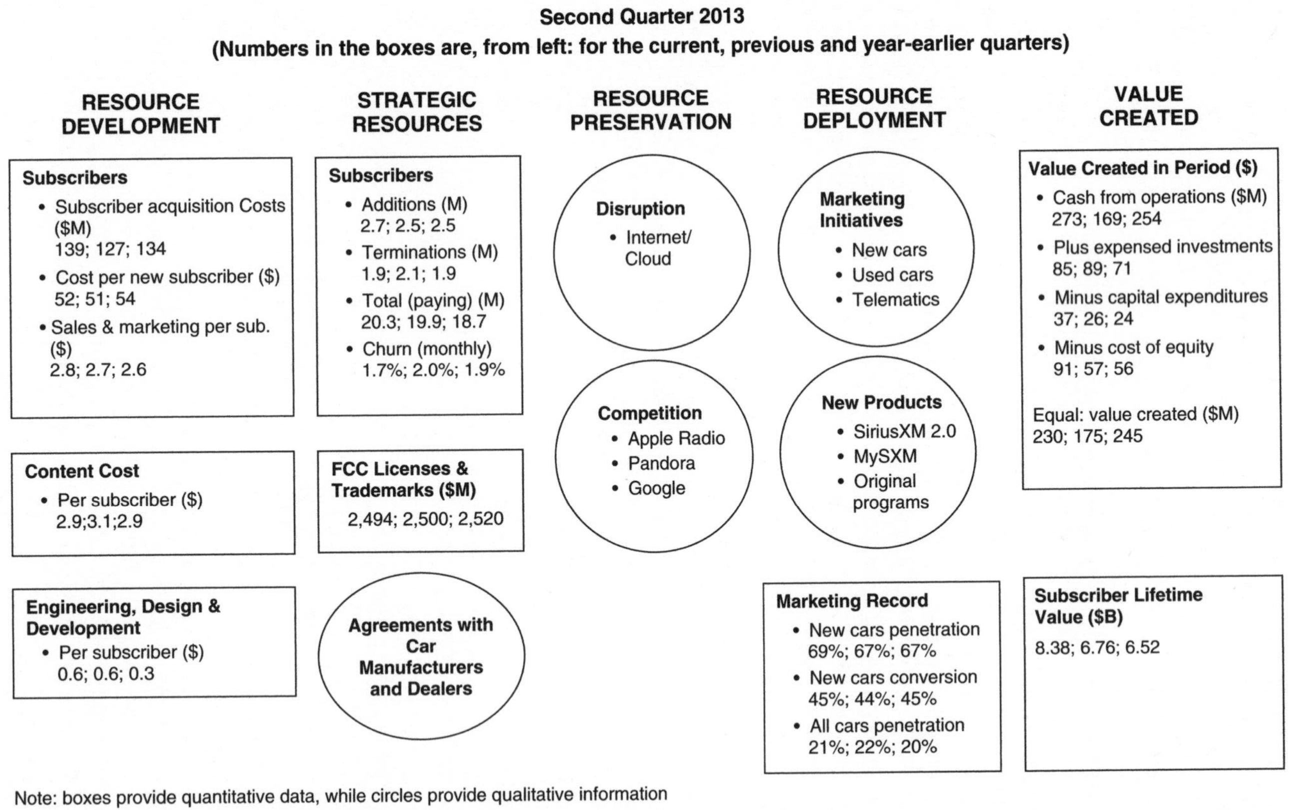

Second Quarter 2013

(Numbers in the boxes are, from left: for the current, previous and year-earlier quarters)

VALUE CREATED

Value Created in Period ($)
- Cash from operations ($M) 273; 169; 254
- Plus expensed investments 85; 89; 71
- Minus capital expenditures 37; 26; 24
- Minus cost of equity 91; 57; 56

Equal: value created ($M) 230; 175; 245

Subscriber Lifetime Value ($B)
8.38; 6.76; 6.52

RESOURCE DEPLOYMENT

Marketing Initiatives
- New cars
- Used cars
- Telematics

New Products
- SiriusXM 2.0
- MySXM
- Original programs

Marketing Record
- New cars penetration 69%; 67%; 67%
- New cars conversion 45%; 44%; 45%
- All cars penetration 21%; 22%; 20%

RESOURCE PRESERVATION

Disruption
- Internet/Cloud

Competition
- Apple Radio
- Pandora
- Google

STRATEGIC RESOURCES

Subscribers
- Additions (M) 2.7; 2.5; 2.5
- Terminations (M) 1.9; 2.1; 1.9
- Total (paying) (M) 20.3; 19.9; 18.7
- Churn (monthly) 1.7%; 2.0%; 1.9%

FCC Licenses & Trademarks ($M)
2,494; 2,500; 2,520

Agreements with Car Manufacturers and Dealers

RESOURCE DEVELOPMENT

Subscribers
- Subscriber acquisition Costs ($M) 139; 127; 134
- Cost per new subscriber ($) 52; 51; 54
- Sales & marketing per sub. ($) 2.8; 2.7; 2.6

Content Cost
- Per subscriber ($) 2.9;3.1;2.9

Engineering, Design & Development
- Per subscriber ($) 0.6; 0.6; 0.3

Note: boxes provide quantitative data, while circles provide qualitative information

FIGURE 12.1 SIRIUS XM Inc.: Resources & Consequences Report

2.0 percent. Note that this non-GAAP customer information portrays a different, more positive, performance picture than the anemic 1.5 percent earnings growth—particularly the substantial increase in new subscribers and the churn rate decrease—providing a certain justification for the CEO's cheerful opening of the conference call. Importantly, the SUBSCRIBERS box provides a comprehensive insight into the company's major strategic asset: development during the quarter, as well as end-of-quarter position.

As there is generally no free lunch, the 2.7-million (gross) customer increase came at a cost: The Resource Development column (left hand) tells us that total subscriber acquisition costs increased from $127 million to $139 million in the second quarter, a 9.4 percent rise, translated to an increase in acquisition cost per new subscriber, from $51 to $52.[3] These costs include commissions paid to automakers as incentives to purchase and activate satellite radios (carrying Sirius) in new cars, and subsidies to radio manufacturers to install satellite service. As the Report shows, other customer acquisition costs, like sales & marketing (divided by total customers), were almost flat in the second quarter. So, from a cost–benefit perspective, the net gain of 700,000 new subscribers in the second quarter came at a relatively low price, particularly considering that, in contrast with accounting procedures, this cost isn't a period expense, rather an investment (asset), providing a stream of future monthly subscription revenues. Given Sirius's annual subscription charge of about $180, the 700,000 net new customers will cover the $139 million acquisition costs in a little over a year, and the low churn rate (1.7 percent per month) indicates that the new customers will stay with Sirius for almost five years, on average, yielding a considerable gain over acquisition costs.[4]

INVESTOR'S INSIGHT

Note how the information in the Resources & Consequences Report allows users: (1) to relate costs (customer acquisition) to benefits (customer growth), (2) to assess the return on investment in franchise building, and (3) to evaluate the success of the customer strategy of Sirius. It is not possible to glean any of this information from accounting-based financial reports, and none of it is really competition-sensitive, precluding disclosure.

This leads us to the bigger question: How did Sirius manage to gain a substantial number of subscribers without a commensurate increase in sales & marketing expenses? Managerial mojo? Howard Stern magic? Not entirely. The second quarter of 2013 saw a substantial increase in new-car sales in the United States. In fact, 2013 was the best car sales year (over 15 million new cars sold) since the low of 2007. Given Sirius's high new-car installation rate—almost 70 percent (see the Report's Resource Deployment column)—much of the subscribers rise in the second quarter was driven by the increase in new car sales and didn't require substantial marketing expenses. But the high installation rate in new cars is obviously driven by Sirius's strategy. This, then, turns the spotlight to the marketing strategy of installing Sirius service in new and used cars.

IT'S THE STRATEGY, STUPID

So, what is Sirius's strategy? How did it get nearly 21 million paying subscribers to its services by 2014? And is this strategy sustainable—namely, does it confer a sustained competitive advantage? These are key questions for investors (and managers, too). Don't look at the financial reports for answers to these fundamental questions. All you'll find is that Sirius's second-quarter total revenues were $940 million. But which managerial strategies and actions yielded these revenues, and which failed? That information is nowhere to be found. Reporting consequences (revenues) without causes is one of the major limitations of accounting-based information. Obviously, without a thorough understanding of Sirius's strategy—its business model—no reliable assessment can be made about manager's performance and the sustainability of current revenues. No wonder that in Sirius's four 2013 quarterly conference calls that we studied there was not a single analyst question about revenues or earnings, but many questions about strategy. That's what matters.

Absent a comprehensive strategy articulation, we managed to cobble up parts of Sirius's strategy from multiple sources, including management presentations and answers to analysts' questions, as well as media sources, and present it in the Resource Deployment column of the Resources & Consequences Report (second column from right). This column summarizes in bullet points the focal points of Sirius's strategy—marketing initiatives and new products—highlighted by performance data (Marketing Record box). In the real Resources & Consequences Report, these strategic indicators would be the basis for a comprehensive discussion of the strategy by management, emphasizing challenges and new initiatives, and elaborated on in the narrative section of the Report (depicted by circles).

As indicated in the Resource Deployment column of the Report, Sirius's marketing strategy revolves around new and used cars. Agreements with car manufacturers to install a six-month trial Sirius service in new cars are very successful (69 percent penetration rate, see Marketing Record). Growth can thus be expected from increases in new car sales (beyond Sirius's control) and an increase in penetration rate. But, at currently almost 70 percent, large penetration gains will be hard to come by, as indicated by the relatively stable 2012–2013 penetration record. The used car market is substantially larger, but more dispersed and difficult to target. Here, Sirius's efforts are aimed at new car sellers offering preowned (euphemism for "used") cars, as well as used car dealers—but those numbers are in the thousands. Agreements to install Sirius's services are also reached with certain dealers servicing used cars. This three-pronged strategy—new, used, and car servicing—is the marketing strategy pursued by Sirius's management. How successful is this strategy? As the quantitative information in the Marketing Record box indicates, the new car penetration rate is high (close to 70 percent), but rather stable, indicating that this rate is close to maturation. Growth can come from increased conversion rate (subscribers who sign for a paid service after the trial period, unlike one of the authors), but this rate is stuck at 45 percent, apparently at a steady state, too.

This leaves the challenging used-car market as the major potential growth driver. But here, too, the stability of the overall penetration rate over 2012–2013—around 20 percent for all cars—indicates significant challenges in the used-car market. All in all, subscribers' growth is undoubtedly the toughest challenge facing Sirius, and it obviously weighs heavily on investors: Despite a rise in the first half of 2013, Sirius's stock remained rather flat since then, lagging the overall market. Now you know why.

Growth, of course, can also come from exciting new products and services. Indeed, in answers to analysts' questions, Sirius's managers mentioned several products under development (Sirius XM 2.0, mySXM), as well as development of original programs and telematic services (two-way convenience and security services). How serious is Sirius's commitment to product development? Lack of data makes this hard to know, but an examination of the CONTENT and ENGINEERING boxes in the Resource Development column (left hand) of the Report isn't reassuring. Expenditures on programming and content are rather low ($2.9 per subscriber vs. $2.8 for sales & marketing), and are not growing. R&D expenditures (engineering, design, and development), at $0.6 per customer, are also low. Management obviously keeps a tight lid on costs, which contributes nicely to accounting earnings ($377 million in 2013), but such tight lid apparently comes at the expense of product development and other growth initiatives. It is questionable, therefore, whether new products will provide considerable revenue boost. Growth is undoubtedly Sirius's Achilles' heel.

INVESTOR'S INSIGHT

Note how the information in the Strategic Resources and the Resource Deployment columns of the Report enable an in-depth analysis of Sirius's strategy, its execution, and the drawing of inferences about future growth. You now have the information needed for a long-term investment decision.

DISRUPTION THREAT

Absent obvious considerable growth prospects, is Sirius's dominant position assured? On the bright side, Sirius's brand is well known; it's practically the only game in town for satellite radio, it has a large and slowly growing subscriber base, and it features some big-name exclusive artists. It seems impregnable. And yet, as the Resource Preservation column of the Report suggests, in this industry with fast-changing technologies and low barriers to entry, competitive and disruption threats can never be dismissed. Indeed, the media carry occasional articles on threats to Sirius's dominance,[5] and many of analysts' questions in Sirius's conference calls revolved around potential competition. The main concerns focus on an Internet strategy as an alternative to satellite radio—wi-fi in the car—and the entry of "big players," like Apple and Google into the car streaming market. In answer to analysts' persistent questions about threats from disruption and competition, Sirius's managers talked somewhat obliquely about developing a double strategy for Sirius: satellite and Internet. But they were obviously reluctant to get into details, and the very low R&D expenditures do not indicate a concerted investment in innovation. This doesn't build investor confidence. The extent to which Sirius will be able, in the long run, to maintain its overwhelming competitive advantage against the likes of Apple, Google, and others aiming at the lucrative wi-fi-in-the-car market is still an open and challenging question. Long-term investors should clearly focus on this issue, and seek more information from management and the board.

VALUE CREATED

This brings us to the last aspect of the Resources & Consequences Report—the actual value created during the quarter by Sirius's strategies (right-hand column). Our computation of value created deviates significantly from accounting-based earnings. As outlined in Chapter 11, we start with Cash Provided by Operating Activities, to abstract from managerial estimates, projections, and occasional manipulations (cash flows are much harder to manipulate than earnings): $273 million in Q2–2013 for Sirius XM (see top righthand box in the Report). We add back investments that were expensed in the income statement (and thereby affect cash flows): Programming & Content, Design & Development: $85 million.[6] We further subtract capital expenditures: $37 million,[7] and a quarterly charge for cost of equity capital: $91 million.[8] Total value created by operations in Q2–2013 at Sirius is thus $230 million.

Abstracting from the unusually low value created in Q1-2013 ($174 million), a $230 million quarterly value created seems representative, a reasonable value, even relative to Sirius's market value of roughly $20 billion. Sirius is clearly a consistent value-creating business.

Finally, we provide a new indicator: an estimate of the lifetime value of Sirius's subscriber franchise—the main strategic asset of the company. This is important, since the value created computed above (as well as accounting earnings) does not include changes in strategic asset values, which are part and parcel of value added. A convenient way to approximate franchise value is to compute the monthly margin per subscriber (monthly revenue-per-subscriber minus operating costs) and multiply it by the inverse of the churn rate. This is the lifetime value of one subscriber; multiplying it by the total number of subscribers yields the overall lifetime subscriber value (assuming no significant subscriber growth). For the second quarter of 2013, this value was $8.38 billion (see Report), an almost 30 percent growth from a year earlier, and a considerable part of the total market value of Sirius (roughly $20 billion in 2013), dwarfing the balance sheet book (equity) value of $3.2 billion.[9]

A REALITY CHECK

It is important to note that our analysis of Sirius was constrained by the limited strategic information we were able to collect from informal sources. A real-life application of our proposed analysis will be based on a comprehensive Strategic Resources & Consequences Report released by the company and reviewed by independent auditors, providing the following information in addition to that in our mock-up Sirius report: a detailed statement of company strategy to increase subscribers, preferably with expected milestones; an articulation of the efforts to develop new products and content; steps taken to maintain Sirius's long-term competitive edge (wi-fi in the car strategy); costs breakdowns between investments and expenses to enable a more precise computation of the value created and life-time customer value; and other information relevant to the competitive position of Sirius. Absent all this, and based on the limited information we have, here is our summary analysis for investors:

> *Sirius XM is a well-run operation. Moderate subscriber growth in the second quarter, 2013 (700,000 net new subscribers), mainly due to an overall increase in new car sales, coupled with tight cost controls produced a reasonable (about 5 percent of market value, annualized) value created, coupled with a substantial growth in the life-time (franchise) value of customers. Sirius's dominant competitive position was maintained in the quarter and appears to be secure for the short-to-medium term. Regarding the long term, two concerns loom large: (1) relatively slow growth (new-car penetration is already high and seems to plateau, and the penetration of the used car market is slow), and (2) competitive threats from strong players in the Internet space (Apple, Google). It's not clear at this stage to what extent Sirius management will be able to cope with these challenges. Accordingly, Sirius stock is a good fit for investors looking for safety and diversification, but questionable for investors looking for significant growth and capital gains.*

BUT IS THIS REALLY WHAT INVESTORS NEED?

In Part II of the book, we elaborated on the main causes of accounting's relevance lost: the absence in financial reports of relevant information on intangibles—the strategic resources of the enterprise, heavy reliance on managerial estimates and forecasts, and the failure to reflect important, nontransactional business events. Notably, these three stumbling blocks are absent from our Resources & Consequences Report. Rather than ignoring intangibles, the Report is built around the company's strategic resources (mostly intangible), highlighting the major value drivers of the enterprise. Furthermore, the Report abstracts from estimates or managerial subjective judgments: Number of new customers, churn rate, or patents and trademarks are all factual data easy for auditors to verify. Moreover, all important developments, whether recorded by the accounting system or not, like new contracts with car manufacturers, or products under development, are highlighted in the proposed Report. This is obviously a far cry from accounting-based financial information.

Importantly, rather than a short-term, backward-looking, and often biased record of the quarter or year that just ended (current financial

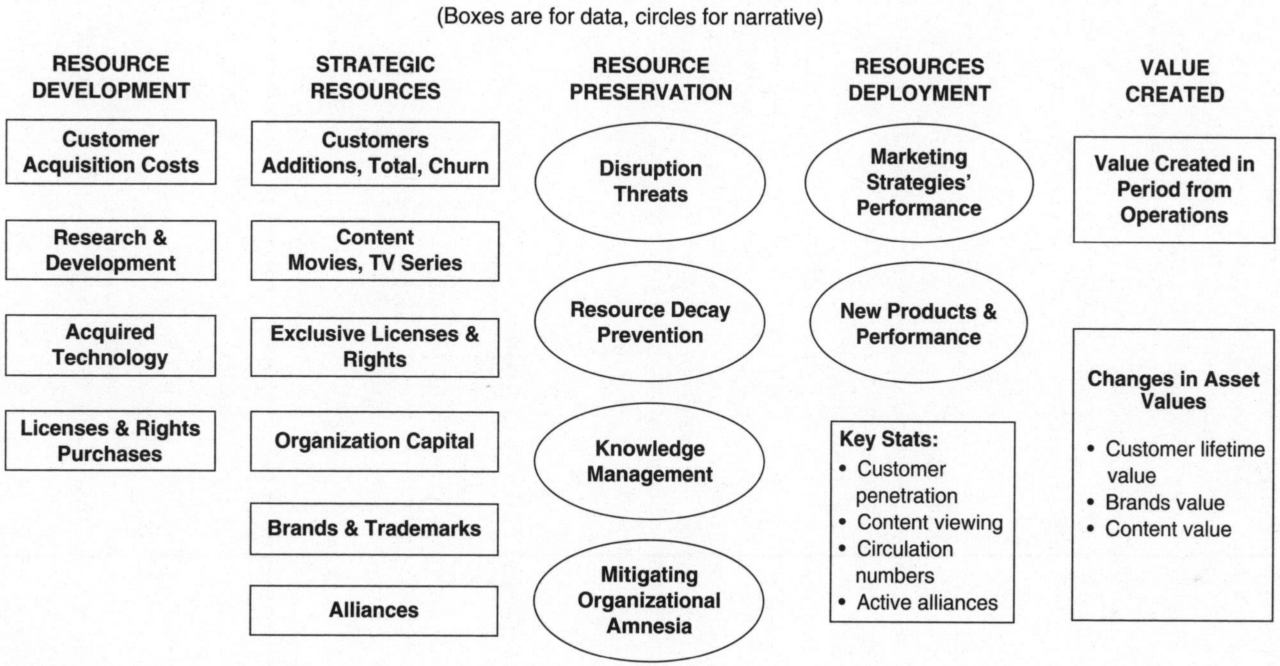

(Boxes are for data, circles for narrative)

RESOURCE DEVELOPMENT	STRATEGIC RESOURCES	RESOURCE PRESERVATION	RESOURCES DEPLOYMENT	VALUE CREATED

Customer Acquisition Costs

Research & Development

Acquired Technology

Licenses & Rights Purchases

Customers
Additions, Total, Churn

Content
Movies, TV Series

Exclusive Licenses & Rights

Organization Capital

Brands & Trademarks

Alliances

Disruption Threats

Resource Decay Prevention

Knowledge Management

Mitigating Organizational Amnesia

Marketing Strategies' Performance

New Products & Performance

Key Stats:
• Customer penetration
• Content viewing
• Circulation numbers
• Active alliances

Value Created in Period from Operations

Changes in Asset Values
• Customer lifetime value
• Brands value
• Content value

FIGURE 12.2 Media and Entertainment: A Strategic Resources & Consequences Report

143

information), the forward-looking Resources & Consequences Report enables a focus on the enterprise's strategy and its execution and particularly facilitates a long-term assessment of the enterprise's ability to maintain competitive advantage. A focus on the bottom line—investors' preoccupation with earnings—is replaced by a panoramic view of the company's strategy–execution–value creation.

The ultimate skeptic may still ask: How do we know that the information in the proposed Resources & Consequences Report really satisfies investors' needs? In fact, we do know. Recently, one of us with two colleagues performed an extensive research on media and entertainment subscription-based companies—telecom, cable, Internet, software, print media, and so on, which, like Sirius XM, charge a subscription fee for their services.[10] A major research question was this: What are the attributes of these enterprises that investors consider essential for security valuation, namely what information affects stock prices? A statistical (regression) analysis relating stock prices and returns of subscription-based enterprises to financial report variables (earnings and book value), as well as to certain key nonaccounting data presented in the Resources & Consequences Report—like number of new subscribers, the churn rate, and revenue-per-subscriber—revealed that indeed, most of the latter, nonaccounting indicators affected stock prices beyond earnings and equity.[11] Investors clearly need and use the information in our proposed Report.

FINALLY, A REPORT FOR THE SECTOR

We conclude the proposed disclosure paradigm for media and entertainment companies with a generalized report (Figure 12.2, previous page) that can be readily adapted to every company in this sector.

NOTES

1. We chose Sirius XM for demonstration because the company, in contrast with many others in the industry, consistently and voluntarily provides many of the strategic indicators called for by our Report. The data in this chapter's examples and those in the following chapters were obtained by us from various sources (earnings calls, company presentations) so that a few errors, misreadings, or inconsistencies are possible. The idea is to demonstrate the potential of the proposed Report, not to analyze a specific company.
2. The numbers in the report are (from left) for the current (second quarter, 2013), previous, and the year-earlier quarters.

3. However, acquisition costs per subscriber decreased dramatically from $82 in the first quarter of 2008 to $52 in 2013. The subscriber acquisition cost of $139 million, includes a couple of adjustments made by the company to the $130 million GAAP costs.
4. A monthly churn (termination) rate of 1.7 percent implies that, on average, a customer stays with Sirius 59 months: "Customer life" = 1/churn = 1/0.017 = 58.8 months.
5. For example, James Brumley, "Sirius XM Is Facing Some Serious Competition," *InvestorPlace* (January 6, 2014).
6. Strictly speaking, since we consider these items investments, or capital, the amortization of the excluded, capitalized expenses should be considered an operating expense. For simplicity, we abstract here from this amortization, which will somewhat reduce our measure of the value created.
7. For simplicity, we subtract the quarterly capital expenditures, rather than a 3- to 5-year average.
8. Based on 2.5 percent (10 percent annual) cost of capital times average Q2-2013 and Q2-2012 ending shareholder equity book value. The 10 percent is, of course, only a convenient proxy for cost of capital. Sirius "systematic risk," or β value is quite high: 1.65 according to Yahoo! Finance. Accordingly, a 10 percent cost of equity capital may be somewhat understated.
9. A comprehensive valuation of customer equity for six companies in the sector found our value to be remarkably close to their estimated values, see Barak Libai, Eitan Muller, and Renana Peres, "The Diffusion of Services," *Journal of Marketing Research*, 46 (2009): 163–175.
10. Massimiliano Bonacchi, Kalin Kolev, and Baruch Lev, "Customer Franchise—a Hidden, Yet Crucial Asset," *Contemporary Accounting Research*, 32 (2015): 1024–1049.
11. The strongest effect on share price was recorded when the nonaccounting variables were combined into a lifetime customer value measure.

CHAPTER 13

Strategic Resources & Consequences Report: Case No. 2—Property and Casualty Insurance

The insurance industry is classified into three segments: property and casualty (PC), life and health (LH), and reinsurance (entities insuring other insurance companies). This chapter presents the Strategic Resources & Consequences Report for the first segment—property and casualty—the largest segment of the industry in terms of number of companies and customers. The PC business is fiercely competitive and its risk is high relative to other insurance segments, particularly due to catastrophic risks. Smart investors in this industry, as in others, focus on the company strategy and its execution, and particularly on the most important strategic asset—the customer franchise. All this is fleshed out by our proposed Report.

The insurance industry doesn't need extensive introduction. Practically everyone is a customer, and most are disgruntled (too expensive, overly bureaucratic, frequently deny claims). But this is just the not-so-pretty face of your insurance company. Most, except for experts, know next to nothing about the business of insurance. If corporate financial reports are generally opaque, insurance companies' reports are outright incomprehensible. We will clear the mist, focusing on the crucial information for investors.[1]

SECTOR SYNOPSIS

The insurance industry is classified into three segments: *property and casualty (PC)*—damage or loss to cars, homes, or businesses; *life and health (LH)*—life and health insurance; and *reinsurance*—entities selling insurance to insurance companies, relieving the latter (ceding companies) from some or all of their risk. We will focus in this case study on the first segment—property and casualty (PC) companies—which is the largest segment of the industry in terms of number of companies and customers. These entities profit from underwriting (selling) insurance to customers, and given the generally long time between receipt of premium from customers and payment of claims, they also gain from investing the substantial funds they accumulate (about 65 percent of insurers' total assets, mostly invested in fixed income securities). These investments provide a major source of income for insurance companies, often surpassing the insurance income.

The PC business risk is high relative to other insurance segments, particularly due to catastrophic risks (earthquakes, terrorism, floods, asbestos claims). That's where reinsurance comes handy. The industry is regulated in the United States at the state level, including regulation of insurance prices. Competition, particularly in the consumer segment of the business is fierce, evidenced by the substantial amount spent by insurance companies on advertising (Geico's gecko, Progressive's Flo). There are several large but not dominant firms in the industry (State Farm, Geico, Allstate). Insurers face two major issues: in the economists' parlance, adverse selection and moral hazard. The former refers to the tendency of individuals or companies with high risk (e.g., seriously ill people) to obtain more coverage than low-risk persons, and the latter refers to the tendency of the insured to engage in riskier behavior (neglect house maintenance) relative to uninsured, and, at the extreme, to fake claims. Both of these hazards are mitigated by smart customer management, as you'll see shortly. The industry as a whole is quite profitable, as indicated by the S&P Insurance Select Industry Index, which slightly lagged the S&P 500 over the 10-year period 2006–2015 (7.84 percent vs. 9.14 percent, average annual return), yet edged the S&P 500 in the latter five years (15.37 percent vs. 13.11 percent average annual return).

Investors in insurance companies, as in other sectors, focus on the company's strategy to create value and growth, and the execution of the strategy. This was made clear in the 2012–2013 conference calls of the 10 insurance companies we studied in detail. For example, in Progressive's 2013 investor meeting (May 16, 2013), both the CEO and CFO presentations were fully devoted to the company's strategy and business model, elaborating on the primary objective of management (to grow as fast as possible, subject to 96 percent or less "combined ratio"—expenses over revenues), and the extent to which this objective was achieved. Analysts' questions were similarly strategy-focused in Progressive's calls, as in the other calls we studied. Financial report (accounting) information plays a limited role in such strategic analysis because it is virtually silent about the main factors that matter: strategic assets and their development (customers, in particular), the fundamental drivers of the value created (like changes in insurance rate, or the frequency and severity of insurance claims), and the company's strategy to manage risk and preserve the strategic assets. Fragments of the strategic information are presented in management's voluminous discussions accompanying the financial reports (MD&A, for example), but they are often buried in hopelessly long-winded and frankly boring statements (Allstate's 2013 report to shareholders is a tome of 294 dense pages). The information is incomplete (some companies provide information on policy renewals, or churn, while others don't), and the measures reported are not standardized and comparable across competitors. This creates the acute need for our compact and standardized Resources & Consequences Report.

IT ALL STARTS WITH STRATEGIC ASSETS

These assets are the drivers of corporate value and sustained competitive advantage: To recap, they generate a stream of net benefits, they are rare (the pool of low risk, loyal insurance customers is limited), and they cannot be easily imitated by competitors (Geico's leading brand cannot readily be recreated by a newcomer). For insurance companies, *customers* are the most valuable strategic asset, as noted by Peter Drucker, the management guru who said that the aim of a business is to create a customer. Much of insurance companies' strategy and operational success revolves around customer management: acquiring the *right* customers, not just any customers, and convincing them to stay with the company (renew policies). Information about customer management—totally absent from financial reports—is thus key for investors to assess company performance and chart its future growth. Other strategic assets are brands (Allstate's Esurance), intellectual property (patents on new products, like Snapshot, Progressive's plugged-in-the-car device to track individual driving behavior and offer personalized premiums), and dedicated, productive agents. Back to customers.

What are the "right" customers assuring sustained competitive advantage? These are persons with low adverse selection and moral hazard (defined earlier), namely, low-risk (safe drivers), and careful (property maintaining) customers. Successful strategy (referred to as book management) is aimed at targeting such customers (Hartford, for example, teamed up with AARP, the dominant retirees association, to market insurance to AARP members—older people are, on average, conscientious, low-mileage drivers, carefully maintaining their cars), and holding on to them as long as possible with attractive rates and good customer relations (claims management). Keeping a high-quality "book" is of the essence. Insurance companies change rates (premiums) frequently—the industry is known to regularly experience competition-driven *underwriting cycles,* where rates and profits rise and fall. Rate decreases draw both good and bad customers, and successful customer management quickly weeds out the latter during successive policy renewal cycles.

The basic tension, or balancing act of customer (book) management is to healthily grow the company—add customers—at relatively low customer acquisition costs (advertising, agent commissions), then hold on to the good customers, and maintain low operating costs (few and inexpensive claims). Regrettably for investors, the quarterly/annual earnings of insurance companies often portray a distorted picture of customer management, particularly in the peaks and troughs of the underwriting cycles. For example, when a company decreases rates to enhance growth, reported earnings will often be depressed, or even negative, because of the low new premiums and losses from the poor (high-claims) customers attracted to the low rates. But these low earnings don't necessarily indicate management failure. It takes time to stabilize the book and reap the benefits of the policy change.[2]

Insurance companies' reported earnings are also distorted by poor expense–revenue matching: Reported earnings often include adjustments made to prior-year reserves (estimates of future claims) without corresponding revenues, and the main expense item—insurance losses (current and expected payments to customers)—is subject to considerable uncertainty due to the long time lag between insured events (car accident, work injury) and the final settlement of claims, which may take years. The large component of *estimated* future payments on claims in the insurance losses item renders the reported earnings of insurance companies less certain and more volatile than the earnings of companies in most other sectors.[3] This, of course, reflects the nature of the insurance business (long-tail claim), and in fairness, PC companies provide substantial information about estimated future payments. Nevertheless, insurance companies' reported earnings are not the most reliable indicators of enterprise performance and growth potential. Enter the customers segment of the Resources & Consequences Report.

THE RESOURCES & CONSEQUENCES REPORT: CUSTOMERS

Figure 13.1 is the "customers box" in our proposed insurance companies' Resources & Consequences Report. The numbers in the box, for

---

Policies-in-Force (000)

- 32,831; 33,062; −0.7%

Written Premium ($M)

- 6,625; 6,463; 2.5%

Average Premium Written ($)

- Auto: 462; 452; 2.2%
- Home: 1,115; 1,065; 4.7%

New Policies (000)

- Auto: 570; 542; 5.2%
- Home: 113; 101; 11.9%

Renewal Ratio (%)

- Auto: 88.7; 88.0; 0.8%
- Home: 87.0; 87.4; −0.5%

FIGURE 13.1 Customers' Box

demonstration purposes, are for Allstate Corp., from left to right: first quarter 2013, first quarter 2012 (year-earlier quarter), and the percentage change.[4]

Allstate is a large and mature company, so don't expect big year-to-year changes. The data on policies-in-force—a measure of customer size—indicate a slight decrease in the number of policies (0.7 percent) over the 12 months examined, but the line below reveals that, nevertheless, there was a 2.5 percent increase in total written premium.[5] The resolution to this seeming contradiction (lower policies-in-force, but higher written premium) is found in the third item in the box: rising average premium written, which increased over the 12 months by 2.2 percent for auto and 4.7 percent for homes. Thus, an across-the-board rise in Allstate's insurance rates, rather than in number of effective policies (customer size), led to the modest (2.5 percent) increased revenues (written premium).[6]

A rise in "combined ratio"—the ratio of expenses (the sum of claims payments and operating expenses) to revenues—generally triggers rate increases as a company seeks to maintain profitability. (Progressive, for example, responded in 2012 to a combined ratio increase by upping auto rates by 6.5–10 percent.) The downside of a rate increase is, of course, customer defection. But Allstate's renewal (retention) rate data, at the bottom of the box, lays this concern to rest for auto: renewals increased by 0.8 percent. However, the larger (4.7 percent) rate increase for homes apparently trigged a negative effect: home renewals decreased by 0.5

percent.[7] Overall, Allstate managed to drive in the quarter a modest car rate increase, improving the top line somewhat, without a significant customer defection, but the higher homeowners rate increase adversely affected the customer base. Obviously, Allstate's rate-increasing policy margins are razor thin. We don't know, of course, how many potential customers were deterred by the higher rates, but the data on "new policies" for the quarter (see box) are encouraging: 5.2 percent increase for auto and a substantial 11.9 percent for homes. Intriguingly, Allstate increased new homeowner policies in the quarter, but also lost more customers (effective advertising?).

INVESTOR'S INSIGHTS

Considering Allstate's customers franchise, the concern is that there was no volume (policies-in-force) growth during 2012, and that the meager top line (revenue) growth (2.5 percent) came from rate increases. In the very price-competitive PC industry, increasing rates isn't a winning, sustainable strategy. Much of the competition is about offering lower rates and customer savings ("15 minutes will save you 15 percent," says Geico's catchy slogan), compensated by enhanced operational efficiency. Indeed, answering analysts' questions in the 2013 earnings call, Allstate's management announced a slowdown of the rate increase. Growth is obviously a concern for Allstate, as well as for most other large insurers.

So, where will growth come from? Allstate's management points at Esurance, the online insurance segment of the company, a pioneer in the industry. Esurance's written premium growth was a healthy 30.5 percent in the quarter, albeit from a relatively small base.[8] But this growth faces a stiff headwind: Customer acquisition costs in Esurance (mainly advertising) is high, still rendering the segment a "loss leader," and competitors are quickly catching up with their own online insurance offerings. This clearly demonstrates the need to sustain innovation to maintain growth.

NEW PRODUCTS—INNOVATION

Most industries generate growth by penetrating new markets as they innovate with new products or services, create new demand (e.g., handheld devices, cosmetic drugs), or poach from competitors. However, foreign markets are not an option for most insurance companies, and competitors quickly imitate innovations in financial services, including in the PC insurance marketplace. Such was, for example, the case of the device plugged into cars to track drivers' habits and adjust insurance rates accordingly. Progressive has its Snapshot, personalizing each driver's policy after 30 days. The company even has six patents on it, but that didn't deter Hartford from developing its own in-car device, "True Lane," or Allstate from its "Drive Wise" car device, which it claims resulted in average premium reduction of 14 percent. The future lies, say PC managers, in telematics devices that will enable ongoing, two-way communication with drivers to improve their driving behavior.

Other innovations include *comparative raters,* allowing agents and customers to compare the company's rates with competitors', and "mobile quoting," enabling customers to get insurance quotes on handheld devices. Progressive claims that mobile quotes increased 8 percent in 2013. Service centers, where customers can interact directly with company representatives, are also a recent innovation. Innovation in the form of new services provides an important, albeit relatively short-lived, competitive edge for targeting the roughly 10–15 percent of customers who switch companies every year, as well as attracting new customers. Obviously, an insurance company must quickly keep up with the leading innovators, which Allstate is clearly doing. Accordingly, information about company innovation and its effects (e.g., new business from service centers) should be provided in the New Products box of the Resource Development column of the Resources & Consequences Report (at chapter end). This will help investors assess the sustainability of the company's competitive advantage.

AGENTS—STILL IMPORTANT

Although direct (online, phone, mail) insurance sales are increasing, the traditional agent channel still generates considerable business. There are two types of agents: dedicated and independent; the former work with one company only, while the latter offer customers a menu of insurance solutions. Dedicated agents are obviously a strategic resource (see Agencies box at end of chapter Report), and details on the number of agents, their productivity (agent-driven new and in-force policies), the quality of the customers they generate (e.g., average losses on agents' customers relative to the company's other customers), and the commissions paid to agents, are important information items to evaluate the company's agency strategy. In its conference calls, Allstate managers touched on agencies, but rather obliquely.

They, for example, mentioned changes made in 2012 to agents' incentives and bonuses, without data, saying that the incentive changes led to a certain decrease in the number of agents. Not much to go by, but other companies disclosed even less. Obviously poor disclosure, but the generally meek analysts in the calls didn't press executives for improved transparency. It is hard to see any competitive threats from disclosing information that enables investors to assess the performance of insurance agencies.

Overall, given the relatively small market slice over which all companies compete (about 10 to 15 percent of the insured, as well as new customers), and the similarly small margins for rate decreases (for most companies, insurance costs already exceed 90 percent of revenues), investors can't expect dramatic top-line (revenue) changes for medium and large companies. Smaller, local companies, exploiting niches, and new entrants to the industry can grow, of course, at a faster rate.

Operational efficiency (effective claims management, information technology) can also generate bottom-line growth and serve as a major source of value creation and competitive advantage. Such operational efficiency, to which we now turn, is mainly generated by the company's "organization capital," namely, the systems, processes, methods, and knowledge employed by the enterprise to perform its assigned tasks in the most efficient way.[9]

OPERATIONS—RESOURCE DEPLOYMENT

Property and casualty insurance operations are quite complex, involving the acquisition of new customers, maintaining the quality of the "book," and handling customers' claims in the least painful way for the insured, all while economizing on the company's resources, maintaining and developing the company's brand, managing risk—how much of the company's exposure to cede to reinsurers, and other risk management techniques—incentivizing employees and agents, and running the huge back-office operations smoothly. This is a mouthful of activities and a serious challenge for managers. Running a tight ship significantly affects the value created and allows the company to reduce rates and stay competitive, and we accordingly devote special attention to this issue. By all accounts, Geico, a subsidiary of Warren Buffett's Berkshire Hathaway, is the best-run major US insurance company.[10]

In the insurance sector, financial report information on operating efficiency suffers from the usual accounting deficiencies, but it is magnified for PC insurers by the unusually large proportion of expenses made up by estimates of future claim payments (loss reserve), and the frequent adjustments of previous-years' loss reserves, included in current expenses, all increasing

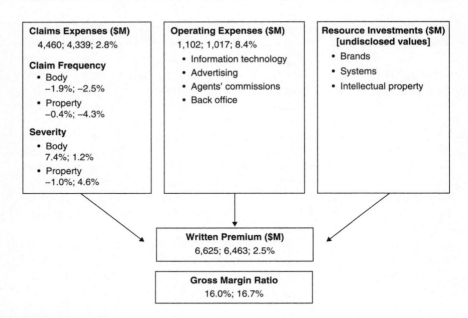

FIGURE 13.2   Insurance Company Operations

the uncertainty of reported earnings and decreasing the revenue–expense matching. Absent from financial reports are insights into the fundamental *causes* of expense changes, impeding investors' assessment of the operational efficiency of the company's organization capital. Needed is a system that relies less on subjective managerial estimates and forecasts, sometimes "managed" by executives, and more on verifiable facts.[11] Such a system, part of the Resources & Consequences Report, is presented in Figure 13.2 (numbers are for Allstate, first quarters 2013 and 2012).

The Operations box in Figure 13.2 focuses on three inputs that support the companies' output (revenue, written, or earned): *Claims expenses*, that is, payments on customers' claims, by far the largest expense item; *operating expenses*, namely, the cost of running the business; and the periodic *investments* in strategic resources—brands, IT, and intellectual property, which accountants lump with regular operating expenses in the income statement. These three inputs support (indicated by arrows) the revenues (written premiums) at the bottom of the box, leading to the gross margin (revenues minus claims and operating expenses) and the gross margin ratio—the "bottom line" of the firm's operations.

We are limited in demonstrating the full potential of the proposed operations analysis, because the expense data in PC companies' income statements mix regular expenses and investments and often don't provide separate information on key expenses (IT, advertising), and are, therefore, inadequate for an in-depth operating analysis. In a real-life Resources & Consequences Report, information would be provided on claims expenses, excluding changes in estimates of prior year reserves, and the reserve for future claims will be discounted, or at least separated from the actual payments on claims, and the main operating expenses, such as advertising and IT, would be split between current expenses and investments (generating future benefits). For example, Allstate's advertising campaign during the first few years of its online Esurance service was obviously an investment in the brand rather than a regular expense. Only current operating expenses, along with claims expenses, should determine the gross margin and be used for assessment of enterprise cost control. Resource investments (right-hand box) should be analyzed separately, relating them to consequent benefits (e.g., effectiveness of an advertising campaign by the consequent business).

PENETRATING THE COSTS BLACK BOX

The reported total *claims expenses* (top left box in Figure 13.2)—$4,460 million and $4,339 million, respectively, a 2.8 percent increase—don't really tell us much about the dynamics of this major expense item of PC insurers. What were the main determinants of the claims, and what do the numbers say about the management of the customers' "book"? The breakdown of claims determinants to accidents' *frequency* and *severity*, provided by a few insurers only, is revealing. Claim frequency—which is affected by vehicle technology, road safety, and drivers' competence and attention (texting while driving) for auto insurance, and the quality of building materials for homes insurance—slightly decreased at Allstate in the first quarter: −1.9 percent for body and −0.4 percent for property, continuing Allstate's 2012 frequency downward trend. In contrast, severity—the amount of claimed damage—jumped for the more serious bodily damage by 7.4 percent in the first quarter of 2013, a significant uptick.[12] Of concern, Allstate's call presentations show a constant increase in body severity growth dating back to 2011: The severity increases in the last three quarters of 2012 were 3.4 percent, 6.8 percent, and 5.2 percent. This obviously should be disconcerting to investors—particularly the negative trend—because body (injury, death) claims are the heaviest cost driver of total claims.

Over time, the inflation of medical costs affects severity, but this cannot fully explain Allstate's fast 2011–2013 growth. In the earnings call, management didn't elaborate on the severity growth—no one asked about it, a sad commentary on analysts' acumen—but the severity growth may indicate a deterioration in the quality of the customers' book. High-risk, careless drivers committing serious accidents aren't being winnowed by the company, and the quality of the book deteriorates. Perhaps, this is an unintended consequence of the sharp growth (30.5 percent) of Allstate's online customers (Esurance).

Proof of concept: Do investors actually need information on claims frequency and severity, as we argue? To prove they do, we collected quarterly data on frequency and severity for 10 companies that provided this information, over the four years 2010–2013. We then regressed (correlated) the quarterly stock returns of these companies on their earnings growth (relative to same quarter a year earlier)—a stock return driver—and the changes in accidents' frequency and severity during the quarter. The regression coefficient estimates of frequency and severity were statistically significant (at the 2–3 percent level), confirming that changes in these two nonaccounting indicators indeed affect stock prices—namely, they are relevant to investors.

INVESTOR'S INSIGHT

Note how GAAP's focus on total claim payments obscures underlying serious developments that should be aired out with management. Allstate's reported total claims inched up during the quarter by 2.8 percent, barely higher than the 2012 inflation rate (2.1 percent), a seemingly innocuous cost rise. Digging deeper, however, shows that a major cost driver—body severity—continued, and even accelerated its rising trend. Management should provide reasons, along with what it is doing to reverse the trend. Allstate, to its credit, voluntarily provided consistent frequency and severity data, which cannot be said about most other insurers we have examined. Investors should obviously demand this information.

We wish we could have analyzed in similar depth the remaining two boxes: *operating expenses* (which "healthily" grew 8.4 percent) and *investments*, but we couldn't find the required details in Allstate's, or any other company's reports. The "big costs" of PC insurers requiring close scrutiny are advertising and IT. In the earnings call (Q1–2013), Progressive executives mentioned that advertising costs were up 15 percent annually for the past 15 years (obvious to everyone who watches Flo with her shticks on TV). But what's important for a strategic cost–benefit analysis are the corresponding performance measures (benefits). For example, do Progressive's 15 percent annual advertising hikes generate similar increases in requests for quotes by potential customers? We know from Progressive's reports that year-on-year revenue growth was about half the advertising growth rate. Did Progressive's advertising reach the stage of diminishing marginal returns? Should the advertising increases slow down, perhaps? Or, for Allstate's Esurance, which is also advertised heavily, it would be instructive to correlate the advertising growth with the number of views of the Esurance site, and the rate of conversion (viewers turned to customers). Perhaps Esurance, too, passed the point of increasing marginal returns and the advertising expenses should slow down. Similarly with agents—their costs should correlate positively with the amount of business they generate.[13] Investors should demand this, and similar strategic information from management to properly evaluate operational efficiency. Financial report totals—Allstate's 8.4 percent operating expense increase—are, at best, a starting point for a serious analysis. The Resources & Consequences Report, accordingly, calls for substantially more insightful cost disclosure.

The right-hand side of the *Operations* box exhibited in Figure 13.2 focuses on investments, in contrast with operating expenses. Insurance companies aren't radical innovators, like pharma or software companies, but they invest substantial amounts in their organization capital, namely in business systems and processes enabling an efficient use of company resources. It's therefore important to focus on brands, IT, and human resource (training) investments, as well as on innovations (plug-in car devices to customize the driving experience, or online claim resolution) to gauge the company's investment rate in future growth. Regrettably, we cannot provide examples of such analysis and inferences because none of the ten companies we have examined in depth provided relevant information on strategic investments.[14]

Concluding the resource deployment (operations) analysis, a cost–benefit comparison is made at the bottom of the box, deriving the gross margin ratio (ratio of the difference between premiums and expenses to premiums), yielding for Allstate a year-to-year slight decrease of gross margin from 16.7 percent in the first quarter of 2012 to 16.0 percent in the first quarter of 2013. This is not alarming, but an issue for investors to watch for.[15]

RESOURCE PRESERVATION

This part of the Resources & Consequences Report is particularly relevant for insurance companies, where the main thrust of resource preservation is managing the risk of the franchise and maintaining a high quality of the book (customers): winnowing high-risk customers and preventing competitors from poaching quality customers. We have discussed customer management, so let's turn to risk. By its nature, insurance is a risky business:

An insurer *buys* risk from the insured, literally "sitting" on pools of risks, and managing this pool is a prime activity directly affecting the company's value created and competitive advantage.

Three types of risks affect insurance operations:

1. *Underwriting risk* is the risk that the premiums collected from customers will fall short of the claim payments to them. This risk is particularly high, since the extent of large liabilities, like asbestos or pollution liability cases is not known at the time the policies are written. Those catastrophic claims can easily mushroom into billions of dollars (the 2012 Hurricane Sandy claims). Underwriting risk rises when competition among insurers intensifies and companies react by lowering rates, thereby attracting low-quality, high-risk customers, among others.

2. *Investment risk* is the risk related to stocks and bonds price fluctuations. Since insurance companies maintain large investments in securities and rely on investment income to fill their coffers, they are subject to the risks of investing in capital markets, such as the impact of unexpected interest rate changes on bond prices, default of borrowers, or adverse changes in stock prices.

3. *Regulatory risk* results from regulators' power to deny or constrain rate increases, to force insurers to cover certain risks they wouldn't have covered otherwise (earthquake or flood damage), or change capital requirements and other solvency-related regulations.

Insurance companies use multiple risk management tools to manage and contain their underwriting risk exposure, particularly potential losses from catastrophic events. These strategies include offering policies that limit the insurer's risk exposure ($1 million max umbrella liability insurance), diversifying exposure across geographic areas and industries, sharing risk with other companies (underwriting pools), or issuing to the public catastrophe bonds (*cat bonds*), which, in case of a catastrophic event, allow the insurance company to retain the bond principle. Reinsurance, however, is the major means of risk management, where part or all of the risk of an insurance portfolio is transferred to a reinsurance company for a portion of the premium received from customers.[16] Some reinsurance contracts involve an "excess-of-loss" clause, where the reinsurance kicks in when the company's loss exceeds a predetermined limit.

Traditional tools of investment risk diversification come into play when managing the risk of the investment portfolio: avoiding high-risk investments (junk bonds), using financial derivatives (hedging), and investing in insured bonds (most of insurance companies' investments are in fixed-income securities). Finally, regulatory risk is largely managed through lobbying the regulators and legislators.

The Resource Preservation part of the Resources & Consequences Report (mid-column) should accordingly provide sufficient information enabling investors to evaluate the effectiveness of the company's risk management, and the extent of risk exposure. Narrative, but not boilerplate, discussion of management's risk mitigation strategies, with quantitative indicators, like proportion of exposure and premium ceded to reinsurers, along with traditional risk measures, such as VAR (value at risk) should be provided in the Resources & Consequences Report. As for regulatory risk, relevant information includes the status of major rate increase applications and regulators' moves to impose new coverage on the company.

Here, as elsewhere, it's important to perceive the proposed Report as an *integrated system*, rather than a list of disparate indicators. Accordingly, other information in the Report, particularly on patterns in the frequency and severity of claims and customer's rate of renewing policies, also shed light on important insurance risk dimensions. A pattern of increasing claims' severity, for example, indicates an increase in underwriting risk. From analysts' questions in the conference calls we studied, it is clear that investors have a keen interest in insurance risk issues, and yet we didn't see any systematic and relevant (nonboilerplate) risk disclosure by the companies, and the answers to analysts' questions were patchy at best—a missed opportunity to inform investors. That's where the potential of our Resources & Consequences Report is manifested: in organizing and standardizing an integrated investor-relevant information system.

VALUE CREATED

Insurance companies' reported earnings and cash flows seem quite hefty. Allstate's 2014 net income was $2.85 billion, 8.1 percent of total revenues, and cash from operations were $3.24 billion. However, these earnings abstract from the cost of equity capital—a necessary cost of doing business—and given the relatively large equity (book value) of insurance companies, their real profits are, in fact, substantially lower than reported. For example, Allstate's average book equity during 2014 was $22 billion. The company's systematic risk is relatively low, due to the size and stability of its operations (beta value of 0.81), so an 8 percent cost of capital seems appropriate. This yields an annual cost of equity capital of $1.76 billion ($22B × 0.08), leaving a 2014 value created of $1.48 billion (3.24 - 1.76), or about 5 percent of market value (around $30 billion). This is a reasonable value creation for a large and mature insurance company.

We conclude the property and casualty insurance analysis with a schematic, comprehensive Resources & Consequences Report (Figure 13.3).

(Boxes are for data, circles for narrative)

RESOURCE DEVELOPMENT

Customers ($)
- Acquisition
- Advertising costs
- Service centers

Information Technology ($)
- Expenditures

Brands ($)
- Advertising
- Brand acquisition

New Products ($)
- Development expenditures

Organization Capital ($)
- Employee training
- Consulting fees

Business Acquisition ($)

STRATEGIC RESOURCES

Customers
- Policies-in-force (000)
- Written premium ($M)
- Average premium written ($)
- New policies (000)
- Geographic footprint
- Renewal ratio (%)
- Rate changes (%)

Agencies
- Number
- New policies written (000)
- Incentives ($)

Intellectual Property
- New products
- Patents, trademarks
- Brands, market share

RESOURCE PRESERVATION

Reinsurance (%)
- Exposure ceded
- Premium ceded

Maintaining Book Quality
- Strategy
- Indicators
- Concentration risk

Competitors' Actions
- New products
- Pricing strategies

Underwriting Risk
- Mitigation

Regulatory Actions
- Approved requests
- Pending

Investment Risk
- Strategy + Risk measures

RESOURCE DEPLOYMENT

Claims Payment ($M)
- Frequency (%)
- Severity (%)

Operating Expenses ($M)
- Advertising
- IT
- Agents pay

Written & Earned Premium ($)
- Rate and quality changes

Gross Margin Ratio (%)

VALUE CREATED

Value Created in Period ($)

Lifetime Value of Customers ($)

FIGURE 13.3 Property & Casualty Insurance: A Strategic Resources & Consequences Report

NOTES

1. Our discussion of the insurance industry benefited from the excellent study of the industry by Columbia University Professor Doron Nissim: "Analysis and Valuation of Insurance Companies" (Columbia Business School, Center for Excellence in Accounting and Security Analysis, 2010).
2. More seriously, the prospects of depressed quarterly earnings and missing the consensus estimate may deter managers from making rate reduction decisions when necessary.
3. The fact that these expected future payments are not discounted when included in current expenses adds to the earnings distortions.
4. Of the 10 insurance companies we examined closely, Allstate was the one providing adequate customer data, and was therefore chosen for demonstration. We remind the reader that the data in the boxes were obtained from several sources (earnings calls, company presentations, etc.), so that some misreadings and inconsistencies are possible.
5. "Written premium" is the total premium on the policies issued by the company during the quarter. This measure is different from the premium amount (revenue) on the income statement—"earned premium"—which prorates the total premium on policies written during the period among the quarters (years) over which the policy is effective. We prefer to consider written premium because it matches better than earned premium with the underwriting expenses—the cost of acquiring customers, although insurers defer some acquisition costs to future periods. Furthermore, written premium is a leading indicator of earned premium. Stated differently, the ratio of written-to-earned premiums—0.98 for Allstate in the first quarter of 2013—is a growth measure (a ratio below 1 indicates negative future premium growth).
6. Earned premium also increased over the 12 months by 2.1 percent.
7. Regarding the decreasing homeowner retention, it would be instructive to learn how many policies were canceled by the company—improving the book quality by derisking it—and how many were canceled (not renewed) by customers; this from an author whose policy was recently canceled.
8. Reassuringly, in the earnings call, Allstate's management stated that Esurance's new customers are not cannibalizing other lines of Allstate, but come from competitors.
9. On organization capital and its measurement, see Baruch Lev and Suresh Radhakrishnan, *Organization Capital*, working paper (New York University, 2015).
10. Progressive included in its 2013 Investor Relations Meeting materials several industry rankings on performance indicators, where Geico ranks first, closely pursued by—who else?—Progressive.
11. See Nissim on "management" of insurance companies' reserves.
12. The percentages quoted are for auto insurance.
13. In its 2013 investor relations meeting materials, Progressive provided graphs showing that the business generated by agencies lagged relative to business generated directly. Were there any measures—incentives revamp, say—taken to prop up the agency business?

14. Dissatisfaction with accounting-based indicators is widespread. Allstate's management, for example, talks about the "economic combined ratio," where, as in our analysis, the investment in the brand is excluded from operating expenses.

15. Remember that we are using deficient accounting numbers, for want of better ones. The more realistic gross margin, based on claim payments net of adjustments of past reserves, and operating expenses net of investments in brands and technology, will likely be different from those in the box.

16. Several of analysts' questions in the conference calls we studied indeed revolved around reinsurance and the extent of ceding risk to reinsurers.

CHAPTER 14

Strategic Resources & Consequences Report: Case No. 3—Pharmaceutics and Biotech

Drug companies hold the record for research and development (R&D) spending: 12–15 percent of sales for large companies, and 15–20 percent for smaller biotech entities. In addition to such substantial in-house innovation, large and medium drug companies often acquire smaller outfits to bolster their in-line, and particularly R&D capabilities. The only GAAP-based information currently provided by pharma companies on their vital R&D activities is the innocuous R&D expense. The major strategic resources of drug and biotech companies are in-line products and their underlying patents, the product development pipeline, trademarks and other intellectual property, and key human resources. Drug companies provide certain information on products and pipeline in supplements to financial reports and presentations accompanying earnings calls, but such non-GAAP disclosure is often haphazard and inconsistent from period to period, and across companies, and hence of limited value to investors. Enter the Strategic Resources & Consequences Report.

As in the preceding case study of insurance companies, practically everyone is a customer of drug or biotech companies. Few, though, are satisfied customers. Many complain about exorbitant drug prices, and the socially conscious question the justification for extended patent protection of essential drugs, particularly in Third World countries. If that's not enough, drug manufacturers are often blamed for focusing research on potential blockbusters, leaving rare diseases unresearched. While spending substantial funds on image-improving and public relations,[1] the strategic focus of pharmaceutical companies is on gaining and maintaining sustained competitive advantage by successful innovation.

STRATEGY AND STRATEGIC RESOURCES

Pfizer's CEO, Ian Read, succinctly summarized his company's strategy in the Q3–2013 (third quarter, 2013) earnings call as: "...[achieving] progress across the businesses by enhancing the quality of the [product] pipeline, demonstrating fiscal discipline on how we deploy our capital, and executing on our business plan in order to drive greater value for our shareholders." By no means Shakespearian, but clear and to the point.[2] Merck's CEO similarly stated in the Q2–2013 earnings call: "... we will build shareholder value by prioritizing investments in our best commercial growth opportunities with key in-line [on the market] products and in innovative R&D... making disciplined decisions regarding the allocation of resources and managing our cost effectively." In short, pursuing drugs' and medical devices' innovations, subject to cost constraints. Sounds good, but how is such a strategy executed?

INVESTING IN INNOVATION

Drug companies hold the records for R&D spending: 12–15 percent of sales for large companies, and 15–20 percent for smaller biotech entities. In addition to such substantial in-house R&D spending, large and medium drug companies often acquire smaller outfits to bolster their in-line, and particularly R&D capabilities. Thus, for example, on February 5, 2015, Pfizer announced the $17 billion acquisition of Hospira, Inc., and AstraZeneca acquired Actavis also on February 5, 2015 (a good day for investment bankers), which, in turn, acquired Auden McKenzie less than a month earlier. Sometimes companies just acquire a product line, as in KYTHERA Biopharmaceuticals, which, on February 11, 2015, purchased the worldwide rights from Actelion to clinical compounds and key intellectual property (patents) for novel treatment of hair loss (not too soon for the authors). The strategy behind these acquisitions is either to facilitate the entry into a new therapeutic line (franchise) or broaden existing lines. Innovation investments are also driven by the acute need to fill gaps arising from patent expiration of leading drugs, often creating serious revenue "holes." The patent on Pfizer's cholesterol-reducing blockbuster Lipitor, with over \$10 billion annual sales expired in November 2011, leading to a 19 percent earnings drop in the first quarter of 2012. All this spending on internal and acquired R&D and products is, of course, subject to promising product market opportunities—existing or creating demand for new drugs and devices—and funds availability.

Cost control is of the essence, as undisciplined research can easily turn into bottomless cash-burn pits. The large firms, with multiple products on the market, have ample cash flows to support innovation investments—Johnson & Johnson's 2013 cash from operations was a whopping \$17.5 billion—but smaller startups and biotech outfits often run out of research funds and look for strategic partners or to be acquired.[3] Tight cost control, particularly of sales and marketing, the largest expense item of drug companies (typically, 25–30 percent of sales), is of great importance. Despite the obvious focus of drug companies on the long term—the average development and approval period for novel drugs is 8–10 years—there is a need to satisfy shareholders with ongoing profits and often dividends. This simultaneous short- and long-term balancing act is a constant challenge in the pharmaceutics industry.

THE RESOURCES & CONSEQUENCES REPORT: RESOURCE INVESTMENTS

The only GAAP-based information currently provided by pharma companies on their vital R&D activities is the total R&D expense. This is of little use to investors. Compare Johnson & Johnson with Pfizer: The former's annual R&D expenses for 2013, 2012, and 2011 were \$8.2, \$7.7, and \$7.5 billion, respectively, whereas Pfizer's R&D expenses in those years were \$6.7, \$7.5, and \$8.7 billion. Totally different trajectories, with Johnson & Johnson increasing R&D and Pfizer continuously cutting this lifeline (23 percent over the three years). This was an obvious strategic change at Pfizer, bucking the general industry trend of increasing R&D, but what exactly was the new strategy? In mid-2013, Pfizer announced a reorganization, creating three business segments, but how is this change supported by cutting almost a quarter of R&D? Absent strategic articulation by management, speculations abound: On February 1, 2011, Reuters claimed, "Pfizer Inc. Chief Executive Ian Read is slashing the massive research budget at the world's largest drug maker to deliver on a 2012 profit forecast... "[4] One can only hope that there were better reasons for laying off more than 2,000 researchers at Pfizer, but a clear articulation of the R&D shift was hard to come by in the financial reports and accompanying material we read. Accordingly, the Resources & Consequences Report calls for a comprehensive and clear disclosure of the enterprise's resource investment strategy.

Two aspects of R&D operations are essential for investors to assess corporate innovation strategy and execution: How much of the total R&D

is in "R" (research—the original development of novel drugs or medical devices), and how much is "D" (development—the tweaking of current drugs and technologies)?[5] This distinction is of great importance because the risks and rewards of the "R" and the "D" are substantially different, with both generally higher for "R" than "D." Consider, for example, AstraZeneca's drug Prilosec, a blockbuster for controlling stomach acid. When the Prilosec patent expired in 2001, AstraZeneca faced a substantial hit to earnings. But rather than yielding the market to generic manufacturers, AstraZeneca created a closely related drug, Nexium, for which it received a new patent, and with the help of smart marketing, got a new lease on life in the acid reflux market.[6] Such "follow-on" patenting—an obvious "D"—is a low-risk strategy, relative to embarking on entirely new and untested therapeutic areas, which is the essence of "R." So, it's of considerable importance for investors' assessment of R&D strategy and execution to receive information on the nature of the company's R&D activities.[7]

The second R&D aspect of importance to investors is the allocation of total research funds to various therapeutic market segments, like primary care, oncology, vaccines, animal health, or medical devices. Acquisitions, such as the above example of KYTHERA acquiring hair loss prevention clinical compounds, offer investors a peek at the direction and focal points of the company's research efforts. Other than that, no information is generally disclosed about the intensity (financial commitment) of innovation directions. Important strategic questions, like how much of the company's research budget is targeted toward existing crowded markets, like cholesterol reducing drugs, and how much to new therapeutic areas are left unanswered by current disclosure.[8] This, then, leads us to the Resource Investment column (left-hand) of the Pharma Resources & Consequences Report (Figure 14.1).

INNOVATION

The Innovation box of the Resources & Consequences report (top left column) starts with internal R&D: $489 million in Q3–2013 for the biotech company Gilead Sciences versus $384 million in the same quarter a year earlier—27 percent growth, compared with a 15 percent sales growth. Evidently, there are attractive R&D opportunities at Gilead, but where exactly is the R&D-enhanced drive aimed?[9] In Gilead's extensive presentation accompanying the earnings call, one encounters the comment: "Higher R&D expenses in Q3–2013 over Q3–2012 driven primarily by: ongoing growth across all therapeutic areas and progression of clinical studies in oncology and HIV." Fine, but surely the company emphasized certain areas over others. Furthermore, is this significant rise in R&D temporary (to accommodate projects in advanced clinical tests, say), or long-term? We couldn't find answers to these pertinent questions.

Ideally, as the Innovation box shows, R&D expenditures should be disclosed by major therapeutic areas to indicate the thrusts of these

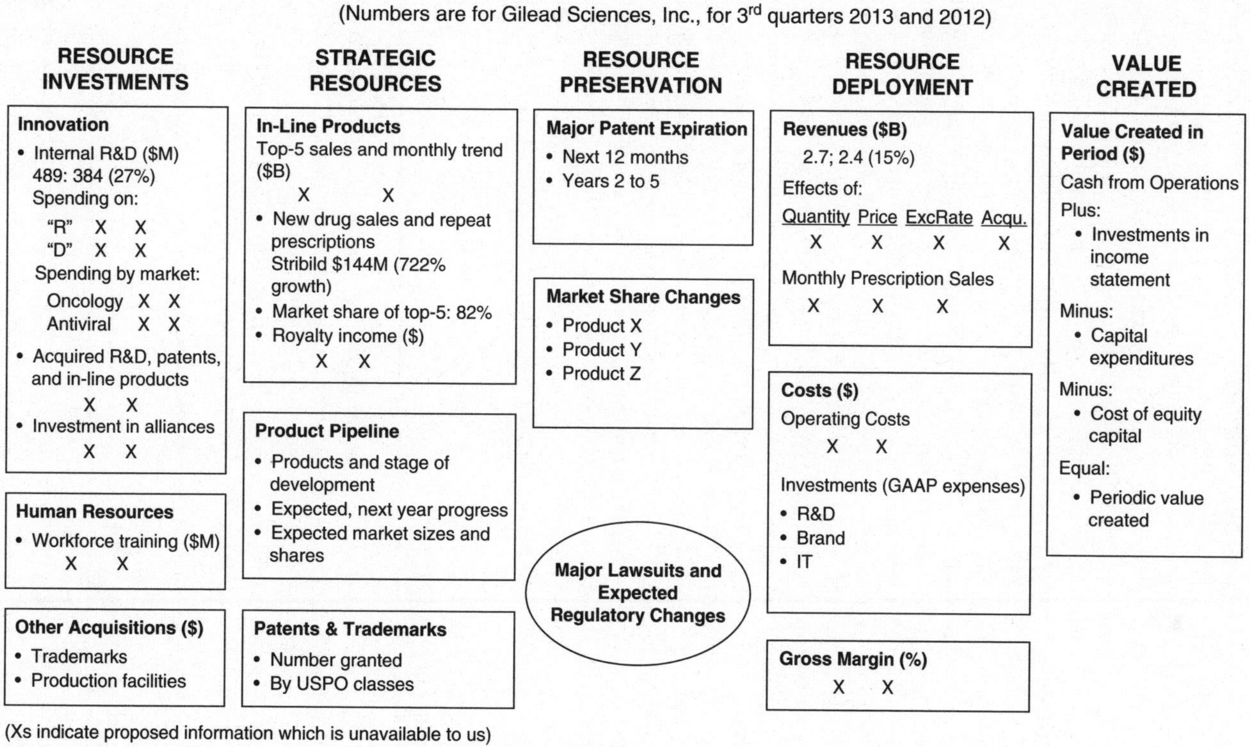

(Numbers are for Gilead Sciences, Inc., for 3rd quarters 2013 and 2012)

RESOURCE INVESTMENTS

Innovation
- Internal R&D ($M) 489: 384 (27%)
  Spending on:
  "R"   X   X
  "D"   X   X
  Spending by market:
  Oncology   X   X
  Antiviral   X   X
               X   X
- Acquired R&D, patents, and in-line products
- Investment in alliances

Human Resources
- Workforce training ($M)   X   X

Other Acquisitions ($)
- Trademarks
- Production facilities

STRATEGIC RESOURCES

In-Line Products
- Top-5 sales and monthly trend ($B)   X   X
- New drug sales and repeat prescriptions
  Stribild $144M (722% growth)
- Market share of top-5: 82%
- Royalty income ($)   X   X

Product Pipeline
- Products and stage of development
- Expected, next year progress
- Expected market sizes and shares

Patents & Trademarks
- Number granted
- By USPO classes

RESOURCE PRESERVATION

Major Patent Expiration
- Next 12 months
- Years 2 to 5

Market Share Changes
- Product X
- Product Y
- Product Z

Major Lawsuits and Expected Regulatory Changes

RESOURCE DEPLOYMENT

Revenues ($B)
2.7; 2.4 (15%)
Effects of:
Quantity Price ExcRate Acqu.
   X   X   X   X
Monthly Prescription Sales
   X   X   X

Costs ($)
Operating Costs   X   X
Investments (GAAP expenses)
- R&D
- Brand
- IT

Gross Margin (%)
   X   X

VALUE CREATED

Value Created in Period ($)
Cash from Operations
Plus:
- Investments in income statement
Minus:
- Capital expenditures
Minus:
- Cost of equity capital
Equal:
- Periodic value created

(Xs indicate proposed information which is unavailable to us)

FIGURE 14.1 Pharmaceutical and Biotech Companies: A Strategic Resources & Consequences Report

activities, and classified by "R" (research) and "D" (development), to highlight the R&D strategy and risks involved. Since many companies augment their internal R&D with acquired patents and research capabilities (in-process-R&D), information should also be provided on these acquisitions. Finally, to share the heavy costs and risks involved in developing new drugs, many companies form alliances and joint ventures, sometimes even with competitors (Merck and Pfizer jointly develop SGLT2—a type-2 diabetes drug). The alliances item closing the Innovation box informs on such investments, preferably, augmented by supplementary information on the directions and expected deliverables from such intercompany activities. Notably, the information in the Innovation box is particularly important for detecting and understanding strategic shifts, like the one mentioned earlier leading to a one-quarter cut in Pfizer's R&D during 2011–2013.

The remaining boxes in the Resource Investment (left) column inform on human resources and non-R&D acquisitions, like brands. Drug companies' sales force (those smiling and sharply dressed youngsters roaming doctors' offices with large carry-ons, while you wait there aching) is an important strategic resource. Typically, pharma companies spend on marketing and sales even more than on R&D, a fact that often riles critics. Sales-force training is an important investment (Gilead disclosed in the earnings call that it conducted a three-months sales training program for a new product—HCV, hepatitis treatment) and therefore should be tracked by investors: total costs as well as certain training details.[10] The bottom box informs on other strategic resource acquisitions, like M&As, or production facilities. This concludes the Report's disclosure on resource investments.

INVESTOR'S INSIGHT

Pay special attention to trends in the *composition* of research and development activities: away from, or into basic research (the "R" of R&D), as well as the new therapeutic areas penetrated by the company. This information is much more revealing about future growth than next quarter's earnings guidance which analysts commonly request.

STRATEGIC RESOURCES

The major strategic resources of drug and biotech companies are: in-line (on-the-market) products and their underlying patents, the product development (in-process) pipeline, trademarks and other intellectual property, and key human resources (star scientists of biotech companies).[11] Drug companies provide certain information on products and pipeline in supplements to financial reports and presentations accompanying earnings calls, but such non-GAAP disclosure is often haphazard and inconsistent from period to period, and across companies, and hence of limited value to investors. Thus, for example, in its Q3–2013 presentation, Gilead Sciences provided the following pertinent information on its HIV drugs' market share: of all US HIV infected persons, 82 percent are diagnosed, of which 73 percent are on antiretroviral treatment, and 82 percent of those are treated by Gilead products. Very informative and impressive, both from disclosure and market dominance points of view. In contrast, for Amgen Inc., a larger biotech company, we couldn't find consistent market share data in the earnings calls we examined. Gilead also provided detailed and comprehensive product pipeline information, whereas Amgen disclosed pipeline updates ("Phase 3 psoriasis studies are completely enrolled… "). On the other hand, Amgen disclosed expected (next year, 2014) pipeline developments, while Gilead did not. Obviously, it's very difficult for investors to conduct a thorough, comparative analysis from such patchwork and inconsistent information.

Here, as elsewhere, a major objective of the Strategic Resources column (second from left in the Resources & Consequences Report) is to provide relevant, consistent, and *uniform* information, enabling a thorough analysis and intercompany comparisons. Return to the Strategic Resources Column of the Report (page 167, second column from left).

In-Line Products Box

The key information on in-line products are sales trend for the top-sellers, market share, and patent expirations. Since a company's four or five top drugs often generate most of its sales, it's important to provide information on revenue patterns from these top sellers, preferably monthly, to alert investors to within-quarter trends in drug sales. Thus, for example, Amgen, with over $5 billion quarterly sales, provides a table with information on its top sellers: Neulasta, $1,444 million in Q2–2013 (7 percent increase from a year earlier); Enbrel, $1,157 million (9 percent of increase); Aranesp; $524 million (2 percent decrease); Epogen, $502 million (4 percent decrease), and so forth.[12] Sales and related data (repeat prescriptions) are particularly important for new drugs to track market penetration. For example, in its Q3–2013 earnings call, Pfizer noted that Xeljanz, a rheumatoid arthritis drug launched in 2013 is a "first-in-class product" (a drug with a novel mechanism of action aimed at a specific therapeutic target) and is already prescribed by 3,000 doctors, with 75 percent repeat prescription. Market share data are also important for investors to track brand value changes.[13]

These data are widely known within the industry, and hence their disclosure to investors doesn't pose a competitive threat. Finally, loss of exclusivity (patent expiration) information is crucial for investors to assess longevity of the leading products. Some of this information can be obtained from vendors or from the Patent Office, but this requires costly search that many investors cannot afford.

Still in the In-Line Products category (top box, second from left column) is information on royalties received from other companies on jointly developed products (Gilead receives royalties from Roche for the drug Tamiflu), and royalty income from the sale or licensing of patents and brands, including cross-licensing agreements.[14] To appreciate the power of the Resources & Consequences Report, just imagine the benefits to investors of receiving all of the above information in a succinct and uniform manner and on a regular basis, avoiding the need to extract bits and pieces of data from vendors or from managers in earnings calls. Once more, there are absolutely no competitive concerns in releasing the information specified in the Report—a common excuse for not informing investors. The multitude of company examples we give throughout this chapter attest to the fact that certain drug companies indeed provide such information and lo and behold, are still competitively viable. Remember: Your industry peers track all this, and more, information. Why not share some of it with your owners–investors?

Product Pipeline

This (middle box, second column from left) is the core of drug companies' strategic resources, and the most relevant information to investors, since the product pipeline, in contrast with the historical accounting information, is *forward looking*, informing about the most important future developments. Pharma's product pipeline is particularly revealing and comparable across companies, because the various drug development stages are well defined and uniform throughout the industry: starting with preliminary target identification, through preclinical (laboratory and animal) testing, to the critical Phases I, II, and III clinical tests on increasing samples of humans, and ending with the FDA review process, and—hopefully—drug approval and marketing. The wealth of past pipeline test data provides useful statistics for investors, like: roughly 70 percent of all investigational new drugs pass Phase I clinical tests, 30 percent pass Phase II, 27 percent Phase III, and 20 percent get FDA approval. Such sequential statistics facilitate investors' assessment of the value and potential of a company's product pipeline. Coupled with statistics on successful marketing likelihood—average probability of getting to market settles out at 10 percent of projects passing Phase I, 19 percent of Phase II, and 64 percent of projects passing Phase III—and market sizes, the product pipeline provides a clear and quantifiable picture of the value of the company's research efforts and their expected contribution to future sales and competitive edge.[15]

Thus, for example, the following Gilead (partial) product pipeline summary (Figure 14.2) disclosed in the October 27, 2015, earnings call materials, indicates a high potential value of the pipeline of Hematology/Oncology drugs: 10 projects under development; 5 in Phase III, 2 in Phase II, and 3 projects in Phase I clinical tests, as portrayed in the accompanying figure. A rich oncology pipeline, with most projects at a relatively advanced and hence low-risk, high-potential stage. In contrast, Gilead has relatively thinner pipelines of Inflammation/Respiratory and other products. Thus, the product pipeline and data on expected progress in the next 12 months (new products on the market),[16] along with estimates of target market share and market sizes for the various drugs or devices under development, allow investors to forecast future company revenues and growth. Such forecasts, based on detailed pipeline information, are much more reliable and long-term than conventional analysts' earnings forecasts, which are primarily based on historical accounting data, lacking the depth and richness of the product pipeline.

Pipeline potential is always coupled with risk: Development *risk diversification* is an important aspect of operations revealed by pipeline information. The development of drugs and medical devices is very risky; products under development are exposed to both feasibility (Is the drug effective?) and marketability (How will it fare against competitors?) risks. One way to diversify this risk, akin to investment portfolio diversification, is to develop drugs in several, unrelated therapeutic areas. Gilead's product pipeline reveals the existence of such diversification: various drug developments in the HIV/AIDS, liver diseases, oncology, respiratory, and cardiovascular areas. This is quite a diversification and consequent risk reduction.[17]

Proof of concept: Various studies established the relevance to investors of pipeline information by empirically validating share price reaction to pipeline news. For example, FDA drug approvals and rejections were found to have a significant effect on companies' shares, with losses from rejections outweighing gains from approvals. Investors were also shown to react to announcement of changes in the drug approval process, and a study on biotech IPOs found that IPO share prices are higher for companies with advanced product pipelines.[18] Obviously, product pipeline information is very relevant to investors' decisions.

Finally, the bottom box of the Strategic Resources column informs on the company's patents and trademarks—in particular, the number of new patents and trademarks granted during the period, as well as the technological classification of those patents. Patents are classified by the US

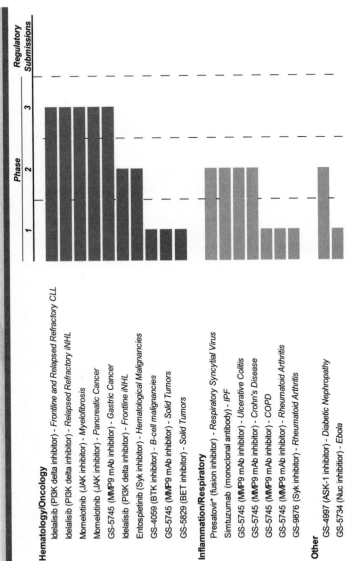

FIGURE 14.2 Pipeline Product Candidates

Source: Gilead Sciences, Inc.; third quarter 2015 earnings call material.

Patent Office (USPO) to a multitude of scientific and technological classes (e.g., in medicine: electrotherapy, magneto therapy, radiation therapy, ultrasound, etc.). A company's penetration into new patent classifications provides investors with perhaps the most reliable and long-term information about its strategic directions. Furthermore, the number and growth of new patents indicate the company's ability to translate ideas and concepts to early-stage products. Studies have documented a significant correlation between the number of patents granted a company as well as other patent attributes (forward citations, scope) and its future profitability.[19]

INVESTOR'S INSIGHT

Pay special attention to the overall state of product pipeline: how many in Phase I, II, and III clinical tests, and FDA submission. The maturity of the pipeline (most products in advanced stages) is an important risk and growth potential indicator. Peer companies can be evaluated on the basis of their relative product pipeline maturity. We haven't seen such in-depth growth potential assessment in the analysts' reports we examined.

RESOURCE PRESERVATION

Three threats (detailed in the middle column of the Report) loom large on pharma and biotech companies: competitors gaining market share, important drug expirations, and adverse regulatory actions.

Losing Market Share

In the Q3–2013 call, a Merck executive frankly stated: "We are losing a little bit of market share each month [diabetes drugs], but you would expect that with four competitors." Not to panic, the company still seems to have (as of 2013) a formidable 70 percent of the diabetes market share, but a creeping loss to competitors is disconcerting. Investors should be informed about significant market share changes and what the company is doing to counter losses (Merck said it pushes harder to expand foreign market sales of diabetes drugs, but supporting this statement with clear data and targets would have been even more helpful).

Patent Expirations

The second major risk factor is *patent expirations*: In the case of leading drugs, patent expiration poses a serious problem.[20] We mentioned Pfizer's hit to sales and earnings from the expiration of Lipitor's patent. Investors should accordingly be informed about prospective expirations of the top sellers, and what are the company's plans to soften the blow. A successful example, already mentioned, is AstraZeneca's extension of the expired blockbuster Prilosec by the slightly modified Nexium. Some companies strike a "cease and desist" agreement with generic-drug manufacturers, while others resort to lawsuits to protect their intellectual property, like Amgen, winning in January 2011 a lawsuit barring the leading generic-drug manufacturer Teva from selling a generic version of Amgen's kidney drug Sensipar before its patent expiration in 2018.[21] Strategies to protect the company's resources, and in particular its intellectual property, are complex and sophisticated, and to the extent it doesn't compromise company secrets, they should be articulated to investors, along with specific results: winning/losing lawsuits, striking agreements with competitors, and so on.

Regulatory Changes

As for the third risk factor, *regulatory changes*, a comprehensive, non–boiler-plate articulation of pending regulatory and legal actions threatening the company's products, prices, or market share, such as FDA drug decisions, Medicare/Medicaid rulings, or state consumer protection actions is very relevant to investors.[22]

RESOURCE DEPLOYMENT-OPERATIONS

GAAP total sales—the income statement top line—is here, and elsewhere, of limited relevance to investors without a breakdown to the four main sales drivers: volume, price, exchange rate effects, and impact of M&A (detailed in the second-from-right column of the Report). Surprisingly, GAAP doesn't require even this rudimentary disclosure to investors. Start with exchange rates: The share of international sales is large for most pharma and many biotech companies, resulting in a generally high sales exposure to exchange rate fluctuations. For example, Merck's Q3–2013 sales decreased 4 percent from the same quarter a year earlier, and fully half of this decrease, said management, was due to exchange rate fluctuations. Obviously, managers have no control over this risk factor, but because its impact is often temporary, identifying its effect on the overall sales change is important for investors to assess managers' performance and future sales growth. Separating the volume from price effects is also important: Volume changes primarily reflect the effectiveness of the company's marketing and sales force activities, whereas the price impact on sales is determined by pricing decisions, and increasingly by regulatory constraints (Medicare/Medicaid price rulings). Finally, identifying the M&A effect on total sales is of considerable importance, since acquisitions automatically increase sales in the short-term. Organic sales growth, net of acquisitions, is the meaningful measure of sales growth. Regrettably, very few of the companies we examined disclosed even partially the volume/price/exchange rate/M&A sales breakdown. We wonder why. What competitive threats are raised by such disclosure?

We now turn from revenues to costs: In its Q3–2013 earnings call, Merck disclosed that it had decreased the number of production plants from 95 to 58, and expects to reduce 2014 costs by $2 billion to $5 billion (quite a range). Cost containment is at the core of pharma companies' strategy, but the cost information generally disclosed is patchy at best. Recall that, in contrast with accounting rules, we don't consider *investments* in strategic resources—like R&D, brand enhancement, or employee training—as regular expenses. It would, therefore, be helpful if—in addition to R&D expenses, which have to be separately disclosed—the company would provide information about material investments in strategic resources, such as brands, IT, and employee training, included in the income statement. This would enable investors to better focus on the company's innovation investments separately from its real expenses (net of investments). Finally, for startups and small biotech companies with no meaningful revenues, the (non-GAAP) *cash burn rate*—monthly or quarterly net cash outflows relative to liquid assets and guaranteed cash reserves—is an important indicator of sustainability and solvency. Investors should be informed how long can the company operate within its financial means. As in the previous cases, the Resource Deployment (operations) analysis culminates with the gross margin.

VALUE CREATED

To conclude our pharma Resources & Consequences Report, we need to compute the periodic value created, similarly to the preceding case studies: cash from operating activities, plus investments (R&D, brands, human resources, IT systems, etc.) expensed in the income statement, minus capital expenditures, and minus full financing costs, including the cost of equity capital. Since none of the 10 companies we examined in detail provided a breakdown of accounting expenses to costs and investments, we cannot provide numerical examples of pharma value-created computation.[23] Related to revenues, a few drug companies provide an important, non-GAAP measure we call "innovation revenues," namely, the percentage of total revenues generated by products introduced in the past three to five years.[24] This important measure, shown by researchers to predict future company and stock performance, indicates the enterprise's ability to both innovate and expeditiously bring products to the market. This revealing performance indicator should be reported more frequently.

INVESTOR'S INSIGHT

Note that the pharma Resources & Consequences Report enables an important attribution of research benefits to costs by relating the periodic progress of the product pipeline (how many projects advanced from Phase I to Phase II, from Phase II to Phase III, etc.) to R&D expenses. Growth in R&D (both internal and acquired) with no (or slow) progress of the product pipeline, suggests ineffective R&D spending. The same holds for growth of R&D and only few new patents granted the company. In contrast, accounting-based data do not allow an assessment of the effectiveness of the companies' innovation efforts. Here, as elsewhere, a major benefit of the Resources & Consequences Report comes from relating the various dimension of the Report to each other—a holistic analysis.

NOTES

1. The pharmaceutical industry leads all other industries in lobby spending: a staggering $228 million in 2014, and over $3 billion during 1998–2014 (www .opensecrets.org/lobby). Not all of these funds are spent on image-building, of course. Much goes to secure favorable legislation and regulation.
2. Notably, the CEO didn't even mention any financial (accounting) results in his call's opening statement.
3. In the 1980s, several pharma companies attempted to raise R&D funds by securitizing their research—namely, to sell shares backed by their R&D and patent portfolios. This novel way of financing research didn't pan out, however, apparently due to investor concerns that promising patents will be kept by the company, while the less-promising ones will be securitized.
4. Ransdell Pierson, "New Pfizer CEO Slashes R&D to Save 2012 Forecast," Reuters, February 1, 2011.
5. A different and more general question is, what's in R&D? There is no satisfactory accounting definition of R&D, and some companies take the liberty of including

in reported R&D all sorts of "related" expenses, like maintenance and quality control, to portray themselves as major innovators.

6. See "Zombie Patents," *The Economist* (June 21, 2014), p. 72.

7. Readers who wonder whether companies can distinguish between the "R" and "D" should note that the annual R&D and Innovation Survey, conducted by the U.S. Department of Commerce and the U.S. Census Bureau, which is answered by practically all companies conducting significant R&D, includes the following questions:

   ▪ What percentage of your R&D was directed toward product lines that are new to your company?

   ▪ What percentage of your R&D involved science/technology that was new to your company?

   ▪ What percentage of your R&D was for R&D in science/technology new to the market in which your company operates?

     And, in particular:

   ▪ How much of your R&D was for *research* (the planned systematic pursuit of new knowledge or understanding) and *development* (the use of research to produce new goods, services, or processes)? Research should be broken down to applied and basic research. Percentage of scientists and engineers of all R&D personnel. So, R&D companies routinely provide these data to the government; why not disclose some of it to their owners?

8. Many drug and biotech companies voluntarily provide detailed information on their product pipeline, informing investors on the various therapeutic areas the company targets. But this information often doesn't include the *financial commitments* in each area, so it's impossible to assess the major thrusts of the company's research.

9. Interestingly, Gilead Sciences was ranked first in *Barron's* 2015 America's Top 500 Companies in terms of performance and growth (May 4, 2015). Nevertheless, *Barron's* mentions that the company faces a shareholder proposal asking Gilead's board "to increase transparency around the management and mitigation of the business risks associated with the company's pricing strategies in the face of rapidly increasing... efforts by payors, prescribers, and regulators to contain these costs." This supports our call to include in the proposed Report relevant information about threats to the franchise (Resource Preservation section).

10. Corporate financial reports are notorious for commonly declaring early on that "our employees are our most important asset," proceeding to ignore altogether their personnel investment and record (turnover, etc.).

11. For the significant contribution of star scientists to the growth of biotech companies, see Lynne Zucker and Michael Darby, "Star Scientists and Institutional Transformation: Pattern of Invention and Innovation in the Formation of the Biotechnology Industry," *Proceedings of the National Academy of Sciences*, 93 (November 1996): 12709–12716.

12. We didn't see similar comprehensive product information released by the major drug companies we examined. There can be no competitive reasons for this lack of disclosure, because weekly prescription sales of most drugs are available from

commercial vendors, though for a stiff price. So, each company's competitors have access to one another's detailed within-quarter sales data.

13. Allergan, in its Q4–2013 call, provided the following market share data: The market for ophthalmics is approximately $20.2 billion, growing at a rate of 12 percent; Allergan market share is 16 percent. The market for glaucoma approximates $5.3 billion, growing at 3 percent; Allergans' market share approximates 27 percent. This is an excellent market share disclosure, rare among drug companies.

14. Interestingly, Johnson & Johnson in its Q3–2013 call told investors that royalty income is included in "Other Income and Expense" item, leaving out the actual amount of royalty income. Go figure.

15. Certain information on companies' clinical trials can be obtained from the website ClinicalTrials.gov, but the comprehensiveness of this source is questionable.

16. For example, Amgen, in the Q2–2013 call, disclosed that Phase 3 test of AMG 145 (cholesterol reducing) is expected in Q1–2014.

17. Given the company's R&D expenditures in each therapeutic area (often not disclosed), a Herfindahl-type measure (sum of squares of relative shares) will quantify the extent of pipeline diversification for cross-company comparisions.

18. The studies cited in this paragraph are: Anurag Sharma and Nelson Lacey, "Linking Product Development Outcomes to Market Valuation of the Firm," *The Journal of Product Innovation Management*, 21 (2004): 297–308. Salil Sarkar and Pieter de Jong, "Market Response to FDA Announcements," *The Quarterly Review of Economics and Finance*, 46 (2006): 586–597. Rejin Guo, Baruch Lev, and Nan Zhou, "Competitive Costs of Disclosure by Biotech IPOs," *Journal of Accounting Research* 42 (2004): 319–355.

19. For example, Ya-wen Yang, "The Value-Relevance of Nonfinancial Information: The Biotechnology Industry," *Advances in Accounting*, 23 (2007): 287–314.

20. "Between 2010 and 2014, about $78 billion was lost in worldwide annual sales of branded drugs whose patents had expired," *The Economist* (November 7, 2015), p. 59.

21. Similarly, in its Q4–2013 call, Allergan disclosed that " . . . regarding LUMI-GAN 0.01 percent, the District Court in Texas ruled that Allergan's five patents are valid until their expirees, the last of which is in 2017."

22. On the latter, see an article on the proliferation of state consumer protection actions in the August 8, 2011, issue of *Rx Compliance Report*.

23. Interestingly, many pharma companies routinely provide proforma (non-GAAP) earnings, eliminating various expense items from earnings, such as intangibles' amortization, and one-time items. For example, Merck eliminated from its Q3–2013 GAAP earnings the following expenses: acquisition-related and restructuring costs, amortization and impairment of intangibles, M&A integration costs, employee separation costs, and costs related to actions under a global initiative. We prefer the clear separation between *expenses* (no future benefits) and *investments* (promising future benefits) over an ad hoc elimination of expenses.

24. For example, GlaxoSmithKline (GSK) noted in its 2014 annual report that £1.5 billion (of total sales of £23 billion) came from new products sales.

CHAPTER 15

Strategic Resources & Consequences Report: Case No. 4—Oil and Gas Companies

The oil and gas industry supplies the major source of energy to individuals and businesses–the lifeblood of all economies. The highly volatile and unpredictable environment within which oil and gas companies operate–wide price fluctuations and geopolitical upheavals–complicate the management of these companies, large and small, as well as investors' valuation of oil and gas enterprises. Oil and gas resources are exposed to a higher level of threats and risk than the resources of most other companies. The operations of oil and gas companies consist mainly of exploration, production and sale of oil and gas products, and–for the integrated enterprises–also oil refining and various other chemical activities. These operations are capital- and labor-intensive, so that cost containment and operating efficiencies are of the essence. The Resources & Consequences Report for the sector focuses on strategic assets and the efficiency of their deployment.

The oil and gas industry doesn't need a lengthy introduction; it is constantly in the news and often shapes national and international policies. The industry supplies the major source of energy to individuals and businesses—the lifeblood of all economies. But the general familiarity with the oil and gas industry is deceiving. The industry is exceedingly complex, and only few are familiar with the inner workings of oil and gas companies. While Exxon is a household name in the United States, Royal Dutch Shell and British Petroleum in Europe, and China National Petroleum in—where else?—China, these companies' vast properties, operations, rich mineral reserves, intricate governmental relationships, and political and technological risk exposures fly under the radar of most people, even investors in these companies. The big oil corporations—known as integrated companies—are among the largest enterprises in the world: Sinopec of China (at no. 2), Royal Dutch Shell (at no. 3), China National Petroleum (no. 4), Exxon Mobil (no. 5), BP (no. 6), Total (no. 11), Chevron (no. 12), and Phillips 66 (no. 23), populate the top 25 largest enterprises in the 2014 *Fortune Global 500 Companies*. These companies engage in exploration and production of oil and gas—known as *upstream operations*—as well as refining and marketing of oil products (*downstream operations*), and some have chemicals, R&D, and other related operations.[1] Managing such a varied, worldwide portfolio of activities for the long term—securing competitive advantage and sufficient oil and gas reserves for years to come—as well as for the short term, generating adequate quarterly and annual sales and earnings, is among the toughest managerial challenges of all industries, particularly in the current (2016) price-depressed environment. Even the medium and small oil and gas companies, focusing on either the upstream or downstream and having more localized operations, are fairly complex organizations. The highly volatile and unpredictable environment within which oil and gas companies operate—wide price fluctuations and geopolitical upheavals—further complicate the management of these companies, large and small, as well as investors' valuation of oil and gas enterprises.

ACCOUNTING LIMITATIONS

The unusual oil and gas business challenges and complexities tax the limits of the accounting and financial reporting system. The balance sheets and income statements of oil and gas companies fall short of articulating the underlying and crucial constant strategic repositioning of these enterprises—*dynamic portfolio management*—where resources are frequently bought and sold to enhance the quality and productivity of the asset portfolios. Moreover, a company can report increasing sales and earnings, even beating the consensus earnings estimates—pleasing shareholders—while depleting its long-term resources. Exxon disclosed on February 21, 2016, that for the first time since 1994 it failed to find enough oil and gas to replace its production in the previous year. Important arrangements with subcontractors, such as Schlumberger's (a leading oil services company) SPM arrangement, where the servicer shares with the exploration company—takes an equity position—the risks and returns of exploration, aren't captured by the accounting system. Similarly, long-term efforts at cost containment, crucial for maintaining competitive advantage, are reflected in financial reports after a considerable delay, and important business relationships, such as joint ventures with other companies and contracts with governments—major value-creating assets in the industry—aren't flagged on the balance sheet. The accounting system is simply unable to capture the intricacies of the oil business.[2] True, specific oil and gas regulations by the FASB and the SEC, requiring disclosure (though not the audit) of proved (proven) reserves and their discounted cash flows, as well as data on productive wells, among other information items, are definitely helpful but insufficient for a comprehensive strategic assessment by investors of the operations of oil and gas companies and their growth potential.

This became clear from our detailed examination of the earnings conference calls and investor day presentations of the 10 oil and gas companies, large and small, that we have studied. Most of analysts' and investors' questions revolved around the companies' strategic moves (buying and selling properties), the consequent growth potential of the resources portfolio, seismic results and exploration plans, the impact on the companies' performance of oil and gas price fluctuations and governmental actions, as well as nonfinancial data on rig and well counts.[3] Very few questions were aimed at information items disclosed in financial reports. As in our preceding case studies, analysts clearly focused on the companies' strategic resources and their deployment. Accordingly, the proposed oil and gas Strategic Resources & Consequences Report (displayed at the end of chapter) aims to get a clear handle of the company's strategy and its execution, piercing the thick veil of complexity of oil and gas operations and enabling investors to assess the performance of companies and their ability to maintain long-term competitive edge. Let's start with the main driver of oil and gas operations: investment in strategic resources.

RESOURCE INVESTMENTS

The most important activity of oil and gas companies, and the most difficult for investors to comprehend, is the continuous repositioning of the resources portfolio. Oil and gas companies constantly purchase and sell properties, often termed *dynamic portfolio management,* which, in the words of Royal Dutch Shell CEO (Q3–2012 earnings call), is " ... aiming overall to optimize both capital efficiency and growth potential." From an investor's point of view, successful, long-term investment in the shares of oil and gas companies is obviously predicated on a comprehensive understanding of the enterprise portfolio strategy and the success of its execution by management. Is management adding to (and at what price?) or depleting company resources? Is the quality (mineral grade) of the resources portfolio enhanced by the disposal of seemingly inferior properties, or were they sold to generate short-term cash and profits? Are new investments increasing or decreasing risk exposure? With but few exceptions, the financial statement disclosure of the portfolio strategy and even managers' responses to analysts questions in earnings calls are patchy and inconsistent over time, often precluding a comprehensive grasp of companies' portfolio strategies. One wonders whether this is a case of "constructive confusion" on the part of managers.

Devon Energy Corp., a mid-sized oil and gas company, is an exception to the general opaqueness of investment strategy.[4] In its Q4–2013 earnings call, John Richels, CEO, stated: "Looking beyond our reported results, we also made some exciting portfolio changes at Devon during 2013." And what were those changes? A strategic combination of Devon's US midstream assets with Crosstex Energy (operating pipeline, processing plants and storage facilities) to form EnLink Midstream, aimed to improve diversification, capital efficiency, and growth trajectory of midstream holdings.[5] As stated by Devon's CEO, this combination increased enterprise value by $3.5 billion, or $8 per share. In addition, the company acquired the Eagle Ford assets, a light-oil acreage position in North America, at a price, according to the CEO, " ... well below our current EBITDA multiple." To balance these acquisitions, Devon sold its entire natural gas Canadian Conventional business (referred to as noncore) for $2.8 billion. According to the CEO, this sale was also made at an attractive price of seven times 2013 EBITDA. Note the clarification of the strategic moves of Devon, away from the price-declining natural gas and into light-oil, while strengthening the company's midstream operations, allowing investors to clearly assess the repositioning of the portfolio to face the 2013–2014 and beyond oil and gas environment, as well as to assess the share value impact of the transactions. Articulating Devon's strategy further, the CEO stated:

> So the new Devon has greater focus of our retained asset base with five core development plays, three of which reside in some of the most attractive oil-prone basins in North America .... Each of these core oil assets represents a low risk and high margin production growth opportunity.... The retained liquid-rich gas component of the new Devon is anchored by our Barnett and Anadarko Basin assets. These core areas currently generate large amounts of free cash flow and provide significant gas optionality.... Devon emerges with a formidable and balanced portfolio positioned to deliver multi-year same store sales oil growth of around 20% per year.

This is unreservedly optimistic, but the explicit and verifiable forecast of 20 percent annual production growth adds certain credibility to the CEO's strategic statement.[6]

It is, of course, easier for a mid-sized company like Devon to so succinctly articulate its portfolio strategy and execution than for the large, integrated oil and gas enterprises. But this is a difference of degree, not of fundamentals. Articulating the overall portfolio strategy of large companies will obviously require a higher degree of aggregation—by geographical areas, say, rather than Devon's location-specific disclosure—but a comprehensive clarification of the portfolio strategy is essential for investors, as made clear by questions of insistent analysts on the subject in the examined earnings calls, such as: "Firstly, on your portfolio strategy, going back to North America. You have talked about trying to match acquisitions and disposals by geographic or asset type. You have spent $2 billion buying acreage in Permian. You have added many positions in the last 12 months. But I haven't seen specific announcements on asset disposals in North America" (Royal Dutch Shell, Q3–2012 earnings call).[7] Thus, big or small, oil and gas companies need to clearly articulate their portfolio strategy, as outlined in the left column—Resource Investments—of the Resources & Consequences Report (chapter end), and shown in Figure 15.1.[8,9]

The top box, Portfolio Strategy, informs about the dynamic portfolio management: investments (acquisitions, explorations, and development), classified by product type (oil, gas) and geographic areas, as well as resource disposals. At the bottom of the box, information is provided on exploration activities, in terms of the numbers of production wells and rigs, started and completed, preferably classified by geographic areas.[10] Hess Corp., for example, in its Q1–2013 call announced plans for 175 new wells, which triggered an analyst question: "175 wells seems fairly modest given the opportunity set." And Royal Dutch Shell (Q3–2012 call) disclosed that in North America the on-shore rig count is "about flat" at 36–37 rigs, but dry gas rigs were reduced from 31 to 15 (presumably in response to gas price decreases).

The last item in the portfolio strategy box (top) is Retained Proved Reserves.[11] These data inform investors of the consequences of the portfolio repositioning in terms of one of the most important capacity indicators—proved reserves. Did the portfolio repositioning by the end of the day increase or decrease the overall company resources? Devon's data in the box indicate a slight decrease. A breakdown of proved reserves to, for example, oil, gas, and unconventional, is revealing. An important metric related to proved reserves is "Finding and Development," indicating the cost of converting undrilled locations to proven developed reserves. At Devon, in 2013, these costs came to $18 per Boe (barrels of oil equivalent), but since some of Devon's competitors don't disclose this indicator, it is not particularly meaningful.

The lower boxes in the Resource Investments column inform on other important investments: mergers and acquisitions, joint ventures, and key agreements with businesses and governments. In each case, a quantitative indication should be given about the investment incurred (cost), as well as the benefits, in terms of acreage, proved reserves, or cost savings. This completes the first dimension (column) of the Resources & Consequences Report.

Portfolio Strategy ($M)

Investments:	2014	2013		Oil	Gas	Unconventional
• Acquisitions	$6,387;	238	(2,584%)	X	X	X
• Explorations	$ 322;	595	(−46%)	X	X	X
• Development	$5,463;	5,089	(7.3%)	X	X	X

By major geographic areas (2014):	United States	Canada
Acquisitions	$6,386	$ 1
Explorations	$ 270	$ 52
Development	$4,400	$1,063

Disposals:	2014	2013			
Divestitures	$5,120;	419	(1,122%)	X	X

Exploration:

Productive wells completed during the year:

2014	2013	
670;	831	(−19.4%)

Retained proved reserves (million Boe):

2014	2013	
2,754;	2,963	(−7%)

Mergers and Acquisitions
  Location, acreage, proved reserves

Joint Ventures and Alliances
  Purpose, partners, investment, acreage

New Important Agreements

FIGURE 15.1   Resource Investments
Data in the column, for demonstration purposes, are for Devon Energy for the years 2014 and 2013.

INVESTOR'S INSIGHT

Get a solid grip of the company's resource portfolio strategy, the major determinant of future growth and competitive edge. Managers will always sweet-talk you to believe that they are doing the right thing. But, do they? Do the geographical shifts (from South to North America, say) make sense? Are they consistent over time or erratic? In line with competitors or not? Are the resource disposals (sales) strategic, or aimed at boosting short-term earnings (capital gains from sales) and cash flows, or—worse yet—funding share buybacks? Do the shifts from gas to oil, or vice versa, make sense (and what about unconventional resources)? At the end of the day, did the portfolio shifts enhance total proved reserves? And what was the impact of the shifts on the company's geopolitical risk exposure (more or less exposure in Russia, say)? Only with answers in hand can you then decide whether you are comfortable holding equity in an enterprise with such a geographical resource portfolio mix and risk exposure. Furthermore, does this enterprise diversify other oil and gas investments you have, or just mimic them? Does the enterprise promise a growth boost to your overall investment portfolio? Note how different and more consequential are these long-term considerations than a mere comparison of quarterly earnings with analysts' consensus.

STRATEGIC RESOURCES

The major strategic assets of oil and gas companies are, of course, their mineral properties (owned or leased) in which they conduct their exploration and production (E&P) activities. These properties are characterized by multiple important attributes: their location (North America, Indonesia), size (generally in terms of acreage), total investment in the area owned, intended product (crude oil, natural gas, unconventional),[12] number of rigs and wells on the property, and, importantly, proved reserves, namely, the value of the resource, both in quantitative (barrels of oil) and monetary—expected cash flow—terms. These resource attributes are presented in the Strategic Resources box in Figure 15.2.

Certain investor-relevant information about mineral resources is currently provided in the financial reports of oil and gas companies, but it is generally scattered over scores of pages and the extent of disclosure is often not uniform across companies. An important benefit of our proposed oil and gas Resources & Consequences Report is that it organizes the information investors need in a manner that is both compact and comparable across companies, ready for use by investors. Consider the following Strategic Resources box (Figure 15.2 with examples, and in the second-from-left column in the overall Report at chapter end), presenting succinctly the major attributes of the company's mineral resources (the values in the box, for illustration, pertain to Devon Energy, for the years 2014 and 2013). The top line—mineral acreage—presents the total area (in thousands of acres) controlled by the company through owning or leasing, and classified by developed (2,317) versus undeveloped (3,926) thousands of acres. Thus,

Minerals

I.   **Mineral Acreage (000)**

	2014	2013	%
Developed	2,317	4,328	−46.5
Undeveloped	3,926	8,411	−53.3
Total	6,243	12,739	−51.0

By major geographical areas:

U.S.	4,666	5,805
Canada	1,577	6,934

Energy type:

Oil   gas   unconventional

II.   **Proved Reserves (million Boe)**

2,754;   2,963   (−7%)

Discounted Cash Flows (billions)

$20.5; $15.7   (31%)

III. **Total Productive Wells and Rigs (2014)**

	Wells	Rigs
Oil	7,165	X
Gas	11,124	X

By geographical areas:

X   X   (X)

Refining Capacity and Usage

Patents and Trademarks

Key Governmental Agreements and Inter-Company Alliances

FIGURE 15.2   Strategic Resources

Devon's footprint (acreage) at the end of 2014 decreased significantly (51 percent) from a year earlier, likely as part of the reorganization. But Totals—like total acreage owned—generally obscure important information, such as the geographical distribution of the footprint and the type of energy (oil or gas), which is stated in Figure 15.2 underneath the total acres owned (most of Devon's acreage decrease was in Canada).

Footprint size obviously doesn't fully inform about the value-creation potential of the mineral properties. For this we move to the second item of the box—proved reserves: the quantities of energy (oil, gas, NGL) estimated to be producible, with reasonable certainty, from the reservoir. Two indicators of the proved reserves—volumetric and monetary measures—are provided: the former, in millions of Boe (barrel of equivalent oil), a unit of energy combining oil and gas reserves into a single measure, and the latter—discounted cash flows—reflecting the present value of the net, of costs, proceeds expected to accrue from producing and selling the proved reserves.[13] Changes in proved reserves are mainly caused by acquisitions and exploration, increasing reserves, and by production (oil extraction) and property sales, decreasing reserves. Devon's data shows a 7 percent decrease in proved reserves in 2014—a much milder decrease than that of acreage—perhaps, an indication of a somewhat reduced growth potential.

A useful indicator, particularly for cross-company comparisons, is the *reserve life index*, calculated as the ratio of proved reserves to annual production. In Devon's case, our calculation shows that with proved (2014) reserves of 2,754 million Boe and reported 2014 production of 673,000 Boe per day, or 242.3 million Boe per year, the reserve life index is: 2,754 million Boe divided by 242.3 million Boe to give 11.37 years. Thus, Devon's end-of-2014 proved reserves would last 11.37 years, under current production level and no new acquisitions. Changes in the discounted cash flows from the proved reserves are an important forward-looking indicator of company value and growth potential, unique to extractive industries. These changes are affected by varying estimates of future energy prices, in addition to acquisitions, production, and disposals. Interestingly, despite the decrease in the quantity of proved reserves during 2014, Devon reported a 31 percent increase in discounted cash flows. Obviously, this indicator is very sensitive to changes in underlying assumptions. Yet another important indicator of the potential value-creation of the company's properties is the extent of its productive (energy extraction) activities, measured by the number of wells and rigs operating on the properties, and classified by oil and gas, as well as by geographic areas.

Summarizing, the three indicators reported in the Strategic Resources top box—acreage, proved reserves, and productive activity—classified by major geographic areas and types of energy, as well as the forward-looking discounted cash flows metric, provide a succinct and comprehensive picture of the company's major strategic asset, namely its mineral resources. Very important information for investors. The three bottom boxes of the Strategic Resources column (second-from-left in the Report) inform on nonmineral resources: refining capacity, important patents and trademarks, as well as key agreements and alliances, and commodity trading. Here, as elsewhere, the Resources information gains relevance to investors when compared with previous years and against peer companies.

Proof of concept: Various empirical studies have established a significant correlation between oil and gas reserve data and stock prices, confirming our claim that these data are relevant to investors. For example, Boyer and Filion (2007) report that growth in proved reserves, among other indicators, is correlated with stock price rise; and Magliolo (1986) documented that a significant portion of share price is attributed to expected cash flows from proved reserves.[14] Oil and gas reserve information in our report is obviously of considerable relevance to investors due to its predictive power.

INVESTOR'S INSIGHT

Intercompany alliances and joint ventures are an important source of revenues for oil and gas companies. This corporate connectivity often falls below investors' radar: In our examination of earnings calls transcripts, we rarely encountered analysts' questions on alliances. Investors may be missing on an important corporate activity, potentially creating a competitive edge. Most important is an assessment of the return (ROI) on joint ventures, relating investment to expected cash flows or cost savings. As an aside, ROI on connectivity isn't only absent from investors' dashboard, most managers aren't privy to this information, either. Since alliances are relatively easy to form, yet costly to maintain, it would be instructive to know, periodically, the percentage of alliances that are operative at the end of the period, and those terminated, along with their costs and benefits.

RESOURCES THREATS

Oil and gas resources are exposed to a higher level of threats and risk than the resources of most other companies, hence the importance of this third column (from left) of the Report. At the extreme, oil and gas assets in certain geographical areas can vanish overnight, as in the 2012 Argentine nationalization of its leading oil and gas company YPF, majority owned by Spain's Repsol. Even short of an outright nationalization or expropriation, oil and gas operations in certain countries are subject to constant rift and dislocations—evidence BP's travails in Russia over the past twenty years. Safety issues are a constant concern, too. Damages from oil spills and refinery accidents can be catastrophic, like the 2010 BP oil spill in the Gulf of Mexico, for which the company provided in its accounts $43 billion for expected restitutions, as of the end of 2014 (Bloomberg, October 28, 2014). Regulatory changes around the world are also a constant threat to oil and gas companies. Thus, for example, in Ohio, in May 2013, the Youngstown city council considered a proposal to ban fracking in the city, but, fortunately for frackers, turned it down. Similarly, the Niles city council passed a fracking ban in August 2013, yet rescinded it the following month (Wikipedia, Hydraulic Fracturing in the United States). And don't forget the constant harassment of oil, gas, and particularly coal companies by environmentalists. No love lost for energy companies. Long-range planning and the substantial fund commitments required in the oil and gas industry are a particular challenge in such a volatile, political, and regulatory environment.

Given the heightened threat level to which oil and gas resources are exposed, a clear, specific statement to investors—not the standard risk boilerplate in companies' financial reports, written by lawyers[15]—detailing ongoing and expected threats, along with estimates of losses, should be disclosed in the Resources & Consequences Report, focusing on the following types of risks: company properties currently subject to ownership challenge, adverse regulatory actions by local authorities, and major contracts currently considered for terms revisions or expected to be challenged in the near future, to the extent, of course, that such disclosure doesn't enhance legal exposure. In short, rather than a meaningless list of all possible risk factors, a specific, concise report of current and expected challenges to the company's resources, accompanied by potential consequences.[16] Finally, an integral part of this report dimension should be a clear description of the measures taken by the company to avoid or mitigate the threats.

Perhaps the most common and ongoing risk to oil and gas operations comes from the large volatility of prices; few other input or output prices are subject to similar gyrations. Just during the 2000s, crude oil prices went from less than $30 a barrel in 2000, to about $140 prior to the 2007–2008 financial crisis, down to about $40 during the crisis, up again to about $120 a barrel in 2011, and down to around $60 in mid-2015, and $28 in early 2016. Such price gyrations strongly affect companies' strategy and financial results—Apache (February 25, 2015, presentation) reported that the recent

38 percent oil price decrease caused a 17 percent decline of cash flows—and puts heavy pressure on exploration and production decisions (shutting off operations when prices drop below breakeven?). It is important, therefore, to provide investors with quantitative risk indicators, akin to VAR (value at risk) financial measures, to indicate the sensitivity of cash flows and sales to expected changes in the prices of oil and gas. You surely don't have to warn investors that oil and gas price volatility affects operations; they know it. But how about quantifying for them the *sensitivity* of operations to prospective price changes, allowing investors to assess the riskiness of operations and the company's future growth? Adopting some of the sensitivity measures prevalent in the banking industry (sensitivity to interest rate changes) would be a step in the right direction. In short, threats to strategic resources are present in any industry, but rarely are they so serious as in oil and gas, and particularly so for the less diversified and integrated medium and small companies.

RESOURCE DEPLOYMENT—OPERATIONS

The operations of oil and gas companies consist mainly of exploration, production and sale of oil and gas products, and—for the integrated enterprises—also oil refining and various other (chemicals) activities. These operations are capital- and labor-intensive, so that cost containment and operating efficiencies are of the essence. In the earnings calls we studied, there were no analysts' questions about cost containment and efficiency drives. Strange. Investors should inquire about unique efficiency mechanisms and drives, as well as unique business processes (employee training, subcontracting) that distinguish the company's operations from its competitors. Operating efficiencies aren't "sexy," but they are vital to companies' success, particularly in hard times.

The Resource Deployment (Operations) column of the Resources & Consequences Report (second from right at chapter's end, and reproduced below), starts with the "top line": production and sales. Occidental Petroleum, for example, disclosed that in 2013 its oil production averaged to 266,000 barrels per day, a 4.3 percent increase from 2012 (*total* production was 763,000 Boe per day), and its total 2013 sales amounted to $20.17 billion, at a level comparable with that of the prior year. Some companies, like Exxon, even guide investors on production. Of considerable importance for understanding the reasons for a reported sales change and assessing its impact going forward is the breakdown of the total sales change to its four drivers: price and volume effects, as well as the effect of exchange rate changes, and the impact of acquisitions and disposals

```
I.    Production (Mboe per day)
          763;     766   (0%)

      Sales  ($ billion)
          20.17;   20.10  (0%)

      Sales drivers
      Price    Volume    Forex    M&A
       X         X         X        X

II.   Reserve–Replacement Ratio
          169%,   X  (X%)

III.  Operating costs

IV.   Gross margin
```

FIGURE 15.3   Resource Deployment—
Operations
Data for Occidental Petroleum, 2013, 2012.

(same-store sales); the latter enables a determination of the organic sales growth without acquisitions (third line in the box in Figure 15.3). Some companies we examined report one or two of the sales drivers (Devon's 2014 10-K report: sales changes due to volume and price were 71 percent and 29 percent, respectively), but rarely do companies disclose all of the sales change drivers. This is strange, since this is very important information for astute investors, and hardly a competitive threat.

Disclosure of company's production and sales naturally raises the important issue of sustainability, since in the extractive industries (oil and gas, mining) production depletes the company's resources. Sustainability and growth require resource replacement, and even addition to the reserves. This depletion/addition feature of operations is captured by the *reserve–replacement ratio,* which indicates the amount of proved reserves added during the period by acquisitions and exploration, relative to the amount of oil and gas produced. Obviously, to maintain enterprise sustainability, the reserve–replacement ratio should be above 100 percent. Occidental reports that at the end of 2013 this ratio was 169 percent, due to the addition of 470 million barrels to reserves. The company also disclosed spending $7.7 billion on finding and developing these reserves, yielding a $16.4 cost per barrel—an important metric for determining patterns over time and benchmarking against other companies.

Data on operating costs, total and per equivalent barrel, conclude the Operations box.[17] Hess, for example, reports for Q1–2013 that its cash operating costs per barrel were $21.2, and its amortization and depletion costs per barrel were $19.2—meaningful when compared with peer companies and market prices. This allows the computation of the gross margin of the company's operations, with particular attention to the *cash* gross margin per barrel (relatively immune to managerial estimates).

INVESTOR'S INSIGHT

"Operating leverage," the ratio of the company's fixed-to-variable costs, is an important attribute often overlooked by investors, focusing on the financial leverage. A high operating leverage means that the company is "stuck" with large fixed costs, such as maintenance, depreciation, or plant and equipment insurance, generally related to heavy investments in long-term assets. When product market conditions change (for instance, demand decreases), fixed costs cannot be lowered rapidly, and earnings plunge. With increases, fixed costs also stay constant (up to capacity) and earnings increase rapidly. Operating leverage, accordingly, is an important contributor to earnings' sensitivity to market conditions. With oil and gas companies' high operating leverage due to large investments in long-term resources, earnings are commensurately sensitive to changing market conditions. The high operating leverage of oil and gas companies is therefore an important risk dimension that investors should consider.

VALUE CREATED

Similar to our previous discussion of value created in other industries, the periodic oil and gas value created equals cash from operations, plus intangible investments expensed in the income statement, minus capital expenditures and cost of equity capital.

We end the oil and gas case with a schematic Resources & Consequences Report (Figure 15.4). Note here, as in earlier cases, how the essential information for valuation purposes is condensed into a compact report, rather than strewn around in hundreds of pages of financial reports and other company statutory filings.

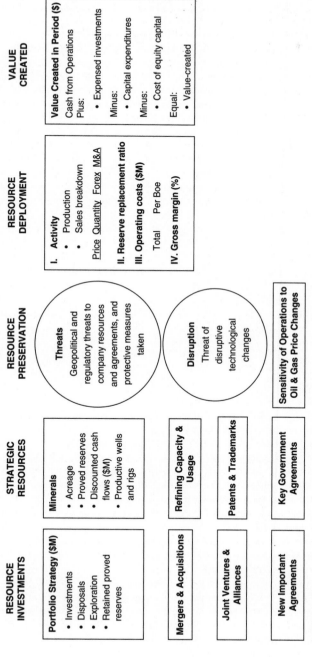

FIGURE 15.4 Strategic Resources & Consequences Report: Case 4—Oil and Gas Companies[*]

[*]Boxes denote data, circles for narrative disclosure

NOTES

1. Some oil companies also engage in commodity trading, but results of these activities are often aggregated with downstream data, adding to the fog surrounding oil companies.

2. The fact that oil companies are allowed to use two procedures for accounting for explorations—"successful efforts": costs of dry wells are expensed, and "full cost": cost of dry wells are capitalized—decreases companies' comparability. Most large companies, though, use "successful efforts."

3. A typical analyst question: "I was wondering as far as the international asset portfolio, is there going to be further rationalization [restructuring] of that portfolio in the future beyond the assets [sales] already announced?" Answer: "There are no current plans for any divestitures." (Hess Corp., Q1–2013 earnings call.)

4. As in the preceding case studies, our choice of company examples should not be perceived as an investment recommendation. Also, the numbers we quote may be subject to misreading and certain inaccuracies.

5. Midstream oil and gas operations generally refer to the transportation, storage, and marketing of products.

6. For added operating clarity and credibility, in Q4–2013 Devon's COO provided a capital expenditures forecast for 2014, classified by areas: "... $1.5 billion in the Permian, $1.1 billion in Eagle Ford, $1.1 billion in our heavy oil projects in Canada, ... $600 million in the liquids-rich areas of the Barnett Shale and Anadarko Basin..." Some other oil companies we studied declined to provide capital expenditures forecasts.

7. Matching purchases and divestments is quite frequent in the industry. For example, Apache (February 25, 2015 presentation) provided an illuminating chart showing that, over the past five years, total acquisitions and divestments amounted to $15.5 billion and $14.8 billion, respectively. An almost perfect match. The chart distinguishes between oil and natural gas.

8. UK companies are required to provide a report on firm strategy and the main performance measures used by management. Of particular interest is the viability statement by managers. An important step in the right direction. The problem: as with financial reports, these strategic reports are generally hopelessly long and cumbersome—BP's 2014 strategic report is 68 pages long—making it very difficult to focus on essentials. Our Resources & Consequences Report, in contrast, is compact, concise, and investor friendly.

9. Data in the column, for demonstration purposes, are for Devon Energy for the years 2014 and 2013.

10. SEC regulations require oil and gas companies to disclose, among other things, the number of productive and dry exploratory wells, and the number of productive and dry development wells.

11. The SEC's (2010) definition of proved reserves: "Proved oil and gas reserves are those quantities of oil and gas, which, by analysis of geoscience and engineering data, can be estimated with reasonable certainty to be economically producible from a given date forward, from known reservoirs, and under existing economic conditions, operating methods, and government regulations."

12. The International Energy Agency (2013) defines: "Unconventional oil consists of a wider variety of liquid sources, including oil sands, extra heavy oil, gas to liquids, and other liquids. In general, conventional oil is easier and cheaper to produce than unconventional oil."

13. Information about the proved reserves and discounted cash flows is required by the SEC and FASB (GAAP) to be provided by US oil and gas companies. Detailed guidelines for the calculation of this information are provided by the SEC and FASB to mitigate manipulation of proved reserves. In contrast with most other data in the Resources & Consequences Report, proved reserves are based on managerial estimates.

14. Martin Boyer and Didier Filion, "Common and Fundamental Factors in Stock Returns of Canadian Oil and Gas Companies," *Energy Economics*, 29 (2007): 428–453. Joseph Magliolo, "Capital Market Analysis of Reserve Recognition Accounting," *Journal of Accounting Research*, 24 (1986): 69–108.

15. Devon's 2014 financial report includes four dense pages of risk factors, most of them obvious: oil and gas prices may change, proved reserve estimates are uncertain, etc. Lacking specificity and focus on real threats, such disclosure is of negligible relevance to investors.

16. An important risk factor, rarely discussed, is the third-party risk in joint ventures, namely the risk born by the nonoperating partners.

17. The SEC requires disclosure of average sales price per unit of oil or gas, as well as average production costs per unit, classified by geographical areas.

Four

Practical Matters

We conclude the book by addressing three practical issues fundamental to its main thesis—corporate financial reports lost most of their usefulness to investors and therefore have to be augmented by a strategic vision and execution disclosure, as prescribed by our Strategic Resources & Consequences Report. These issues are:

- **Implementation:** How can our proposed disclosure paradigm be implemented by the corporate sector?
- **Accounting:** How should the ubiquitous accounting and reporting system be restructured to halt and reverse its loss of usefulness?
- **Investors' operating instructions:** How should investors' financial and securities analyses be changed to best utilize the proposed strategic information for improved performance?

CHAPTER 16

Implementation

In which we outline how our proposed disclosure—the Strategic Resources & Consequences Report—could be implemented by companies to provide investors with action-able information hitherto unavailable in corporate financial reports. Short of new regulations, which we don't prescribe, how could corporate managers, who are already heavily burdened by extensive accounting and financial reporting regulations, be motivated to impart with the information outlined in our Report? Wishful thinking? We think not. In fact, we propose in this chapter an evidence-based, non-coercive way to elicit the required information from business enterprises.

HOW TO ELICIT THE PROPOSED INFORMATION

We outlined and demonstrated in the preceding five chapters the new infor-mation paradigm we propose managers share with investors. We have shown that this information is prescribed by economic theory as key to assessing the performance and success of business enterprises, that this information is indeed requested by analysts in corporate earnings calls, and that upon the release of the information, albeit sporadically and by few companies, it significantly affects share prices. So there is little doubt that this is the missing information investors need for successful investment decisions. So far, so good; but how will investors receive this information on a regular and uniform basis? Realistically, we suspect, corporate managers—already heavily burdened by extensive statutory disclosure requirements—will be less than thrilled to shoulder additional disclosure burden. Indeed, resisting calls for additional disclosure is a Pavlovian managerial reaction.[1] So does our disclosure proposal have a prayer?

The traditional path of eliciting corporate disclosure, be it about product attributes and safety, environmental harms, or financial information, is by coercion—namely, regulation.[2] This is definitely not the path we wish to follow with our proposal. Suffice it to look back at the many diminishing information usefulness graphs we presented in Part I of the book to raise serious doubts about the benefits of mandated disclosure. There must be a better way to elicit from companies useful information to investors; indeed, we believe, there is. Economists dub it *revealed preferences*. Consumers demand the best, most price-effective cell phones or cereal; similarly, investors should insist on getting the best information. Accordingly, our proposed information revelation process should start with investors actively *demanding* the prescribed information, which, as we have shown, predicts enterprise performance and stock prices. To demonstrate that this can be done, we developed the following case study on Pfizer, the leading drug company, and its evolving product pipeline disclosure.

PFIZER RESPONDS TO ANALYSTS' PIPELINE QUESTIONS

More than anything else, for pharmaceutical and biotech companies, the scope and progress of their new-product-development (pipeline) activities are shaping the future course of these enterprises. It stands to reason, therefore, that in this fiercely competitive industry, product pipeline information would be the most treasured and guarded company secret. And yet, Pfizer reports its entire product pipeline development on its website (www.pfizer .com/research/science_and_technology/product_pipeline) and updates this information quarterly, disclosing the development stage of each project, FDA filing status, as well as marketing information. For investors interested in tracking the progress of Pfizer's new drugs under development, this information, in conjunction with Pfizer's real-time press releases of FDA decisions and other breakthroughs, provide a clear view of the company's future growth. As a bonus, Pfizer also lists other business development initiatives that have direct implications for its product pipeline, such as acquisitions, collaboration with other companies, patent licensing, and divestiture. Notably, Pfizer is not the exception in the industry; rather, it is the rule. Most pharma and biotech companies provide regularly detailed pipeline information. Surely the result of a highly effective disclosure regulation, you say. Not really: Product pipeline disclosure is totally voluntary. How come?

A review of Pfizer's pipeline disclosure in 10-K filings starting with the early 1990s reveals that the company used to be far less forthcoming about its product pipeline. For instance, in its 1993 10-K filing, Pfizer disclosed only eight new drug applications under FDA review. But from 1994 on, the company gradually increased the quantity and quality of information about its product pipeline. In the 1994 filing, for example, it mentioned 15 chemical entities in advanced development, and a year later it disclosed that 48 other compounds were under development (some of which must have been started in prior years, yet not mentioned in Pfizer's earlier disclosures). In 1998, for the first time, Pfizer gave the name and disease information for eight drugs in late-stage clinical trials and further expanded pipeline disclosure in the 1999 filing. In its 10-K filing for 2001, Pfizer elaborated on five new drugs, expected to be approved and launched in the United States and Europe within a year, along with two anticipated new filings in the subsequent year. It also started reporting on ongoing collaborations with other companies in new drug development. Continuing the trend, in 2003 it also disclosed its five-year plan to submit 20 new filings. The Pfizer pipeline disclosure progressed until February 2011, when it started posting online pipeline updates each quarter. Table 16A, shown in the Appendix, demonstrates in detail the development over the past 20 years of Pfizer's pipeline exposure.

WHY THE PIPELINE EXPOSÉ?

What motivated Pfizer's managers to part with presumably the most secret product development information? An epiphany that transparency is a good thing? Perhaps, but we think more likely the driving force was analysts' persistent demand for this information, which we carefully document thus:

To examine analyst's demand for Pfizer's product pipeline information, we studied the question and answer (Q&A) section of Pfizer's earnings conference calls with analysts in the first quarters of 2001, 2002, 2003, 2005, 2010, and 2015, to track a trend. We commenced with 2001, since, as Table 16A (Appendix) shows, the years 2001–2003 were the most active in Pfizer's progress toward full pipeline revelation. We examined earnings calls because they provide a unique opportunity for analysts to seek answers from management on important issues of strategy, operating results, and future outlook. Accordingly, for each conference call, we counted the total number of questions raised by analysts and singled out the subset of questions pertaining to the product pipeline.[3] The total number of questions analysts raised in the calls ranged from 20 in 2001 to a high of 30 in 2015. However, as Figure 16.1 vividly shows, the number and percentage of questions concerning Pfizer's pipeline *declined* markedly. In 2001, analysts asked 12 product line questions, accounting for 60 percent of all questions asked in the call and attesting to analysts' intense interest in the status of Pfizer's product development activities (as well as the absence of adequate information in the financial report), but as Pfizer responded to the demand with increasing disclosure, as we have shown in the preceding section, analysts' pipeline questions declined steadily, to only five pipeline questions (17 percent of all questions asked) in 2015. This looks to be a classic case of supply meeting demand.[4]

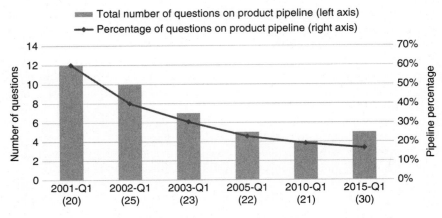

FIGURE 16.1 Number and Percentage of Product Pipeline-Related Questions Raised by Analysts During Pfizer's 2001–2015 Earnings Conference Calls

It seems obvious from our documented chronology that Pfizer's gradual enhancement of pipeline disclosure came mainly as a response to analysts' insistent questions.[5] This is in no way intended to diminish Pfizer's credit for enhanced transparency. No one forced the company to respond so promptly and adequately to investors' questions. The point we are making, and the reason we elaborate on Pfizer's case, is that investors' insistent demand for relevant information is a potent force for eliciting the information from companies.[6] Requesting information is effective because there are serious capital market ramifications to persistent refusal to address investors' questions; a "silence" is generally perceived as the company hiding bad news. "No news is bad news in capital markets," goes the saying. And consistent with the economic principle of "full revelation," once a company discloses certain information, its peers are "forced" to join the bandwagon. Fact is that extensive product pipeline disclosure is now the norm in pharma and biotech industries. So, our vision for the implementation of our proposed Resources & Consequences Report starts with a concerted effort by analysts and institutional investors to elicit this information from public companies. Not heavy-handed accounting regulation, sure to raise manager's antagonism and take a decade or more to implement; instead, just insistent demand for useful information by none other than the company owners. We are not naïve to believe that *all* analysts and investors share the desire for improved transparency. Some well-connected analysts and large investors thrive in the current murky disclosure environment, being able to get their information directly from managers. Nevertheless, we strongly believe that there is a sufficiently large number of analysts and investors who will benefit from improved corporate disclosure, and who will be willing to express their desire for the information we prescribe.

AN IMPORTANT ROLE FOR THE SEC

Investors' information demand is effective in eliciting corporate disclosure, as we have shown, but the going is often slow and the disclosure not uniform across companies. Pfizer's case shows that it took over a decade to get the full pipeline information disclosed, and our proposed Resources & Consequences Report is more extensive. Since we wish to see our proposal implemented in our lifetime, we look for expediters. A nudge by the SEC, and similar regulators in other countries, will hasten this process. To its credit, the SEC is genuinely interested in improving corporate financial disclosure, and over the years it has initiated various efforts to curb information misrepresentation, make corporate reports more accessible to investors (Edgar, XBRL), and improve accounting standard-setting and the content of financial statements. As of this writing, the SEC considers responses to its 2014 call for proposals to improve financial disclosure effectiveness. Our evidence in Part I of the book, however, indicates that these efforts have thus far yielded limited success as far as the *usefulness* of financial information to investors is concerned. The reasons, we believe, were the absence of a specific and empirical identification of investors' changing information needs and tailoring industry-specific information paradigms to meet these needs, as in our Strategic Resources & Consequences Report. This gives us confidence that our proposal, if supported by the SEC, will fare better than previous attempts to enhance corporate disclosure effectiveness. In fact, our proposal is consistent with the SEC's principle of "core disclosure": " ... certain information that does not change as frequently, such as the description of the business ... "[7]

Endorsement of our disclosure proposal, or one similar in spirit, by the SEC will go a long way toward its implementation. Operationally, the SEC could set up industry groups of managers and investors to develop specific Resources & Consequences Reports, like the four we have outlined in Chapters 12–15. Such an SEC initiative will add to our proposal the important element of *comparability*—a uniform report for all companies in an industry, or sector, which is a necessary condition for effective disclosure, since most investment decisions are predicated on the ability to compare a company with its peers. The SEC and comparable regulators in other countries can thus play an important role in enhancing disclosure effectiveness along the lines proposed in this book.

INDUSTRY ASSOCIATIONS COULD HELP, TOO

Industry (trade) associations aren't particularly active in the area of corporate financial disclosure. They generally strive to enhance demand for the industry's product ("Got Milk" advertisement), offer member development programs, and lobby legislators for favorable laws and regulations. Occasionally, though, such associations develop industry-specific financial and valuation indicators, often adopted by members. One well-known industrywide indicator is the *book-to-bill ratio*—the forward-looking ratio of orders received to units shipped and billed—closely watched by technology investors, particularly in the semiconductor sector. Another case in point: The World Gold Council (how does one become a member?) recently formed a working group to establish a new cost disclosure framework, more reflective of miners' costs than accounting (GAAP) information. In June 2013, the Council published a Guidance Note defining new cost metrics, such as the awkwardly named "all-in sustaining costs" (AISC), which traces the costs incurred during the complete mining lifecycle, from exploration to closure.[8] This is a comprehensive measure that includes on-site mining costs, royalties and taxes, community costs, operational stripping costs, exploration and study costs, capital exploration expenditures, as well as general and administrative expenses. One-time items, like impairment and severance charges, are excluded from AISC, rendering it a more recurring cost performance measure than GAAP costs. Dividing the all-in costs by output yields the important indicator of cost per unit of output. We were told by the CFO of a leading mining company that most industry peers report this measure (in addition, of course, to the measures required by GAAP). This is a clear example of the way industry associations, having deep understanding of sector technology and specific circumstances, can contribute to the legitimacy and implementation of our proposed disclosure.

BUT, OF COURSE, MANAGERS' COOPERATION IS INDISPENSABLE

Naturally, a noncoercive disclosure initiative like ours requires managers' cooperation. We believe that, upon reflection and with the right incentives, corporate managers will support our disclosure proposal. Here is why:

Managers are well aware, perhaps more than anybody else, of the fast-diminishing usefulness to investors of financial information. How else to explain the continuous rise in voluntary, non-GAAP disclosure by companies? Take the non-GAAP (proforma) earnings, for example: Their frequency doubled from 20 percent of public companies in 2003 to over 40 percent in 2013.[9] It used to be that non-GAAP earnings were the butt of a joke: They were called "managers' wishful thinking," "Kool-Aid," or "the best non-GAAP earnings is EBE—earnings before expenses." But an SEC regulation (2003) requiring the reconciliation of non-GAAP with GAAP earnings, and empirical evidence documenting that investors respond to non-GAAP earnings *more strongly* than to their GAAP brethren,[10] conferred certain respectability on pro forma earnings and other non-GAAP items.

But whatever the merits of non-GAAP earnings, their proliferation testifies to an increasing number of managers losing faith in GAAP numbers reflecting their companies' operations. And it's not only non-GAAP earnings attesting to managers' realization of the diminishing usefulness of financial information; it's also the constant increase in other voluntary disclosures by public companies, such as the product pipeline of pharma and biotech companies, which opened this chapter, or the proliferation of customer-related information, released by telecom, Internet, insurance, and media companies.[11] The problem, however, with these voluntary information releases is that they are haphazard, inconsistent, and not uniform across the industry, and hence of limited usefulness to investors. That's what our proposal is set to improve.

So, the evidence on the diminishing usefulness of financial information we provide in Part I of the book, along with managers' own intuition to that effect, provide the necessary conditions for managers' support of our disclosure proposals. But that might not be enough to garner managers' full support. They still have legitimate concerns about enhanced disclosure.

COMPETITION AND LITIGATION CONCERNS

We need to allay managers' concerns of litigation exposure and releasing competition-sensitive information raised by our proposal. Legitimate concerns, to be sure, but they do not really apply to our proposal. First, practically all the data in our Resources & Consequences Report are factual and easy to verify: Number of new customers, insurance claims frequency and severity, patents developed and licensed out, or oil companies' number of rigs and wells, among others, are simply facts. They are not hairy estimates or managerial projections, nor speculative (fair value) valuations— nothing that can raise managers' litigation exposure. Unless a company intentionally misstates these facts, there is no basis for litigation concerning our proposed disclosure. Add to this the assurance that the data in the

Resources & Consequences Report can be easily verified by external auditors, and managers' litigation concerns can be safely laid to rest.

As to benefits to competitors from the disclosed information, the many company-specific numerical examples we provided in the four industry cases outlined in Chapters 12–15, indicate that many companies already report substantial elements of our proposal. True, no company discloses all the information in the Report, and in the integrated form we prescribe, but they voluntarily disclose important elements of it, obviously without competitive harm. It is therefore highly unlikely that following our strategic disclosure proposal will cause competitive harm to companies.

Finally, what about the "what's in it for me?" question? Meaningful information disclosure isn't effortless. Data must be organized (not originally collected; any well-run company has all the information we prescribe) and investors' questions answered. It would be helpful, therefore, if these managerial efforts were rewarded; and, indeed, they are. The reward to managers and companies lies in the removal of the detrimental effects on companies of inadequate disclosure and lack of transparency—information asymmetry, in the economics jargon. Simply put, the fast-diminishing usefulness of financial information we documented isn't good for companies and their managers, because it increases investors' uncertainty about companies' growth prospects, as we have shown in Chapter 6, and increased uncertainty translates directly into lower share prices and higher cost of capital.[12] Indeed, extensive evidence links investors' information uncertainty to share price decline and volatility increase, particularly for medium and small companies (thin institutional holdings, low analysts following), for which investors' information is generally constrained.[13] So, it's obviously in managers' best interest to responsibly enhance disclosure to arrest the diminishing usefulness of financial information. Most managers understand this, but they are unsure about the best way to provide such enhanced disclosure. We offer an evidence-based, systematic answer to this quandary.

So, we believe that most corporate managers would support our disclosure proposal; but, being humans (most of them, at least), we feel they may need an additional incentive. Here it comes.

FOR CONSIDERATION: LIGHTEN THE REGULATORY BURDEN

A few years back, while discussing enhanced corporate disclosure, we were told by an astute CFO: "If you want to be taken seriously by executives, whenever you suggest a new disclosure, point at the same time to current reporting requirements which could be eliminated. Just piling up on companies additional reporting won't work." Sage advice. So, how can the current reporting burden be substantially eased to accommodate our proposed disclosure? By now you have become used to our reform proposals, which are all but timid. But this one is so radical, we don't dare to put it forth as a recommendation; just for consideration.[14]

Consider eliminating quarterly reporting, leaving semiannual (every six months) and annual reporting only. Importantly, to keep investors apprised of the company's operations during the six months, the company should report every three months the results of its basic operations: Sales − Cost of sales = Gross margin. Not a complete quarterly income statement, not a balance sheet, and not a cash flow statement—just quarterly sales and cost of sales. This should come as a big relief for managers: two fewer financial reports, earnings conference calls, and particularly the pressure to meet the quarterly earnings consensus. What a relief.

Will the world come to a stand-still without quarterly reports? We doubt it. The United Kingdom requires only semiannual reporting; likewise for Australia, among other countries. True, the UK economy is substantially smaller than that of the United States, but UK capital markets—the determining consideration for frequency of reporting—are large and very advanced; the number of listed companies in the United Kingdom is only about half of that in the United States. Moreover, we aren't aware of comprehensive research showing that UK capital markets are less efficient or that share prices are less accurate (informative) than on the western side of the Atlantic. Tellingly, UK-listed companies are allowed to report quarterly, but few do, we are told. If investors' demand for quarterly reporting were overwhelming, surely more UK companies would have responded by reporting quarterly.

A significant advantage of abolishing quarterly reporting is to lessen the pressure on corporate managers to deliver short-term results, which, as is widely perceived, adversely affects managers' focus on the long-term growth of the company, and sometimes even leads to earnings management.[15] The shorter the period of performance measurement, the more volatile are earnings (short-term fluctuations smooth out with longer reporting periods), and the greater is the "need" to adjust reported earnings to meet targets (managers' guidance, analysts' consensus). A modest lengthening of the reporting period—from three to six months—will therefore significantly lessen the pressure on managers to calibrate reported earnings to targets, and, as we expect, will mitigate managerial myopia.

Will abolishing quarterly earnings cause a significant loss of information to investors? We doubt it. First, recall our suggestion that in lieu of full-fledged quarterly reports, companies should still disclose their quarterly sales and cost of sales. Investors will accordingly receive a quarterly update of the fundamental performance of the company. Second, and more subtly, reporting *frequency* and reporting *quality* are to a certain extent substitutes. Adopting our proposal of a comprehensive strategic disclosure—the Resources & Consequences Report—will undoubtedly enhance the quality of reporting, compensating, if compensation is needed, for the elimination of full-fledged quarterly reports.[16]

Finally, we asked 25 CFOs of large companies whether eliminating quarterly reports will result in negligible, moderate, or considerable loss of information to investors, and whether it will significantly lighten their administrative load. Only one-third of respondents stated that eliminating quarterly reporting will result in considerable information loss to investors,[17] and 20 of the 25 CFOs stated that eliminating quarterly reporting would result in a moderate to considerable administrative load lightening. A favorable endorsement of our proposal.[18]

TAKEAWAY

Consider how to implement our proposal to annually or semiannually report the company's strategic resources and the efficiency of deploying those resources. First and foremost, investors and analysts have to actively request this information. Our Pfizer case study indicates that, in general, investors' demand for strategic information is met, albeit with delays by companies. An SEC endorsement of such reporting—in line with the SEC continuous efforts to enhance disclosure effectiveness—coupled with the cooperation of industry associations, will encourage companies' response and will add the important dimension of industry uniformity to this disclosure.

Managers, key players in our reporting proposal, are already aware of the serious shortcomings of current financial information and are therefore open to, and indeed practice, enhanced non-GAAP reporting, but in a haphazard, inconsistent manner. Our proposal will streamline and make comparable the individual attempts at voluntary disclosure. The strong incentives to reduce investors' uncertainty, thereby increasing share prices and reducing cost of capital, and perhaps even lightening the regulatory burden by eliminating quarterly reporting, will undoubtedly contribute to managers' willingness to adopt our proposal.[19]

APPENDIX 16.1

TABLE 16A Major Enhancements in Pfizer's 10-K Disclosure About Its Product Pipeline, 1994–2014

	Filing Date	Major Enhancements in Pfizer's Disclosure about Its Product Pipeline
1994	3/24/1995	(1) 15 new chemical entities in advanced development with no names given
1995	3/29/1996	(2) 48 other compounds in early development with no names given
1996	3/28/1997	None
1998	3/26/1999	(3) Name and treatment of eight drugs in late-stage clinical programs (4) Collaborations with two entities in new drug development
1999	3/27/2000	(5) Name and treatment of five ongoing or planned clinical trials in new product development program (6) Name and treatment of one discontinued drug development program
2000	3/25/2001	None
2001	3/28/2002	(7) Name and treatment of five new products under review in US/EU with expected launch next year (8) Name and treatment of two anticipated new filings next year (9) One drug in Phase III trial in a collaborative program
2002	3/27/2003	(10) Name and treatment of newly approved products in EU and Japan (11) Specifics of three ongoing collaborations in new product development
2003	3/10/2004	(12) Name and treatment of five new filings in EU and Japan (13) Five-year FDA filing plan for 20 new filings
2004	2/28/2005	None
2005	3/1/2006	(14) Details of acquisition and licensing deals with implications for product pipeline
2006	3/1/2007	None
2007	2/29/2008	None
2008	2/27/2009	None
2009	2/26/2010	None
2010	2/28/2011	(15) Online product pipeline update twice a year
2011	2/28/2012	(16) Online product pipeline update four times a year (once each quarter)
2012	2/28/2013	None
2013	2/28/2014	None
2014	2/27/2015	None

NOTES

1. Late nineteenth century, we were told, the New York Stock Exchange asked the managers of listed companies to regularly disclose their companies' annual sales. "This is very sensitive information, benefiting our competitors," was the justification for managers' refusal to release sales numbers. Managers' frequent reaction to disclosure proposals is now more nuanced: the required information will not benefit investors, it is costly to produce, and the clincher, it exposes companies to shareholder litigation and competitive disadvantage.
2. As of this writing, for example, the FDA proposes rules requiring restaurants to list clear calorie information for pizzas, salad bars, and popcorn. Forgot chicken wings and ribs?
3. Such as, Hen Koyu of Credit Suisse First Boston: "My question relates to Geodon [a bipolar disorder drug]. Could you give us a feel of how the European launch timeline will look for Geodon . . . " (Pfizer's conference call on April 18, 2001).
4. A contextual examination of the earnings calls strengthens our conclusion that Pfizer indeed responded to analysts' requests of information. For example, in the conference call held on April 18, 2001, Hen Koyu from Credit Suisse First Boston asked about the timing of a drug's launch in Europe. In its subsequent 10-K for 2001, filed on March 28, 2002, Pfizer revealed the names and treatment of five drugs expected to be approved and launched in Europe during 2002. Another example: during the conference call held on April 17, 2002, Lynn Gaffe from Bank of America, asked Pat Kelly, Pfizer's Head of World Wide Marketing: "Could you comment a bit on Europe for European approvals too Pat?" Although the response from Pat Kelly was somewhat brief, in its very next 10-K release on March 27, 2003, Pfizer started disclosing information about new drug approvals in specific European countries. Analysts also asked Pfizer's management about the company's view on the value of acquisitions for beefing up the company's product pipeline. In response, starting from Pfizer's 10-K filing for 2005, the company disclosed the specifics of both completed and in-process acquisitions that are expected to enhance its product pipeline.
5. In the early 2000s, one of the authors served on an SEC commission on enhanced corporate disclosure with, among others, Pfizer's then CFO, and clearly recalls the CFO saying: "We generally respond to analysts' information requests with enhanced disclosure."
6. We emphasize: demand for "relevant information." We are not surprised, for example, that politically motivated requests for, say, information on the alleged environmental harms perpetrated by the company, do not elicit a positive response.
7. See Keith Higgins, Disclosure effectiveness: Remarks before the American Bar Association Business Law Section, Spring Meeting, April 11, 2014. US Securities and Exchange Commission.

8. See Tom Whelan, "All-in sustaining costs and all-in costs," Ernst and Young, American Mining & Metals Forum, September 2013.

9. See, Jeremiah Bentley, Theodore Christensen, Kurt Gee, and Benjamin Whipple, *Who Makes the Non-GAAP Kool-Aid? How Do Managers and Analysts Influence Non-GAAP Reporting Policy?* working paper (Salt Lake City: Marriott School of Management, Brigham Young University, 2014).

10. See, for example, Nilabhra Bhattacharya, Ervin Black, Theodore Christensen, and Chad Larson, "Assessing the Relative Informativeness and Permanence of Pro Forma Earnings and GAAP Operating Earnings," *Journal of Accounting and Economics*, 36 (2003): 285–319. Concluding that: "Our analyses... indicate that pro forma earnings are more informative and more permanent than GAAP operating earnings."

11. A participant in a CFO survey we conducted commented: "Most investors I talk to do not understand the accounting, nor do they care." We wonder why.

12. Recall, in particular, the evidence (Figure 6.1) of the increasing uncertainty and ambiguity of analysts' earnings forecasts (dispersion). An effective demonstration of the positive impact of enhanced disclosure is the insurance company Progressive's move in 2001 to disclose monthly income statements. This disclosure significantly tamed Progressive's share price volatility.

13. Mary Billings, Robert Jennings, and Baruch Lev, "On Guidance and Volatility," *Journal of Accounting and Economics*, 60 (2015): 161–180, providing evidence that earnings guidance decreases investors' uncertainty and reduces share price volatility.

14. The FASB has been recently engaged in attempts to simplify certain disclosure requirements. A laudable effort, to be sure. But, to the best of our knowledge, so far these attempts didn't yield substantial reductions in regulatory burden.

15. A recent addition to the burgeoning literature on manager's short-termism: William Galston, 2015, Clinton Gets It Right on Short-Termism, *The Wall Street Journal*, July 29.

16. The empirical evidence on the merits of quarterly reporting is very sparse and mixed. One study (Arthur Kraft, Huai Zhang, and Renhui Fu, 2012, "Financial Reporting Frequency, Information Asymmetry, and the Cost of Equity," *Journal of Accounting and Economics*, 54: 132–149) reports that quarterly statements enhance corporate transparency (investors' information), but the main findings of this study come from comparing quarterly to annual reports. Our suggestion maintains semiannual reports. On the other hand, a research on Singaporean companies found: " ... mandatory quarterly reporting does not reduce information asymmetry ... " (Peter Kajüter, Florian Klassman, and Martin Nienhaus, *Causal Effects of Quarterly Reporting—An Analysis of Benefits and Costs*, working paper (University of Muenster, Abstract, 2015).) Also, a study on monthly disclosures documents no positive effects on transparency of such frequent reports (Andrew Van Buskirk, "Disclosure

Frequency and Information Asymmetry," *Review of Quantitative Finance and Accounting*, 38 (2012): 411–440).

17. However, we didn't include in our questionnaire the requirement to report quarterly sales and cost of sales. We just asked about total elimination of quarterly reporting.
18. In the spirit of "natural experiments," which certain governments and institutions experiment with, the SEC could abolish quarterly reporting for a few industries only and observe the consequences over several years, before applying it to all companies.
19. In our survey of 25 CFOs, 19 of the 25 respondents said that in lieu of a quarterly report, they will expand disclosure about their companies' business model.

CHAPTER 17

So, What to Do with Accounting? A Reform Agenda

In which we propose far-reaching changes to the current accounting and financial reporting system (GAAP) to arrest the fast-diminishing usefulness of financial information, which we have documented in Part I of the book. We propose a three-pronged substantive overhaul of the system, which is a far cry from the common "fine-tuning" of accounting regulators. Nothing short of this, we believe, will reverse the declining usefulness trend of financial information.

REVITALIZING ACCOUNTING

Having established earlier in the book that, in recent decades, accounting-based financial reports lost most of their relevance to investors, followed by the identification of the major reasons for the relevance lost, and outlining our proposed strategic corporate report to respond to current investors' needs, the remaining question is: How can historical-based accounting and financial reporting be restructured and rejuvenated to provide investors' needs and complement our proposed forward-looking disclosure on company strategy and execution?

The gradual, fine-tuning approach of accounting regulators to enhance information effectiveness failed, as we have shown in Part I of the book. But don't just take our word for it. A recent exhaustive examination of the Financial Accounting Standards Board's (FASB) 40-year regulatory record corroborates our verdict.[1] Four accounting researchers examined the impact on investors of 147 accounting regulations enacted between 1973 and 2009—many of them with extensive implications on how assets, liabilities, revenues, expenses, and cash flows should be accounted for and publicly disclosed—and reported sobering results: A whopping 75 percent of the regulations had no impact on investors whatsoever. If new accounting and reporting rules enhance transparency and reduce investors' uncertainty about companies' operations, as accounting regulations are advertised to do, companies' cost of capital should decrease and share prices increase as a result of the improved information environment. And yet, the researchers found that for 75 percent of the FASB's standards, the share prices of the companies impacted by those accounting rules didn't budge around the rules' deliberation and enactment dates. Worse yet, 13 percent of the standards actually reduced shareholder value, while only 12 percent of the rules improved investors' lot. So, an almost 40-year extensive and costly accounting regulation effort was, in fact, a washout as far as investors—its main beneficiaries—are concerned.[2] Doesn't this call for a major accounting soul searching and overhaul?[3]

A new direction of accounting and financial reporting is obviously in order: We propose: (i) Accepting reality, that the value-creating resources of business enterprises are increasingly intangible assets that have to be recognized as such in accounting; (ii) That accountants shouldn't be in the business of asset valuation, which by its nature is subjective and speculative; and finally (iii) Internalizing the fact that financial information's increasing complexity and obscurity is diminishing its usefulness to investors. Essentially, accounting and financial reporting should predominantly be about facts, and facts that matter. A return to fundamentals, so to speak.

We elaborate below on these three major changes, which we hope will be considered seriously and with an open mind by capital markets and accounting regulators, as well as by managers and academics. Rest assured, the following is a carefully thought through and operational proposal that benefited from comments and suggestions from some of the best accounting minds.

I. TREAT INTANGIBLES AS ASSETS

In the United States, a poorly reasoned, 40-year old accounting rule (SFAS No. 2, 1974) that predates the software, biotech, Internet, energy alternatives, wireless, nanotech, and other intangibles-intensive industries still governs the accounting for R&D—the driver of many intangibles. It mandates the immediate expensing of practically all internally generated research and development efforts.[4] And not just R&D. Practically all other internal investments in intangible assets—brands, know-how, business systems—are immediately expensed. The folly of this wide-ranging accounting rule is made clear by looking once more at Figure 8.1 (p. 82) portraying the total corporate investment in tangible and intangible assets. Ironically, most of the investments reflected by the fast-rising curve—intangible assets—are denied assets status by accountants, whereas those on steep decline—tangible assets—proudly populate corporate balance sheets. Even the government-produced National Income Accounts (issued by the Bureau of Economic Analysis) now consider most intangible expenditures—primarily on software, R&D, and brands—as investments rather than expenses for purposes of national economic accounting.[5]

We know what you, accountants, are now thinking: Intangibles are uncertain and notoriously difficult to value, so how can we report their values on the balance sheet? Don't we have already enough questionable estimates in corporate reports? Here is our answer:

We don't suggest to value intangibles by their *current* purchase or sale prices (fair values). Rather, in line with the treatment of these assets in the national income accounts, we propose to *capitalize* the investment in these intangibles, using their objective original costs. We leave intangibles' valuation to appraisers and just propose properly accounting for the facts—that is, the costs of intangibles. After all, that's exactly what's done in accounting for tangible, physical assets. But, you'll riposte (we know, because we heard these arguments for years): what good will it do to report the historical values of intangibles on the balance sheet? What can investors learn from these numbers? Answer: What they learn now from balance sheet values of tangible assets (property, plant & equipment): the original spending on these resources. Not much, we admit, but better than the complete absence of intangibles from the balance sheet. Importantly, the main reason to capitalize intangibles isn't to enhance the realism of the balance sheet—very few, if any, investment decisions are based on asset values anyway—rather, its aim is to restore the income statement to the status of a meaningful indicator of operating results, by properly separating investments from current expenses, thereby substantially improving the measurement of business performance.[6]

Consider: A fundamental tenet of accounting used to be that enterprise performance, reflected by periodic income or earnings, is properly measured if revenues are carefully *matched* against all the costs (expenses) incurred in the process of generating the revenues. This matching principle ensures properly measured performance. But if, for example, Verizon's total acquisition costs of a new wireless customer (commission paid to retailers) who is expected to contribute to the company's revenues over the next three-to-four years are charged (expensed) against this year's revenues, an obvious revenue–cost *mismatch* occurs (four years of cost charged against one year of revenue), leading to an earnings distortion.[7] Similarly with the installation of a major software security system, expected to be used over the next four to five years, whose total costs are charged to current revenues. R&D is, of course, an extreme case of such revenue–cost mismatch: The costs of R&D are typically larger than most other intangible investments, and the duration of benefits longer. Accordingly, the immediate expensing of R&D for a company with a positive R&D growth rate burdens current revenues with an expense (R&D) whose benefits will be reflected by future revenues—a serious distortion of *both* current and future earnings.[8] Even more seriously, such understatement of reported earnings, from the expensing of R&D, likely has an adverse effect on the actual R&D expenditures by companies. Indeed, a recent study on UK data shows that companies that switched from R&D expensing to capitalization *increased* significantly their R&D outlays.[9] Improved accounting has positive consequences.

Thus, the immediate expensing of intangible investments plays havoc with reported earnings as indicators of enterprise performance, particularly for growing or declining enterprises, namely most businesses in a dynamic economy. The intricate effects of intangibles' expensing on reported earnings, sure to mislead investors, were discussed in Chapter 8. Generally, for companies with increasing rates of investment in intangibles, immediate expensing depresses their earnings and book values relative to capitalization and amortization of intangibles, but often inflates their profitability ratios (ROE, ROA), because their denominators are missing the intangibles' capital, and vice versa (earnings overstatement) for companies with decreasing rates of intangibles investment. The adverse effect of intangibles' expensing on reported profitability is substantial. Thus, for example, Google, with an increasing rate of R&D expenditures, reported a hefty 2013 earnings of $12.9 billion, and its return-on-equity (ROE) that year, based on reported numbers, was 14.8 percent. If Google's R&D were capitalized and amortized (say, over five years), its reported earnings would have been $16.6 billion (29 percent higher than GAAP earnings), and its ROE would be 18.4 percent (24 percent higher than GAAP ROE).[10] For Google, an investors' darling with massive earnings, such distortions aren't critical, but for the multitude of companies with lower earnings or even losses, many of which are leading innovators, intangibles' capitalization will have a big impact on investors' decisions.[11] At the national level intangibles' capitalization had a significant effect on economic statistics, it will have a similar effect at the corporate level.[12]

Capitalization of intangibles raises, of course, the issue of amortization for assets with restricted life. Amortization/depreciation even of physical assets is, of course, an estimate, since it depends on forecasts of future asset use and technological changes. Regarding intangibles, those with clearly specified duration, like patents (20-year), copyrights, or other restricted-life legal rights will be amortized over their remaining life. Where industry standards are well established, like the useful life of software products (three to five years), those amortization standards can be used for amortization purposes (e.g., Cisco reports amortization rates for acquired intangibles—33.3% for Metacloud Technology, for example—in footnotes to its 2015 annual report). For other restricted-life intangibles, like brands, an annual test of impairment (loss of value) should be applied, such as the one currently mandated by GAAP for goodwill.[13] These are sensible and practical amortization rules, as reliable as those currently applied to physical assets. Overall, given the large number of intangibles owned by companies, while the life of some intangibles may be overestimated, it will be largely offset by underestimations of other intangibles. Importantly, the estimates of the useful lives of intangibles that underlie their amortization should be disclosed, allowing investors to benchmark against competitors.

Finally, the empirical evidence is strongly in support of our proposed intangibles' capitalization in financial reports. Thus, early studies (e.g., Lev and Sougiannis, 1996) showed that investors consider the reported R&D expense in the income statement an asset that increases share value, rather than a value-reducing expense, and recent studies (Oswald, Simpson, and Zarowin, 2015) confirm and extend this finding.[14] Studies on brand value, software, or organization capital similarly documented a positive association of these intangibles with share values. More recently, research on capitalized development costs (the "D" of R&D), mandated by the international accounting rules (IFRS), substantiated that these capitalized R&D values are indeed recognized by investors as valuable assets, on par with physical and financial assets.[15] Even the oft-mentioned abnormally high uncertainty associated with intangibles, and R&D in particular, to justify their immediate expensing, is a gross generalization. A recent study documented that, in general, R&D risk is no higher than that of tangible assets, except for the risk posed by the infrequent and transformative disruptive innovations.[16]

Summarizing, given the compelling logic of capitalizing intangible investments—as well as the partial R&D capitalization already required by the international accounting rules (IFRS), and the capitalization of intangibles in the national income accounts, what else, we wonder, is required to convince US accounting regulators to scuttle the dated intangibles expensing rule and move accounting to the twenty-first century?

Improve Disclosure of Intangibles

The capitalization of certain intangible investments, just proposed, will undoubtedly improve the quality of reported earnings, but much more is needed to provide relevant information on intangibles to investors. Most companies provide extensive footnote disclosure to reveal information on physical and financial assets, so, why aren't any details provided on the far more consequential intangible assets? Why isn't even the cost of most intangibles separately reported, rather than buried in large expense items, such as cost of sales and SG&A? Wouldn't you like to know how much the company spent on information technology, brand enhancement, employee training, customer acquisition, or the development of unique business processes, and wouldn't you like to be able to track the trends in these investments (e.g., is the workforce quality being run down?) and benchmark the data against competitors? Of course you would, but you can't from current financial reports.

Many companies have large patent portfolios, the details of which are sorely missing. For example, investors will find it very useful to obtain the classification of the company's patents by technological areas (e.g., measuring electrical variables, radio direction finding, conductive master, etc.),[17] allowing them a rare glimpse at the technological strategy of the company: which new areas are penetrated and which are abandoned.[18] And within technological areas, patents should be classified according to remaining life, patents underlying products and development efforts, patents sold or licensed out, and those allowed to expire. For many companies, their patent portfolio is their most important asset, but, strangely, GAAP doesn't require any meaningful disclosure about patents.

Regarding R&D, the total periodic expenditure, currently provided, is of limited use to investors. So what if R&D increased 3 percent? Where is the money going to? Missing is any information on the *nature* of R&D: how much "R" (long-term investment in new technology development) and how much "D" (short-term modifications of available technologies)?[19] This is essential information to assess the risk and growth prospects of the company—whether, for example, long-term growth (investment in "R") is sacrificed for meeting short-term targets.[20] Some may argue that such disclosure is excessively intrusive, potentially benefiting competitors, but these very same arguments were made 20 to 30 years ago regarding pharma companies' portfolio of products under development (pipeline), which is now routinely and comprehensively disclosed by most companies, apparently without competitive harm.

An important clarification: if you think that our call for extended intangibles disclosure affects only tech and science-based companies, think again. Intangibles create value in practically all sectors of the economy: brands in consumer's goods, organization capital in producers of oil and gas and in retailers, and IT in financial services. Our proposed accounting change will therefore improve disclosure of practically all public companies. So, in addition to the capitalization (asset recognition) of certain intangibles, particularly those with identifiable benefit streams, we call for an extended disclosure about core intangibles' attributes. Reforming GAAP (the regulated accounting and reporting system) to include such disclosures in the required periodic reports will ensure the crucial attributes of information uniformity and consistency, which are necessary conditions for effective use of information in investment analysis. We move now to our second change proposal.

II. REVERSE THE PROLIFERATION OF ACCOUNTING ESTIMATES

In Chapter 9 of the book, we documented the ever-increasing number of managerial estimates in corporate financial information and identified it as a major cause of the deterioration of its usefulness. Consider: Most of the substantive accounting regulations issued by the FASB in the past 20 years—accounting for assets and goodwill impairment (loss of value), recording the fair values of assets and liabilities, expensing employee stock options, and so on—generate information primarily based on subjective managerial estimates and forecasts. Some of this information is of questionable reliability, like the required marking-to-market of nontraded assets/liabilities, which don't have market prices: an obvious non sequitur.[21] These regulations rank high in detracting from shareholder value.[22] A substantive overhaul of the current accounting and reporting system has to tackle head-on the proliferation of managerial estimates and forecasts, which detract from financial information effectiveness. It is time to reverse the rising trend. If you doubt the need to seriously tackle the estimates proliferation issue, realize that the financial information you are currently using in investment decisions, such as earnings, is a mixed bag of facts (salaries, rent, or cash revenues), certain reasonably reliable estimates (bad debt and warranty expenses), and the rest (asset and goodwill write-offs, changes in fair values of nontraded assets and liabilities, employee stock option expense)—highly speculative, sometimes manipulated values. Worst of all, you have no way to parse out how much of, say, total earnings is fact-based and how much is estimated, or whether the estimated portion of earnings is increasing or decreasing. Truly alarming. No wonder the relationship between earnings and share prices deteriorated markedly (Figure 3.2, Chapter 3).

Our accounting proposals concerning estimates are twofold: abolish certain estimates from financial reports and enhance the reliability of the remaining ones.

Leave Valuation to Investors

Accountants should avoid the periodic *valuation* of assets/liabilities that are *not traded* in active markets. Such assets should be reported at original costs, and their essential *attributes* (ages, nominal values, description of properties) should be adequately disclosed in financial report footnotes, allowing investors who are interested in current values to estimate them.[23] This will come as a shock to accounting regulators who spent most of the past two decades mandating such valuations, but truth be told, accountants have no special expertise in valuation. If there is a strong and sustained investor demand for current values of nontraded corporate assets/liabilities, appraisers and information vendors will surely step in and provide them.[24] Financial reports should stick to facts and "near facts," namely, highly reliable and verifiable estimates. After all, that's what accounting, derived from *counting* (of facts), is all about.[25] A positive byproduct of eliminating unreliable assets/liability valuations: Mitigating the detrimental effect on the informativeness of earnings (sheer noise) from the gains/losses of such periodic valuations.[26]

Enable the Verification of the Remaining Managerial Estimates and Forecasts

The incentives for accuracy of a pollster or a weather forecaster are reasonably strong, because their forecasts can be easily verified against the subsequently observed election results or weather conditions and their reputation harmed by poor forecasting. In stark contrast, corporate managers, who generate the numerous estimates and forecasts underlying financial reports, lack such reputational (and legal) incentives, because, hard to believe, most accounting estimates cannot be verified by investors. Even the most rudimentary managerial estimates, like those for uncollectible receivables, or warranties provisions, cannot be verified after the fact, because no systematic information is available in financial reports comparing specific estimates with the subsequent facts.[27] This is an invitation to careless and even manipulative estimation.

A straightforward and promising suggestion made years ago by Professor Russell Lundholm will do wonders for enhancing the accuracy and reliability of financial information estimates and projections: Companies should be required to periodically provide a comparison of five to seven key estimates that had the largest impact on earnings with subsequent realizations (facts).[28] Managers will obviously be asked to explain large and particularly persistent misestimations (e.g., a bad debt expense that was lower every quarter than the respective debts written off), a highly embarrassing task, and obviously not a recipe for reputation. Imagine the strong incentives for serious and honest estimation created by this requirement. And yet, despite the obvious benefits from this sensible suggestion, which was made years ago and mentioned in various academic writings, it was, to the best of our knowledge, never seriously considered by accounting regulators. We wonder who pushed back against it.[29]

We accordingly recommend the adoption of Lundholm's proposal, to include in annual reports a comparison of key managerial estimates and projections with subsequent realizations (facts), as well as explanation of large and persistent differences. This, along with our first proposal to avoid the valuation in financial reports of nontraded assets/liabilities, will go a long way to restore the reliability of financial information.[30] And now for our third and last proposal.

III. MITIGATE ACCOUNTING COMPLEXITY

Here is the Lev-Gu law of the dynamics of regulation: Regulatory systems strive to be even more complex than the structures or institutions they were charged to regulate. A race to the bottom, so to speak. If you doubt the universality of our law, think of the 1,990 pages of the original 2009 Affordable Health Care Act (Obamacare), ballooning to about 20,000 pages four years later,[31] or the Dodd–Frank Wall Street Reform and Consumer Protection Act, originally at 848 pages, and mushrooming to 13,789 pages as of July 2013 (and still going strong—the length, we mean).[32] And not only in America: No regulatory agency rivals the European Union in scope, intrusion, and complexity of regulation. Accounting is no exception. The organization and operations of business enterprises, particularly the global ones, are obviously quite complex, but the regulations concerning the accounting and reporting on these operations exceed even business complexity. We have never heard managers or investors complain that they don't fathom the business environment or the operations of companies, but we've heard plenty of them, even those with accounting degrees, lamenting that recent accounting standards and the consequent disclosures (e.g., on financial institutions' risk) are beyond their comprehension. As individuals who have to teach this stuff, we fully concur.

The numbing complexity of the statutory corporate financial information system, constantly on the rise, is a major contributor to its deteriorating usefulness, documented in Part I of the book. At the most fundamental level, if it's difficult to understand a message and its underlying logic is unclear, the message will be largely ignored.[33] Think about the convoluted warnings following drug ads on TV. Who even listens to them? And that's exactly what our evidence presented in Chapters 3–6 shows: Investors increasingly ignore financial information. But turning off investors and increasing their uncertainty aren't the only adverse consequences of accounting's complexity. Counterintuitively, regulatory complexity often enhance the complexity of the regulated entities or structures.[34] A vicious feedback cycle. This surely happens in accounting; for example, the various rules of accounting for leases—which leases should be capitalized and presented on the balance sheet—triggered numerous unnecessary changes and increased complexity in lease contracts to avoid the lease capitalization. Accounting and reporting complexity may also have affected the decision of some enterprises to remain private or withdraw from the public market. A mouthful of harms.

Why Accounting Complexity?

Accounting is complex because business is complex, is the standard answer to the above question. But this is a faulty logic. Consider a company's sales: When should a sale be recorded as such in the books? It is hard to believe, but this question led to a 15-year (!) project by the FASB (the revenue recognition project), and despite having been presumably concluded in 2014 with the production of a 700-page rulebook, it was soon delayed for another year because it's apparently not yet ready for prime time.[35] Why the complexity? Primarily because regulators strive to incorporate in the rules any known or conceivable transaction and agreement between parties, even remote and inconsequential.[36] The irony is that this is a futile endeavor. Forms of business engagements are so varied, fluid, and easy to change that, once a specific accounting rule is promulgated, companies that wish to circumvent it will change the terms of engagement to achieve their aim. And when new business arrangements emerge, accounting regulators are back to work, trying to accommodate the new circumstances, further increasing the complexity of the rules. It's an endless chase of the elusive all-encompassing, perfect accounting standard. The cost of complexity—fewer and fewer people, even professionals, comprehending accounting rules, and the constantly increasing compliance costs by public companies—is apparently overlooked by accounting regulators.[37] We, of course, reject the oft-mentioned allegation that accountants like complexity because it creates more work for them and deflects the intervention of reformers who are deterred by its arcanity as shear malice.

The endless chase of the perfect accounting rule is well demonstrated by the accounting for leases. For decades, accounting regulators strove to clearly define lease arrangements that, in substance, resemble purchasing the leased equipment with a loan from the lessor—termed *capital lease* by accountants—to be recorded by the lessee as an asset and a liability. But as soon as new lease accounting rules were formulated, parties to lease arrangements changed the terms of the lease to avoid the recording of assets and liabilities on the balance sheet, necessitating further rule changes. Guess what? After all these years, lease accounting is once more on regulators' agenda.[38]

Fighting Back Complexity

Lease accounting also highlights a practical way to arrest accounting complexity: substitute enhanced disclosure for detailed accounting rules. In the case of leasing, for example, rather than search in vain for the perfect capital lease rule, require full disclosure of a company's future lease payments, by year.[39] No complicated, convoluted rules, just the disclosure of facts. Investors convinced that future lease payments are an obligation, on par with other company liabilities, can easily add to the company's balance sheet debt the present value of the disclosed future lease payment. Those who believe that future lease payments are not a firm commitment, because, for one, leases can be canceled, will not capitalize future lease payments. End of story.

The same should be done with accounting for revenues (revenue recognition rules). A concise definition of a sale as a transfer of control over products or services from a seller to a buyer, with no future obligations by the seller, covers most of business sales arrangements. For sales with future vendor obligations, such as software products sold with seller commitment to maintain and update the product, the rule should specify the need to allocate the total sales price to the value of the service that has already been rendered (to be recorded as a sale), and the value of the future services (to be recorded as deferred revenue). The relatively rare, industry-specific sale arrangements that are not captured by the above concise accounting rule will have to be fully disclosed in financial statement footnotes, with a clear description of the way they were accounted for by the parties to the transaction, and attested by auditors as reflecting the economic substance of the transaction. This proposal shifts certain accounting rule making from regulators to managers—a healthy bottoms-up shift, because full information about specific and unusual business transactions resides with managers, not regulators. There is absolutely no need to rule on any conceivable seller–buyer arrangement. It's futile to do so anyway, evidenced by the constant updating of accounting rules.

We are cognizant, of course, of the fact that in some cases the complexity of financial information is due to companies, often backed by auditors, that push regulators to rule on the accounting for their specific business transactions in an effort to limit the legal exposure of managers and auditors to allegations of misreporting, since following GAAP is an effective defense against such allegations. In the process, influential companies and industry associations also push for their favored accounting treatment. This is a win–win situation and a form of "regulatory capture," where regulatory agencies " ... eventually come to be dominated by the very industries they were charged with regulating."[40] Accounting complexity can be substantially reduced if regulators would decline to rule on every specific request by companies ("just say no"). A side benefit: Leaving the mode of reporting for infrequent and situation-specific business transactions to the judgment of managers and auditors, backed by a full-disclosure requirement, will encourage experimentation and innovation in accounting, currently sorely missing. After all, that is what the generally lauded, yet never really followed, "principles-based accounting" is all about.[41]

Sadly, current accounting and financial reporting have deteriorated into a compliance activity, where managers and auditors check the very detailed regulatory boxes. There is no room for managers to decide whether the reported item fits the specific aspects of the transaction and the surrounding economic circumstances. Does it make sense, for example, to capitalize (recognize as an asset and a liability) a lease when challenging market conditions increase the likelihood that it will be canceled? Accounting rules should accommodate, even encourage, managers and auditors to fit the reporting of unusual and specific events to reflect the surrounding business and economic circumstances, with full disclosure, of course. Accounting will advance by experimentation more than by dictation.

TAKEAWAY

We strongly believe that a substantive overhaul of accounting and financial reporting regulations (GAAP) in the following directions will significantly improve the usefulness of financial information:

- Adapt accounting to the revolutionary change in the value-creating resources of business enterprises—the continuous rise of intangible capital (Figure 8.1)—by accounting for the *cost* of intangibles as assets, subject to amortization and impairment charges, rather than recording intangibles as current expenses. This should be augmented by extended disclosure of the attributes of intangible assets.
- Avoid the valuation in financial reports of assets and liabilities that are not traded in active markets. Leave valuation to investors.
- Reduce accounting complexity, primarily by avoiding ruling on industry-specific, infrequent transactions. The accounting and reporting on such transactions should be left to the discretion of managers and their auditors.[42]

Corporate financial information thus modified, coupled with the Strategic Resources & Consequences Reports proposed in Chapters 11–15, will adequately respond to investors' information needs.

Finally, no one, even we, likes criticism, and accounting standard setters are no exception. So, regulators could well ignore our reform proposals (naïve, ivory tower). But before they do that, we suggest they seriously consider the accumulating evidence that accounting rules and regulations, by and large, don't benefit investors. A good place to start is the evidence we presented in Chapters 3–7 and continue with the research studies mentioned earlier (footnotes 1 and 3) about the ineffectiveness of accounting standards. Isn't it time for a serious rethinking of financial report regulations?

NOTES

1. Urooj Khan, Bin Li, Shivaram Rajgopal, and Mohan Venkatachalam, *Do the FASB Standards Add Shareholder Value?* working paper (Columbia Business School, 2015).
2. Such a capital markets research doesn't capture potential benefits not reflected in share prices, such as the boon to the accounting (auditing) profession from the ever-increasing accounting regulatory burden and complexity. One man's loss is another's gain.
3. The international accounting standards didn't fare better. A recent study on 44 countries concludes: "We find that the adoption of IFRS [international accounting rules] or US GAAP per se does not make stock prices more informative." Jacqueline Wang and Wayne Yu, "The Information Content of Stock Prices, Legal Environment, and Accounting Standards," *European Accounting Review*, 24 (2015): 490.
4. Judge for yourself how poorly reasoned and out of touch this accounting rule is: Section 41 of its "Basis for Conclusions" states, "A direct relationship between research and development costs and specific future revenue generally has not been demonstrated, even with the benefit of hindsight." (Well, you can't *demonstrate* anything without the benefit of hindsight. Can you?) In fact, multiple empirical studies have documented a strong correlation between R&D and subsequent revenues (e.g., Bronwyn Hall, "Innovation and Productivity," *Nordic Economic Policy Review*, 2 (2011): 167–203, stating: "The conclusion is that there are substantial positive impacts of product innovation [product R&D] on revenue productivity....."). The accounting rule goes on stating (section 44): "The criterion of measurability [of asset] would require that a resource not be recognized as an asset for accounting purposes unless at the time it is acquired or developed its future economic benefits can be identified and objectively measured." Under this rule, even a noncontroversial asset like a security acquired by a company should not be recognized as an asset, because the future benefits (returns) of securities obviously cannot be "objectively measured" at the time they are acquired. And we can't resist one more nugget: " ... at the time most research and development costs are incurred the future benefits are at best uncertain" (section 45). In the current business environment of stiff competition and fast technological changes, aren't the future benefits

of most corporate assets (acquired businesses and related goodwill, say) "at best uncertain"? You've got the drift; these are the underpinnings of the rule governing the twenty-first-century accounting in the United States for internally generated R&D.

5. See, Dylan Rassier, "Treatment of Research and Development in Economic Accounts and in Business Accounts," *BEA Briefing* (March 2014): 1–8.

6. See Anup Srivastava, "Why Have Measures of Earnings Quality Changed over Time?" *Journal of Accounting and Economics*, 57 (2014): 196–217, for the distortions in *reported earnings* caused by the rise of intangibles ("I hypothesize that increases in intangibles intensity reduce earnings quality ....").

7. In a steady state, where there is no growth or decline in the number of customers, it won't make a difference to periodic earnings whether customer acquisition costs are charged directly to revenues or are spread over their useful life. But very few companies are in a steady state, so reported earnings will differ considerably whether those investments are immediately expensed or capitalized and subsequently amortized.

8. Not surprisingly, the previously mentioned examination of all the FASB standards found that the R&D expensing rule was among the highest drivers of investors' losses (see Khan et al., 2015).

9. Dennis Oswald, Ana Simpson, and Paul Zarowin, *Capitalization vs. Expensing and the Behavior of R&D Expenditures,* working paper (New York: New York University, Stern School of Business, 2015).

10. See Baruch Lev, Bharat Sarath, and Theodore Sougiannis, "R&D Reporting Biases and Their Consequences," *Contemporary Accounting Research* (Winter 2005): 977–1026, for the full range of earnings distortions caused by the expensing of intangibles.

11. Yet another objection we heard to our capitalization proposal was: Why capitalize? If investors believe that intangibles are assets, they can easily undo the accounting by adding back to earnings the intangible expenses. Not so fast. As explained in the next section, except for R&D, all other intangible expenses (brands, IT) are not reported separately in the income statement, so investors have no way of adding back these expenses to earnings. Furthermore, even for R&D, if investors "capitalize" it by adding it back to earnings, past R&Ds should be amortized. But, by how much? The short of it is this: Investors cannot capitalize intangibles on their own.

12. "When Germany last year added R&D to its investment statistics for the first time, it led to a 'noticeable' upward shift in gross-domestic-product levels, according to Destatis." See Nina Adam, "Business Investment Is Changing Its Stripes," *The Wall Street Journal* (August 17, 2005), p. A2.

13. A brand loses its value as an asset when its owner can no longer charge a price premium for the product (like Bayer Aspirin does).

14. Baruch Lev and Theodore Sougiannis, "The Capitalization, Amortization and Value-Relevance of R&D," *Journal of Accounting and Economics*, 21 (1996): 107–138. Oswald et al., 2015.

15. Instructively, a recent study shows that, in the process of capitalizing development costs, companies accumulate and report valuable strategic information,

required by the international (IFRS) capitalization rule, such as on the company's financial ability to complete the projects or on the technological feasibility (beta test for software products) of the developed projects, which is of considerable importance to investors. See Ester Chen, Ilanit Gavious, and Baruch Lev, *The Positive Externalities of IFRS R&D Rule: Enhanced Voluntary Disclosure,* working paper (New York: New York University, Stern School of Business, 2015).

16. Baruch Lev, Suresh Radhakrishnan, and Jamie Tong, *R&D Volatility Drivers,* working paper (New York: New York University, Stern School of Business, 2015).

17. The US Patent office classifies patents by roughly 1,000 technological areas.

18. Similar technological change assessment by patent classification is performed on the macro level; see Deborah Strumsky, Jose Lobo, and Sander van der Leeuw, *Using Patent Technology Code to Study Technological Change,* working paper (Charlotte: University of North Carolina, 2010).

19. We have commented in footnote 7, Chapter 14, that this information is available to companies, since it is routinely reported in the annual R&D Survey, conducted by the Census Bureau.

20. A recent study, for example, found that companies engaged in cancer research underinvest in long-term research. Eric Budish, Benjamin Roin, and Heidi Williams, "Do Firms Underinvest in Long-Term Research? Evidence from Cancer Clinical Trials," *American Economic Review,* 105 (2015): 2044–2085. The authors conclude: " ... private research investments are distorted away from long-term projects."

21. An amusing (not at the time) example was Enron, marking-to-market ("fair valuing") 30-year gas contracts in which they were the main market-maker.

22. See, Khan, Li, Rajgopal and Venkatachalam, 2015.

23. A few exceptions might be made for financial institutions, where, due to the unusual complexities of such assets/liabilities, fair values can still add useful information over original costs.

24. A case in point: Prior to the requirement to record an expense for employee stock options (2005), adequate disclosure about such options was given in a footnote to the financial report, and, indeed, some investors used this information to adjust reported earnings for the impact of stock options.

25. A commentator on an early draft of the book applied a cliché "better be approximately right than absolutely wrong" to this case, arguing that accounting estimates, even of questionable reliability, could still be informative. We disagree. First, the evidence we presented in Chapter 9 links the proliferation of accounting estimates to the deterioration in financial information usefulness. So, where is the informativeness of all those "good enough" estimates? Second, as this commentator noted, such estimates could be informative if they are unbiased (managers don't intentionally misestimate) and "the level of noise in the estimate [is] fully understood by investors." Perhaps. But, effective ways of conveying noise in accounting estimates are not available. That's the reason we say that it is better to do without estimates of questionable reliability.

26. For the detrimental effect on earnings of periodic balance sheet valuations, see Ilia Dichev, On the Balance Sheet-Based Model of Financial Reporting, *Center for Excellence in Accounting and Security Analysis* (New York: Columbia Business School, 2007).

27. We know—you find this hard to believe. So, here is an example: Consider the uncollectibles (bad debt) provision. The periodic expense (estimate) can be obtained from the cash flow statement. In subsequent periods, the company reports the total amounts of accounts receivables that were written off (namely, deleted from the books due to customers' default). These write-off amounts, however, cannot be attributed to a specific former uncollectibles estimate to establish misestimation, since the write-offs in a given quarter or year can relate to the estimate of the previous quarter (year) and/or the estimates made two or three quarters earlier. In short, there is no way to attribute facts from published data to respective estimates. Same with the estimates of warranties expenses. The situation is, of course, even worse regarding the multitude of accounting estimates that aren't even disclosed in financial reports.

28. See Russell Lundholm, "Reporting on the Past: A New Approach to Improving Accounting Today," *Accounting Horizons*, 13 (1999): 315–323.

29. In a few cases, like restructuring costs, GAAP requires a comparison between estimates and subsequent realizations. The most comprehensive comparison of estimates and facts can be found in property and casualty insurance companies, which fully disclose annually their claim loss reserve revisions for 10 years. But these are exceptions in accounting. Why not make them the rule?

30. An interesting proposal was advanced years ago by then Carnegie University accounting professor Yuji Ijiri. He proposed providing a triple-column income statement: a column informing on fact-based revenues and expenses, a second to summarize the estimates in revenues and expenses, and a "totals" column, identical to today's income statement (see Yuji Ijiri, *Cash Is a Fact, but Income Is a Forecast,* working paper (Pittsburgh: Carnegie Mellon University, 2002)). No doubt, such a clear separation of facts from estimates will be highly informative to investors.

31. The 1,990-page number is from Computational Legal Studies, November 8, 2009. Rep. Richard Hudson (R-NC.) speaking on "Fox and Friends" on May 13, 2013, said: "Implementation [of Obamacare] has also become a bureaucratic nightmare, with some 159 new government agencies, boards, and programs busily enforcing the 20,000 pages of rules and regulations already associated with this law."

32. Joe Mont, "Three Years in, Dodd-Frank Deadlines Missed as Page Count Rises," *Compliance Week* (July 22, 2013).

33. A demonstration: *Barron's* (July 27, 2015, p. 20) wrote the following about the transportation ticketing company Cubic Corp.: "Earnings are expected to drop 30 percent in the fiscal year ending September .... Much of the decline relates to a noncash *deferred tax asset impairment....* This may be a source of investor confusion." (Italics ours). No kidding. Does anybody, including those who sat through accounting courses, understand the meaning of deferred tax asset impairment causing a 30 percent earnings drop?

34. Point made by Chester Spatt in "Complexity of Regulation," *Harvard Business Law Review Outline*, 3 (2012): 1–9.
35. In July 2015, the Financial Accounting Standards Board voted for a one-year delay of the revenue recognition standard.
36. How remote? An example: The revenue recognition rule includes a large number of industry-specific supplements. Take the one for insurance intermediaries (brokers and agents), who used to record sales when the service was rendered (a policy sold) and customer payment reasonably assured. That's not good enough, because some transactions may include a variable or contingent element (how frequent among insurance brokers?), and for those the new rule states: "Variable consideration should be estimated using the method that best predicts the amount of consideration to which the entity will be entitled: the expected value or the most likely amount. The expected value approach represents the sum of probability-weighted amounts for various possible outcomes. The most likely amount represents the most likely amount in a range of possible amounts." (FASB and IASB, Revenue Recognition Standard, Insurance Intermediary Industry Supplement, July 7, 2015, p. 3.) Our nightmare: that a student will ask us what this means and who cares about it.
37. The FASB claims that it does consider the costs of regulations in setting accounting rules, but the ever-increasing complexity and scope of GAAP render this claim questionable.
38. In February 2016, the FASB issued new guidance on lease accounting.
39. The current requirement for future lease payments disclosure is for *minimum* lease payments, excluding, for example, contingent rentals or not reasonably assured renewal options. Our proposal, therefore, broadens the requirement for future lease payments disclosure, with explanations of contingencies and optionalities.
40. Investopedia. The industry capture concept of regulation was first proposed by the Nobel Laureate economist George Stigler in "The Theory of Economic Regulation," *Bell Journal of Economics*, 2 (1971): 3–21.
41. In fact, the 2002 Sarbanes–Oxley Act recommended a shift to principles-based accounting, evidently with no impact. The study on the effectiveness of FASB standards (Urooj Khan, Bin Li, Shivaram Rajgopal, and Mohan Venkatachalam, *Do the FASB Standards Add (Shareholder) Value?* working paper (New York: Columbia University Business School, 2015) found that principles-based standards dominate rules-based standards in benefiting investors.
42. "An invitation to information manipulation by managers" will be accountants' reaction. Not so. First, not all managers manipulate financial information. And the few that do will always find ways to "manage" financial information.

CHAPTER 18

Investors' Operating Instructions

In this final chapter, we synthesize the main lessons for investors drawn in the previous chapters in the form of a new approach to analyzing the performance and long-term competitive position of twenty-first-century business enterprises. Forget the conventional, short-term analysis you learned in business school, focusing on accounting-based profitability (ROE, ROA) and liquidity ratios. Those are based on flawed data, and their predictive power is negligible. Our proposed analysis focuses on what matters: the strategic assets that determine the enterprise's ability to sustain competitive advantage—bringing to light their availability to the enterprise and the efficiency of their deployment by management. This represents a radically different methodology of securities analysis.

ANALYSIS FOCUSED ON STRATEGIC ASSETS

Imagine, you were just notified by your doctor of an appointment at XI:XLV on VIII-XX-MMXVI. Overcoming the initial temptation to switch doctors, you vaguely recall that you saw similar signs at the end of movie credits and in Super Bowl announcements (up to 2015), but you haven't the faintest idea what they mean. A Google search clarifies: these are Roman numerals, meaning that your doctor's appointment is at 11:45 on 8–20–2016. You should thank the thirteenth-century mathematician

Fibonacci (Leonardo of Pisa) for liberating you of the clunky Roman numeral system inherited from the ancient world, and the picturesque, mysterious abacus (consult Google once more) used by merchants and accountants to get around the awkward Roman numeral system. In his 1202 book *Liber Abaci* (the Book of Calculations), Fibonacci introduced the universally used Arabic numerals (in fact, Indian) to European merchants.[1] Why do we tell you this fascinating tidbit? Because you need a modern-day Fibonacci to free you from the shackles of "ancient," clunky accounting-based investment analysis you learned in business school, like we did, decades ago—an analysis that focuses on the "bottom line," comparing quarterly reported earnings with analysts' consensus estimates, and attempting to predict future earnings and stock prices, primarily based on accounting reports and complex spreadsheets. The depressing performance of such investment analysis drove hordes of investors to give up entirely on analyzing individual companies and invest in index funds. Bye-bye accounting. A new investment analysis is obviously called for.

As we have shown in Chapter 11, what determines a company's ability to grow and sustain competitive advantage—the long-term enterprise goal—is the existence and effective deployment of strategic assets, those resources that are rare, are difficult to imitate, and generate benefits. Consider a successful clinical test of a drug under development, the prospects of an oil field under exploration, trends in the capacity utilization of airplanes, the book-to-bill ratio of tech companies, patterns of policy renewals of insurance companies, or the customer churn rate of Internet and telecom companies. Any of these is a much more reliable indicator of enterprise future performance and competitive advantage than the backward-looking quarterly earnings and revenues you analyze, because such indicators inform directly on the fundamental performance of strategic assets: pharmaceutical patents and pipeline, mineral reserves of oil companies and exploration, airlines' landing rights, and insurance companies' customer franchise.

Traditional securities analysis focuses on *symptoms*, like sales, earnings, profitability (ROE, ROA), and solvency. But these are backward-looking *consequences* of past deployment of strategic assets (e.g., transforming patents into revenue-generating drugs in recent years), having limited predictive ability, as we have shown in Part I.[2] In contrast, our proposed analysis focuses on the *causal factors*—the resources that determine the enterprise's future performance. A drug company's current sales might be high and its earnings might beat the consensus, but if its product pipeline (a strategic asset) is thin, its future performance will soon deteriorate. An insurance company's earnings may be currently low because it is improving the customers' book by weeding out high-risk customers, but future earnings will consequently rise. Focusing on available strategic assets and their future potential, rather than on their past performance, leads to substantially improved investment decisions.

True, our analysis is more complex, multidimensional, and penetrating into the enterprise's business model bowels than the simple (rather simplistic) conventional analysis, and people in general, and investors in particular, tend to focus on heuristics (comparing P/E ratios to past averages), or just on a single indicator or two to assess the situation: GDP growth and the unemployment rate to gauge the state of the economy, sales and earnings to evaluate business performance. This habit follows Occam's razor—the law of parsimony, which is good enough in certain situations[3]—but fails when pitted against complex systems like modern businesses. The current investment reality calls for a more comprehensive, deeper analysis, an analysis that makes extensive use of the Strategic Resources & Consequences Report developed and demonstrated in Chapters 11–15.[4]

ASSESSING ENTERPRISE PERFORMANCE AND COMPETITIVE EDGE: THE NEW APPROACH

Let's be clear: Without strategic assets—those benefits-generating, nonabundant, and hard to imitate resources—a business enterprise will not be able to maintain competitive advantage for long, irrespective of its current sales and earnings, or the size of its tangible and financial assets. Dell is a case in point. Founded in 1984 with a unique and innovative asset—its "build-to-order" business model, where customers design the computer they order, rather than buying what producers designed for them, catapulted Dell to the top of the PC world. Economies of scale carried the company forward for quite a while, but alas, competitors caught up by also offering customers "configure-to-order" features at competitive prices. Dell rested on its laurels, and failed to invest in innovation—its R&D outlays, for example, where among the lowest in the industry.[5] Consequently, it was stripped of its sole strategic advantage, and sure enough, absent other strategic assets, Dell's stock price started to head south in mid-2005, losing half its value by the following year, never to return to its previous highs. Crucial to note: During the early 2000s, as Dell gradually lost its strategic assets and competitive edge, its accounting performance—sales, earnings—was still impressive, totally masking its deteriorating fundamentals.[6] Investors, assessing Dell's performance traditionally—based on financial report information—were, therefore, totally hoodwinked, unaware of the vanishing competitive advantage, as evidenced by the sharp price collapse in 2005–2006. There are few better examples than Dell of the futility of an accounting-based investment decision process. So, what do we propose?

FIRST STEP: TAKING AN INVENTORY OF STRATEGIC RESOURCES

We don't mean, of course, the inventory account on companies' balance sheets (raw materials, work in process, etc.), which in most cases is irrelevant for serious performance evaluation.[7] We propose that investors should start their investment analysis by carefully evaluating the existence and condition of the enterprise's operating strategic assets. An inventory taking, so to speak, of all the assets that matter, yet are mostly missing in action from the balance sheet (and sometimes even from managers' minds); that is, the unique resources that give the company an edge over competitors. Examples of strategic assets for a broad cross-section of industries follow:

- *The customer franchise* of Internet, media, insurance, and telecom companies: Carefully document the total number of customers of the company, the growth rate of new customers, the churn (desertion) rate,[8] and the total monetary value of the customer franchise (see Chapter 12 for calculation). A recent positive growth rate of new customers, churn decrease, and growth in the monetary value of the franchise are positive indicators for investment in the company, and vice versa for decreases in these customer attributes. Recall Peter Drucker's dictum: "The purpose of business is to create and keep a customer." So, for companies whose customers can be tracked, an evaluation of the customer franchise is essential.

- *Product pipeline:* What is the state of the product pipeline of pharma and biotech companies? Record the progress over recent periods in the success of products under development in clinical tests, the number of products/devices in advanced state (Phase III clinical tests, FDA review), the extent of diversification of the development portfolio across therapeutic areas (an important risk measure), and the total size of the market for the main drugs under development (growth potential). These product-development dimensions provide a thorough risk–return profile of the major strategic asset of pharma companies. Regarding products already on the market: consider their therapeutic market share (e.g., HIV drugs) and the patent duration (time to expiration) of the leading drugs. These are the major indicators of the sustainability of the on-the-market drug portfolio. If the size of your investment justifies it, track the monthly prescription rate of the company's leading drugs (available from vendors) to detect early signs of loss of competitive advantage. Such fundamental analysis of the pharma/biotech's two major strategic assets—products under development and those on-the-market—will point at opportunities or vulnerabilities of the stocks in your portfolio, indicating purchase and sale opportunities.

- *Brands* of consumer goods producers, retailers, hotels, leisure providers, and electronic products companies: Most people confuse brands with recognized names. The Polaroid name is still widely recognized but the company went bankrupt in 2001. Xerox is one of the most well-known names in business, but it's questionable whether its products or services are now substantially superior or distinguishable from those of competitors. So, it's not clear that Xerox has a valuable brand. Nike, for example, is a different story. It consistently manages to charge higher prices than competitors and maintains a long-lasting leading market share, as do Apple, Starbucks, and Bayer aspirin. These are brands, because they enable their owners to charge *premium prices* (an implicit seller guarantee for quality or exceptional service) and/or maintain a leading market share. For investors (and managers, too), it is important to determine whether the company has valuable brands and to evaluate their impact on operations. Examining market share for the company's major products and comparing its prices with those of close competitors will indicate the existence of brands and their impact on operations. Brands enable their owners to maintain long-term competitive edge and render these companies attractive investment candidates—for the right price, of course.
- *Unique talent* is crucial in certain sectors: leading scientists in pharma, and particularly biotech companies, stars in entertainment and sport enterprises, successful fund managers and deal makers in financial institutions. When considering investment in these sectors, the monitoring of talent, focusing on long-term relationships, is a key aspect of the investment analysis. Emphasis should be placed on quantitative, objective indicators, such as the scientific publication record and number of citations to it of biotech scientists, or the investment record of fund managers. Inspect the flow of talent to and from the company, paying special attention to loss of talent to competitors.[9] Establishing the existence of talent, particularly for small and medium enterprises, is an important dimension of the investment analysis.
- *Patents* of technology, science-based, and Internet service providers are, of course, a prime strategic asset. But don't be fooled by the number of the company's patents, or the rate of patent grants—most patents are worthless, sunk cost. The question is whether the company's patents support revenue-generating products, the remaining lives of the patents (20 years max), and their scope (Do they in fact cover the attributes of the products they protect?). Furthermore, for patents not supporting products or services, does the company generate revenues from patent sale or licensing? A thorough evaluation of a patent portfolio requires special expertise, so this will only be performed for significant investment in the company or for acquisitions (such analysis requires, of course, cooperation of the company).

Summarizing, a comprehensive documentation and evaluation—inventory taking—of the strategic assets of investment candidates is the first step of a serious investment analysis.[10] Obviously, the absence of significant strategic assets, like Dell in the early 2000s, calls into serious question the investment in such a business. The existence of strategic assets, though, is only a necessary, but not sufficient condition for your investment. These assets have to be maintained and protected; otherwise, they will wither on the vine. This leads to the next step of the investment analysis.

SECOND STEP: CREATING AND MAINTAINING STRATEGIC ASSETS

Strategic assets have to be constantly maintained, adapted, or replaced. Changing customer tastes and behavior (e.g., online purchases), technological innovations (e.g., gas fracking), and competition erode the value and contribution of the strategic assets of incumbents and require continuous investment, modification, and sometimes replacement. Accordingly, a crucial aspect of the proposed strategic investment analysis is the monitoring of the company's ongoing investment in strategic assets: expenditures on product and process R&D, technology acquisitions, brand purchases and maintenance (e.g., promotion, advertising), strategic business acquisitions (e.g., of biotech startups by pharma companies), research and marketing alliances and joint ventures, IT investments and consulting engagements to create organization capital (e.g., recommendation algorithms of Netflix and Amazon), as well as the acquisition of exploration rights by extractive companies and landing rights by airlines.

It's not just the size of the investments that matters—it's mainly their strategic function. In particular, are they really filling the "holes" created by obsolescence (patent expiration of leading drugs), technology changes, or competition, or do investments just increase asset redundancy? In short, is the portfolio of strategic assets maintained, or even growing, despite business and technological challenges, or is it deteriorating? You want to invest in enterprises that not only are well-endowed with strategic assets but that also keep them "fresh" and growing. Seek positive dynamics of strategic assets.

An important aspect of maintaining the strategic assets portfolio is to make sure that assets are well protected against infringement, disruption, and obsolescence. In contrast with most physical assets, strategic assets are exposed to specific threats. You should inquire: Does management regularly monitor its competitors and alliance partners to make sure that its patents, brands, and know-how are not infringed upon, and does management act vigorously when they are? Are disruption threats—a new technology developed elsewhere that threatens incumbent's technology—monitored continuously and effectively?[11] Is the obsolescence of know-how—employee skills, key business processes—avoided by remedial measures (training)? Is tacit knowledge of employees, particularly those soon to retire, made explicit by regular debriefing and knowledge management systems? Are the company's mineral assets threatened by regulators or environmental activists? In brief, has management instituted effective systems to protect and preserve the strategic assets of the company? The pressure of day-to-day operations often distracts managers from the long-term thinking required to institute protective mechanisms for strategic assets. Risk management is now routine in financial and other institutions. Similar strategic assets risk management should be deployed by companies endowed with valuable assets. You want to invest in enterprises that actively protect and grow their strategic assets. Note: when you meet with managers, it's much more important to get informed about strategic assets than on next quarter's earnings.

THIRD STEP: SUCCESSFUL DEPLOYMENT OF STRATEGIC ASSETS

All assets, even strategic ones, are inert; they have to be deployed effectively to create value. This is the third and final dimension of the proposed strategic investment analysis, and the one that comes closest to conventional investment analysis. A successful deployment of strategic assets, along with conventional ones (property, plant & equipment) is indicated by value creation: Primarily organic sales growth (net of mergers and acquisition) and positive residual cash flows (below). Most analysts and investors still focus on reported earnings, despite their glaring deficiencies, as highlighted in Chapters 2 and 5. In contrast, we proposed in Chapters 11–15 to focus on "residual cash flows" to avoid unreliable managerial estimates and projections embedded in reported earnings, as well as the occasional "management" of earnings.[12]

Specifically, we suggested and demonstrated (in Chapter 12) the use of the following residual cash-flow indicator (residual, after subtracting cost of equity capital):

Residual Cash Flows
- Cash flow from operations (Reported in the Cash Flow Statement)
- *Plus:* Investments expensed in the income statement (R&D, IT, brands)
- *Minus:* Normal capital expenditures (3 to 5 years average)
- *Minus:* Cost of equity capital
- *Equals:* Value created during the period

True to our approach throughout this book, we subjected the proposed residual cash-flow measure to an empirical horse race with the leading financial statement performance indicators: earnings (profit) and cash from operating activities. We used the usefulness test displayed in Chapter 2: measuring investors' returns from a perfect prediction of the measures (explained in detail in Chapter 2, Appendix 2.1). The higher the investment returns from predicting a measure, the more useful it is to investors. Figure 18.1, on next page, presents for each year, 2009–2013, and averaged over the five years, the gains from perfectly predicting the following year's residual cash flows (left bar), cash from operations (middle bar), and earnings (right bar). We find—in each year, and on average, with the exception of 2012—that our proposed residual cash flow measure yields the highest gains from predicted values. That is, it beats the other two contenders in investors' usefulness.

Consistently positive residual cash flows indicate systemic value creation by the company—an attractive investment attribute. But note, this is not sufficient for an investment decision. Even our proposed measure, an improvement over the alternatives, is a look-back indicator. For a successful investment decision, you need to combine the residual cash-flows signal with those of the three analytic dimensions outlined earlier in this chapter and conveyed by the proposed Strategic Resources & Consequences Report: availability of strategic assets, new investments in these assets, and the safeguards of assets from infringement, disruption, and adverse regulatory impact. Only positive signals from these three will assure *continuation* of value creation.

TAKEAWAY

The investment analysis we prescribe in this concluding chapter differs significantly from traditional financial analysis. Whereas the latter focuses on the consequences of companies operations (sales, earnings, ROE or ROA)—highlighting the past, with very limited predictive power—our investment analysis focuses on the fundamental drivers of future operations: the company's strategic assets, as well as their nurturing, protection, and deployment to generate benefits. Determining the strengths and weaknesses of these assets and the success of their deployment provides a clear view of future company operations. Ours, evidently, is a more complex and nuanced investment analysis than the traditional one—examining a mosaic of assets and strategies—but it is, we strongly believe, a more rewarding analysis. Obviously, companies' current GAAP disclosures don't provide all the information required for the proposed analysis. For this, you need companies to release the essence of the proposed Strategic Resources & Consequences Reports (Chapters 12–15). But you don't have to wait for that. Start by performing a partial strategic analysis, based on information in earnings calls and companies' presentations, as we did in our extensive examples in

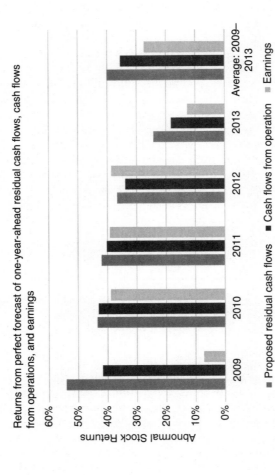

FIGURE 18.1 Residual Cash Flows Measure Outperforms Conventional Ones

Chapters 12–15. Just performing a thorough customer franchise analysis, or gaining a deep understanding of an oil company's "dynamic portfolio management," will considerably enhance your investment decisions. We guarantee it.

NOTES

1. See John Steede Gordon, "The Man Behind Modern Math," *Barron's* (August 24, 2015) (or VIII-XXIV-MMXV), p. 45.
2. Not to speak of the multiple accounting shortcomings and biases (Part II of the book) adversely affecting conventional securities analysis.
3. After the philosopher William of Ockham (c. 1287–1347), stating that among competing hypotheses, the one with the fewest assumptions should be selected. Wikipedia (October 2015).
4. Rules of thumb also fail in other areas of finance, like "chasing winners" in selecting investment funds or vehicles (ETFs); another simple, unidimensional investment decision. Multiple studies have shown that choosing funds by recent performance is a losing proposition because of the widely known, but rarely heeded, phenomenon of "mean reversion." Winners in any field (sport, management, Oscars) are affected to varying degrees by talent and luck, and luck, unfortunately is ephemeral. Thus, erstwhile winners tend to revert (regress) to the mean, namely fall from grace.
5. The average ratio of R&D to sales ("R&D intensity") over 2001–2005 for Dell, Apple, Hewlett-Packard, IBM, and Microsoft were: 0.9, 6.0, 5.1, 5.6, and 16.8 percent, respectively.
6. Dell's sales, in fact, kept rising until 2011, and its earnings increased every year through 2005.
7. The exceptions are large inventory changes that deviate significantly from sales changes (inventory increases 50 percent more than sales), often implying an unexpected sales shortfall, or "dead inventory," or alternatively, managers' expectation of unusually large sales increases. A somewhat muddled signal.
8. Like the rate of policy cancellation for insurance companies.
9. Such an analysis is routinely performed at top universities, quantifying the publication record and scientific impact (citations) of professors, as well as the move in/out record of leading academics.
10. There are, of course, additional, industry-specific strategic assets to those mentioned above, like legal rights (landing rights of airlines, exploration rights of oil and gas companies), that should be considered in the investment analysis.
11. Indeed, we encountered such analysts' questions in the earnings calls we examined.
12. The *Economist* recently discussed earnings management ("The Story and the Numbers," October 31, 2015, p. 66) and noted: "And it remains much harder for firms to fluff up the audited cash flow figures—which measure the cash coming in less the cash paid out—than profits or the balance sheet. Four of the five firms in trouble today have had weak cash flows."

Epilogue: Advocacy Needed

Regrettably, experience shows that even the best of evidence is often insufficient to drive a significant social change. Inertia is strong, existing practices are protected by special interests, and regulators are entrenched and often convinced that they are doing the right thing, making it rare for evidence-based proposals like ours to be quickly implemented. Evidence and proposals for change have to be bolstered by advocacy: Interested parties must push vigorously for change to happen. In our case, such advocacy should come from those who stand to benefit most from our change proposals: investors, standing to gain from improved information, and executives, benefiting from the rewards of enhanced transparency (lower cost of capital, higher share prices, and improved credibility). We urge these interested parties to organize and advocate for changes in corporate disclosure along the lines proposed in this book, and we promise to lend any assistance necessary for this important endeavor.

Author Index

Subject Index

Note: Page references followed by f and t indicate an illustrated figure and table, respectively.